Praise for *Whispers from the Wild*

"*Whispers from the Wild* by Amelia Kinkade is a truly remarkable read on many levels. With pages dripping with nectar from the heart, this book makes abundantly clear Amelia's passion and concern for wild animals. It's a passion we should all share, as you'll come to learn, if you care about reversing the extensive and perhaps nearly irreparable damage humankind has caused our planet. And you won't have to take her word for it; this comes straight from the horse's mouth, so to speak. Various species of animals she communes with in the book have told her so. These interspecies dialogs so amazed me, I had to prop up my jaw from dropping so much. Woven into this amazing narrative are fascinating stories from Amelia's past as a professional dancer and actress, performing with some of the great talent of the time. After reading this book I can't look at animals the same way; I'm now convinced they know more than we do."

— **Andrew Bloomfield**, author of *Call of the Cats*, *Learning Practical Tibetan*, and *How to Practice Vedic Astrology*

"Amelia Kinkade is a modern Dr. Doolittle, bringing more than twenty years of her teaching and knowledge into this new book. *Whispers from the Wild* is written with compassion, love, and humor, giving readers the behind-the-scenes of the amazing animal kingdom."

— **Gary Quinn**, bestselling author of *May the Angels Be with You* and *The Yes Frequency*

"Amelia and her work and books have opened my mind and beliefs to a world of potential for all living things. She has incredible talents and abilities that we can all learn from. Read about her work in her latest book and become her student. You will be grateful for her and her work — and how it changes your life for the better, too."

— **Bernie Siegel, MD**, author of *Love, Animals & Miracles* and *A Book of Miracles*

"In *Whispers from the Wild*, renowned animal communicator Amelia Kinkade provides us with just what we need to deeply and personally reconnect with the fascinating and mysterious world of nonhuman animals — to rewild our hearts. Not only do they need us, but we also need them to thrive and to truly experience our own humanity in an increasingly human-dominated world. *Whispers from the Wild* made me deeply rethink ways in which we could truly honor the presence and essence of nonhuman animal beings, while at the same time saving ourselves from the devastating effects of our alienation from nature and from ourselves."

— **Marc Bekoff**, author of
The Emotional Lives of Animals and *Rewilding Our Hearts*

"Everywhere there is growing awareness that we humans *will* find harmony with nature or we may not be at all. In *Whispers from the Wild*, Amelia Kinkade reminds us that an astonishing level of communication with wild creatures is indeed possible. Her enchanting book helps us resacralize the Earth and its creatures — seeing all life as sacred and deserving of love, respect, and compassion. The beneficiaries are not just the animals but ourselves as well."

— **Larry Dossey, MD**, author of *One Mind: How Our Individual Mind Is Part of a Greater Consciousness and Why It Matters*

"Amelia Kinkade has amazing abilities to communicate with animals and, perhaps more important, humans who love animals. Her depth of experience and wisdom sparkle on every page. Highly recommended."

— **Arielle Ford**, author of *The Soulmate Secret*

Whispers
from the Wild

ALSO BY AMELIA KINKADE

Straight from the Horse's Mouth:
How to Talk to Animals and Get Answers

The Language of Miracles:
A Celebrated Psychic Teaches You to Talk to Animals

Whispers
from the Wild

LISTENING TO VOICES FROM
THE ANIMAL KINGDOM

Amelia Kinkade

New World Library
Novato, California

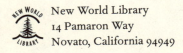

New World Library
14 Pamaron Way
Novato, California 94949

Text design by Megan Colman
Watercolor paintings by Fiona Knox

Library of Congress Cataloging-in-Publication Data is available.
Names: Kinkade, Amelia, author.
Title: Whispers from the wild : hearing voices from the animal kingdom / Amelia Kinkade.
Description: Novato, California : New World Library, 2016. | Includes bibliographical references.
Identifiers: LCCN 2016029886 (print) | LCCN 2016036888 (ebook) | ISBN 9781608683963 (pbk. : alk. paper) | ISBN 9781608683970 (Ebook)
Subjects: LCSH: Human-animal communication. | Animal communication. | Extrasensory perception in animals.
Classification: LCC QL776 .K56 2016 (print) | LCC QL776 (ebook) | DDC 591.59—dc23
LC record available at https://lccn.loc.gov/2016029886

First printing, October 2016
ISBN 978-1-60868-396-3
Ebook ISBN 978-1-60868-397-0
Printed in Canada on 100% postconsumer-waste recycled paper

New World Library is proud to be a Gold Certified Environmentally Responsible Publisher. Publisher certification awarded by Green Press Initiative. www.greenpressinitiative.org

10   9   8   7   6   5   4   3   2   1

To Beatrice Lydecker, my teacher,
who taught me the call of the wild is heard in whispers

In the name of the daybreak
and the eyelids of morning
and the wayfaring moon
and the night when it departs,

I swear I will not dishonor
my soul with hatred,
but offer myself humbly
as a guardian of nature,
as a healer of misery,
as a messenger of wonder,
as an architect of peace.

In the name of the sun and its mirrors
and the day that embraces it
and the cloud veils drawn over it
and the uttermost night
and the male and the female
and the plants bursting with seed
and the crowning seasons
of the firefly and the apple,

I will honor all life
—wherever and in whatever form
it may dwell—on Earth my home,
and in the mansions of the stars.

— DIANE ACKERMAN, "School Prayer" from *I Praise My Destroyer*

Contents

Prologue

IN 2001, A TEAR-STAINED, tattered diary became a book that got published all over the world and turned my house cat's name into a synonym for a forbidden love "that no one else would understand." I called Mr. Jones, my Maine coon, "the sunlight in my universe" and described our relationship as "a love that transcends all space and time." Since the publication of *Straight from the Horse's Mouth*, I've received thousands of emails from all over the globe with readers sending me photos of *their* Mr. Jones. When I open the attachments, I'm surprised to find that the pictures are not always of house cats, but also of horses, dogs, and sometimes even rabbits or birds. But when I read the emails saying, "This is my Mr. Jones" or, sadly, "I just lost my Mr. Jones," you know my tears always come. You all trust me to know what you mean. This new book is a walk on the wild side, but I'm trusting you to continue to know what I mean.

Whispers from the Wild is meant to ambush your comfort zone, because if that zone includes the pain of being unable to assist animals — so conditioned are we to feel powerless to help them — you may enjoy my audacious intervention. This book is designed to challenge that sinking sense of helplessness and then to champion your abilities to be powerful agents of change for this Earth and her animals. But brace yourself for a wild ride.

In these pages, you'll get to overhear my private conversations with wild tigers, lions, elephants, whales, and bees — and, if you have the courage, join me on a roller coaster ride with great white sharks and a black mamba. There's a rebel in me I can't ignore. So I find myself showered in grace when I listen to her wisdom and allow her to steer my life. I've always let her have the last word. In this book, New World Library let her have the last word, too, and they've opened up a new savanna where my wild spirit can run free.

I'm not a scientist, zoologist, or veterinarian, yet owners of sanctuaries let me in with their troubled tigers, lions, and cheetahs, and even let me cuddle their cobras. Wild elephants seek me out in the lobbies of safari parks to kiss my face. I am not technically a tiger expert, nor an elephant expert, and I admit that before researching this book, I didn't know many of the scientific facts documented about sharks, whales, snakes, or bees. Albert Einstein said, "The most beautiful experience we can have is the mysterious. It is the fundamental emotion that stands at the cradle of true art and true science. Whoever does not know it and can no longer wonder, no longer marvel, is as good as dead, and his eyes are dimmed." I hope *Whispers from the Wild* helps open your eyes, no matter how dimmed they may be by discouragement and tears.

The only arena in which I am truly an expert is the realm of the mysterious. I'm just a curious student of nature's mysteries and a witness of God's daily miracles in my life. Every animal is a miracle. And it must be a miracle that I can hear them when they "whisper" to me. I've written this book to share with you some of the techniques that make that magic possible, so that you may hear some "whispers" for yourself. I've also collected facts and figures to accompany my scandalous stories, but these you can easily find elsewhere. What I can give that you will not find elsewhere is access to my soul. Enter at your own risk. It's a jungle in there. Wild animals occupy the sweetest place in my soul. I know that many of you feel the same way. So my highest hope is that I may simply give your wildest love a safe place to live.

Maybe it's hardwired into me to sing love songs to the animals, a remnant of my Cherokee ancestry. On my last safari, as I sat singing quietly to the lions with tears streaming down my cheeks, one of my students asked me the lyrics to my secret song. It's an old Aaron Neville song that I whisper to every one of my patients, be they a lion, tiger, tortoise, elephant, shark, snake, wolf, whale, bear, jaguar, giraffe, gorilla, tarantula, penguin, dog, pig, parrot, alpaca, iguana, eagle, owl, bat, house cat, or Olympic show horse: "I don't know much. But I know I love you. And that may be all I need to know." May this book grant you permission to love the wild ones, too.

1 | Tigers
Lords of the Stargate

We are both their greatest enemy
And their only hope.
They will not put up a fight.
They will not beg for reprieve.
They will not say goodbye.
They will not cry out.
They will just vanish.
And after they're gone
There will be silence. . . .
And nothing you can do will bring them back.
Their future is entirely in our hands.

— Bradley Trevor Greive, from
Priceless: The Vanishing Beauty of a Fragile Planet

"There's something wrong with the oldest tiger's teeth," I said into the camera on the way to the big-cat sanctuary. "All the cats are concerned. They all told me he had a problem with one of his teeth recently, and the leopard said, 'I hope it doesn't happen to me.' I checked in with every big cat last night, and all they wanted to talk about was how worried they are about their eldest tiger. His tooth problem must be really bad."

"Can you tell me which tooth?" asked Bob Faw, a correspondent from *NBC Nightly News*.

I tuned in to the tiger, did a body scan on him, and winced with pain. My left hand automatically shot up to the left side of my jaw. "Upper left. It's an upper-left molar."

"Are you certain?"

"Yes."

"How do you know?"

"I can feel it."

"You feel the tiger's pain as if it's your own?"

"Yeah, I think he just had surgery on one of his teeth." I rubbed my jaw tenderly. The pain was excruciating.

I had never been to McCarthy's Wildlife Sanctuary in south Florida when *NBC Nightly News* flew down to film an Animal Communication seminar I was teaching there and interview me. I had never met any of the exotic cats in person, nor had I even seen photographs of the cats, which, as a professional animal communicator, is the way I usually focus my attention to tune in clairvoyantly. In this instance, I simply reached out with my mind to all the big cats in the sanctuary, enveloped them in my love, and asked them to tell me the biggest news — any recent changes in their home or pride.

Mentally, I begged them, "Look, I need your help! I'm the first animal psychic ever to go on national news in America at this level. These people *don't believe in what I do*. I need to prove to them and all of America that you are a million times more intelligent than humans give you credit for, and I need to prove that you can 'talk' to me and that I can hear you! Please, please, will you help me? Can you tell me something really unusual that's happened out there lately — something evidential — something no one else knows?"

I hadn't done a web search on any of these big cats. I had deliberately gone at it cold. I had only meditated on them the night before, preparing for my day on camera at the sanctuary. I moved my consciousness from pen to pen, meeting all the exotic cats in this magical realm where we have access to each other's thoughts and feelings and can "talk" instantly, silently, nonlocally, but in great detail. As I asked them each to tell me how they felt and what they were concerned about that night, every one told the same story. The tigers, the jaguar, and the mountain lion all had the same issue on their minds. Each cat telepathically told me that nothing mattered more than the trauma their "king" was enduring, and their hearts ached to ease his suffering. There was so much sadness and frustration around the issue; some were afraid for him, some were afraid for themselves, but all were upset and disheartened by the illness of their pride leader.

I was shaking and trying not to stutter as I breathlessly blurted my intuitive impressions into the camera, talking too fast — which happens when the information is coming in from the outside. When I'm downloading data at light speed, stumbling over words in an attempt to keep up with the messages, I experience a physical reaction that indicates the information is coming from another living being, not being manufactured from my own mind at the slower rate of my normal thinking process. This cue was helpful but not comforting enough. I was terrified. I had no way of knowing if I was right. If I was wrong, I would discredit not only myself but all my beloved students and my entire profession. I had asked the news not to just focus the piece on me but also to invite a panel of six or so of the best animal psychics in the world so that they could cross-analyze us, perform double-blind experiments on us, and scientifically prove that if we could agree on mysteriously obtained data, our collective work would have more mainstream credibility. They refused. They wanted to do the piece on me and only me, and they wouldn't consider allowing me to appear with even my most prestigious colleagues or protégés. I agreed because they said that if I wasn't the focus, they wouldn't do a piece on Animal Communication at all.

To make the pressure cooker even hotter, the correspondent they'd assigned to my interview was Bob Faw, a brilliant, hard-boiled journalist who had received two Overseas Press Club Awards, one in 1982 for his coverage of the invasion of Lebanon by Israel, and the other for an *NBC Nightly News* report on Mozambique, which also garnered him an Emmy in 2000. I can guarantee that during his two decades of covering international news, including wars in the Middle East, he'd never been asked to take seriously a woman Leeza Gibbons once called a "doggie psychic" and who at the moment was switch-hitting species to prove herself as a "tiger psychic."

The news producers had been benevolent enough to ask me, though, if I had a teacher I'd like them to interview. I didn't, because my teacher had passed away, but I offered them Captain Edgar Mitchell, the legendary NASA professor and astronaut who left his footprints on the moon. Although Dr. Mitchell hadn't taught me how to telepath with tigers, he may have been the only genius scientist on earth who understood the process and didn't flinch. We were brought together over the love of his very clever old-lady schnauzer, Miss Megs, because even her *very* clever daddy couldn't tell what she was really thinking when she looked up at him with irresistible soulful eyes to beg him for a piece of cheese.

Dr. Mitchell allowed the news crew to come to his home in West Palm Beach and interview him privately. He told me about it later.

"Is she ever wrong?" they had asked him.

"Well, not that I've heard of, but I guess it's possible that everybody has a bad day once in a while. I suppose there could be days when her antenna isn't as sharp as others."

Thankfully, this wasn't one of those days. When we arrived at the tiger sanctuary, I was already sweating in the Florida heat, but the nerve-racking stress of performing for the most prestigious nightly news program in America made my temperature rise what felt like another ten degrees. Dry-mouthed and tense, I walked past the pens of the big cats with the news cameras hot on my trail. Every ounce of my courage, talent, and strength was about to be tested. We passed many of the cats I had already spoken to in my meditation. I greeted each one silently, reverently, and thanked them for talking to me as they mentally directed me to their ailing king.

Suddenly he came into view. There was the most massive, majestic Bengal tiger I'd ever seen in my life, but he hung his huge head in pain. His beautiful upper lip was dripping blood. Mark McCarthy, the wonderful owner of this rescue facility, had silently joined us by this time. He looked into the news cameras and explained:

"This is Rajah. He just had one of his teeth removed to try to get to a cancer tumor in his sinus cavity. We were very concerned about putting him under because of his age. He's our oldest tiger."

"Which tooth was removed?" asked Bob Faw.

"One of his upper-left molars."

Unfortunately, even the most supportive news crews who truly champion psychics are stunned when the magical process happens right before their eyes. At this point, they were probably busy coming up with half a dozen possible explanations for how I had obtained my information.

Could the tiger's health condition have been posted on the web? It hadn't. Could the owner of the sanctuary have told me in advance in private? He hadn't. I'd never met him or spoken to him before. Could I have sent a student or friend to the sanctuary as a spy? I hadn't.

The cats told me. And they told me without my even having a photograph to read. I had no psychic coordinates. I simply entered the sanctuary in my mind and asked the cats directly. Now here I was with them face-to-face. I fought back tears in front of Rajah's cage. Unlike the sanctuaries in Thailand that let me cuddle and play with the world's most dangerous wild tigers, or the cheetah sanctuaries in South Africa that allow me to carefully caress the mighty cheetahs, this sanctuary did not allow me to go into Rajah's pen and hold him. I had to comfort him through the bars of his cage with no stroking or kisses, only healing thoughts and tender words of encouragement. He hung his glorious head in pain as blood dripped down his mane. The cancer in his left nasal cavity was inoperable. He was dying.

One of his last wishes was that a little animal communicator from Los Angeles could explain to her species that animals have feelings, too; their intellectual capacities are monumentally more expansive than humans give them credit for; their emotional scope is broader than we ever dreamed; and our treatment of our fellow beings leaves so much to be desired that they die unheard in cages of diseases we sometimes cause by providing them with insufficient nutrition, compromised living conditions, and emotional suffering. Our primitive medical knowledge of animals and our inability to honor their healing processes can tip the scales so that they feel even more humiliated and betrayed. Add to that the fact that humans are the only species that cannot "hear" other animals, and this can create a recipe for disaster — a sense of isolation, sadness, and hopelessness that leads to depression, and a confused frustration about the only species that has lost its connection to nature: humans.

But Rajah had a small beacon of hope that day shining into the darkness of his desolate future.

"I can hear you," I said to him telepathically. "And I love you. If I lived my entire life just for this moment — for the opportunity to meet you and be here to comfort you — it was all worth it."

He looked up at me and smiled the way all cat lovers know cats can, when their furry lips curl up in a blissful expression of satisfaction. He yawned slightly even with his incredibly sore jaw. He stretched his powerful back in a proud stance, reached his resplendent front legs toward me, and crossed his paws. Then, in an irresistibly cute kittenish flirtatious move, he laid his cheek on his paws and looked up at me, making goo-goo eyes. Those wide blazing emerald laser beams cut right into my heart.

"I crossed the country just to meet you, Rajah," I told him mentally. "And I would have crossed the galaxy for you."

"Thank you. And I for you. I have some messages for your people," he said. "Tell the humans that tigers are still the kings of the jungle, and as the king of this pride I will speak not just for all tigers but for all animals everywhere. Tell your people to treat us with kindness, not cruelty. Tell them they must learn how to honor all the other beings on this planet. Tell them we are their teachers, not their slaves. Tell them that as they destroy all the other species, they will ultimately destroy themselves. Tell them that they need to learn how to *share*."

"Okay, I'll try…but you know they won't listen."

"If not to you, then who?" he asked.

"I'll do what I can. I promise," I said, and I wished him a fond farewell, getting hustled inside to stay on our tight shooting schedule. As I wiped my eyes and walked away from his pen, red drops of blood were still trickling gently from his furry lips. I had to clean up my face and pull it together for the on-camera interview we were about to film, but leaving him was sheer hell. I could have spent every day of my life just gazing at his magnificent face, in awe and gratitude that we humans are allowed to live on a planet alongside such beauty.

The news crew ushered me inside. Powdered and freshened up with new mascara, I sat on a couch in the living room of the sanctuary owner's humble home, took a deep breath, prayed to my spirit guides, and tried to center myself. The news producers had assured me that they truly supported my work no matter how controversial and that the presenter wouldn't "try anything" on camera — no cheap shots, no hidden agendas or sucker punches that so many talk-show hosts consistently spring on their psychic guests just when we least expect a left hook to the jaw.

Despite their promises, I was midway through a nervous rant about why interspecies communication works, what electromagnetic energy is, and how it can be exchanged between living beings to be broken down into frequency patterns and "read" not unlike Morse code, when Bob Faw interrupted me:

"You can read photographs, right?"

"What?"

"Your powers work with pictures, too, right?"

"Um...er...yes, well, they do, but —"

"Then what do you get from *this?*" He pulled a photograph out of his upper-left pocket and smacked it on the coffee table in front of my nose. Ouch. The sucker punch. I fumbled for a moment, explaining that I'd need to go into meditation in a moment of silence and that I hadn't been prepared to read a photo live on camera under such pressure. Then I did the stupidest thing I've ever done in my life — something I've regretted ever since. I asked them to turn the camera off. The camera clicked off, and I sat quietly staring into the eyes of the sweetest female bulldog I'd ever seen.

"This is my dog," he said. "What do you get from *her?*" You could have heard a housefly hiccup if one had buzzed through the room. I had three of my workshop coordinators sitting in chairs around me off camera, watching the interview and silently cheering me on. I felt them all holding their breath. I heard them praying for me inside their own minds. White-knuckled, clutching their chairs, all three women were frozen like statues, eyes full of horror and hope. In the silence of the tomblike room, I prayed to make contact with this precious dog. I love bulldogs. The fact that Mother Nature designed them to have enough skin for *two* dogs always makes me laugh. I mean, really! Was God drunk when He created bulldogs? Why do they have all these wrinkles? What is all this baggy skin supposed to be used for? And what personalities! I just love bull-dogs. And instantly she *knew* it! I felt the dog's joyous spirit reach out and touch mine. Her personality was so spunky and maternal, her happiness so infectious, that I relaxed a little and smiled.

"I'm comin'!" she said. Immediately, I saw her walking painfully down a flight of stairs inside the house. She was trying to make her way to a kitchen with a red brick floor. Her back and hips creaked and ached as she descended the stairs, but her mood was decidedly upbeat.

"What's got you so excited?" I asked her.

"I can't wait to see the new baby!"

I told Bob that she had some pain in her lower back and hips, but he refuted it, saying that most dogs have pain in their back and hips as they age. I told him she loved the kitchen with the red brick floor, and he confirmed that the kitchen floor in her favorite house was made of red brick, and yes, there were stairs in his daughter's house, where she loved to visit.

"Tell him there's a little blonde girl coming at Christmastime! 'I love the little blonde baby! It will be my job to take care of this little girl!'"

I saw the house decorated for Christmas, and I flashed forward in time to see the blonde toddler, older now, playing with the dog by the Christmas tree. The bulldog hovered around the darling child as she unwrapped her Christmas gifts. When I relayed this information to Bob, he looked puzzled, then pale. His eyes were burning holes in me, but his lips formed a grim line.

"Ask her her favorite person," he said quietly. I silently asked the dog in the photo, "Who do you love the most, other than Bob?"

"Rachel. Tell him I spend most of my time with Rachel." When I did, his poker face finally softened.

"My grandmother's name was Rachel!" he blurted out excitedly. Then he immediately began to equivocate. "But lots of people have grandmothers named Rachel, or at least someone in their family named Rachel." I seized the moment. I looked up into the pained, hopeful eyes of my seminar coordinators, who sat in a semicircle around me like stone gargoyles. Jamie coordinated for me in Boston, Connie in South Florida, and Beth in Tennessee. By coincidence, two of the three women were Jewish, and this increased the odds that one of them might have a grandmother named Rachel, being that Rachel is a popular Jewish name.

"Jamie, is your grandmother named Rachel?" Speechless, she shook her head no.

"Connie, is your grandmother named Rachel?"

"No," she squeaked out.

"Beth?"

"Uh-uh." A nervous shake "No." No words.

"Looks like it's just you, Bob," I said, turning the investigative spotlight back on him.

"She says she loves your grandmother Rachel more than anyone in the world other than you and spends a lot of time cuddling in her lap."

"Well, that's not possible because my grandmother passed away some time ago, and it doesn't make sense that the dog's still in the house, because that dog is —"

"*Dead!*" We said the word in unison. He was startled. I was not. He went on to tell me that his daughter was pregnant and that the baby was due around Christmastime. Seven months later, the producer of the show emailed me to say that at Christmas of that year, Bob Faw's daughter gave birth to a beautiful blonde baby girl.

Unfortunately, *NBC Nightly News* never showed the piece they filmed at the sanctuary. Right when it was scheduled to air, the war broke out in Iraq and all the news on TV for months after was about violence and chaos. I hounded the network to show my special, but they never got around to it and the footage was shelved. If it's still gathering dust in a can somewhere, I'll never know. But it was the first and last time America ever put the spotlight on dying tigers telepathing their final wishes for all the human race to hear or dead bulldogs naming grannies and predicting the sex of unborn babies.

Until now. I think it's time we changed all that.

PERHAPS AMERICA WAS NOT YET READY when the interview took place in 2002 to embrace a shaman who could talk to animals, much less heed my advice about tenderness, reconnection with nature, life after death, and the possibilities of magical awakenings inside the brains of an ever-evolving human race. But that time has come — it's now or never. Rajah died within the year. He finally relinquished himself to the cancer. His story went untold. But I made him a promise, and I intend to keep it. Join me in my quest.

THE GOLDEN TIGRESS IS BORN

Some of you may know of a beloved American television comedy called *The Golden Girls*, which starred four spunky older women demonstrating to the rest of us how to go through our "golden years" with a new sense of grace and wisdom, but mostly just a great sense of humor. The naughtiest of the four marvelous old broads was a hot Southern bombshell named Blanche, but to me she was just my aunt Rue. Now that Rue McClanahan is raising hell and holding court in heaven, I can tell a secret I could never tell when she was alive. *Rue, now that you're gone, I'm going to hurt your pride.*

I was living with my hilarious, warm-hearted, animal-loving aunt when I was nineteen years old and had just moved to Los Angeles. She took me in to her sprawling house in the Hollywood Hills, just south of Ventura Boulevard, a stone's throw from Universal Studios. I lived there for one blissful year. Two weeks after I got off the bus in Los Angeles from a boring college life in Oklahoma (where Rue and all my family were from), I booked the lead in the Stray Cats video *Sexy and 17*, which led to a glamorous career as a professional jazz dancer. In my first few years in Hollywood, I was privileged to be a backup dancer for Smokey Robinson, Cher, Sheena Easton, the Four Tops, Mary Wells, Ray Charles, and El DeBarge as I made rock videos; I performed in break-dance movies like *Breakin' 2: Electric Bugaloo* and *Girls Just Want to Have Fun*, and TV shows like *The Motown Revue Starring Smokey Robinson*, *Fame*, and *Dirty Dancing*. I was even flown in a helicopter from gig to gig by Donna Summer. Being one of Donna's two female backup dancers was one of the highlights of my dance career, touring with her in a string of exhilarating concerts.

But even as I danced to "Bad Girls," I didn't realize how far that "bad girl" persona could take me. During this first summer in L.A., I had also begun to take acting classes and had no idea that those meager classes would lead me into a career as a horror queen — a rather scandalous one at that. In my trilogy of cult-classic horror films, I created a character named Angela, Hollywood's first female monster, literally a tiger-bitch-from-hell, and the evidence of it is tattooed all over the bodies of many of my fans. But long before prosthetics ever graced my cheeks, before pineapple-flavored demon tongues, fangs, and cherry blood filled my young mouth, I opened my big not-yet-fanged mouth in a way that made history far more than my short stint as a horror movie star did.

I'm going to tell you two secrets about my aunt Rue that no one has ever heard before, and they both involve tigers. This is Tiger Soul Secret Number One:

One night, just after Rue landed her prize-pig position as one of the Golden Girls, she came home from the set despondent. In their first few weeks of rehearsal, the directors were trying to make Betty White and Rue *both* dumb blondes. Betty's dingy blonde persona was tried and true, perfected over years of masterful blonde ditziness on beloved sitcoms. This was what Betty was famous for — so trying to compete with her was going over like a trap door in a submarine. *The Golden Girls* didn't need two dumb blondes, and Rue had not yet found her sea legs with her character development. I'd never before seen her in tears over a role. We sat in her kitchen late one night sipping at a bottle of champagne. I was nineteen.

At this point, Rue was already an established TV star from her decade of wonderful work on *Maude*, where she did indeed play a bit of a ninny, but a lovable, memorable one. This approach simply wasn't going to work on Betty's turf. I had just launched my career as a video vixen. *Sexy and 17* got my face on many national talk shows as well as the cover of *Life* magazine, where I was honored as one of the "Faces of 1983." But as with most rock-video queens, I'm afraid it wasn't really my face that was getting the most attention. I was no stranger to my own inner tigress, which had already become my selling point. Rue's character on *Maude*, Vivian, was also a bit of a tart. I remember an episode where Bea Arthur knocked on her neighbor Vivian's door and caught Vivian wearing nothing but Saran Wrap. So I knew Rue had it in her.

Finally tired of her whining, I barked, "Hand me that script!" I started poring over her lines. I said, "Rue, I want you to read these lines like your panties are on *fire*!"

She took the cue, reading the very unfunny lines like a snarling tigress, and all of a sudden, everything that hadn't been funny before became wickedly funny. She continued to build the prowling tigress character with hissing Southern-drawl sexual innuendos. When there was a point in the script where the doorbell rang, and Rue's line was "Isss that the possst-man? Ahhhl git it!" or if a thud sounded on the side of the house and her line was "Isss that the pap-uh-boy? Ahhhl git it!" every line was now punched with a sly wink, pucker, and grin. With brains full of champagne bubbles, we sat on the kitchen floor, busting each other up and giggling long into the night. Suddenly Blanche, the sex-crazed bad girl, was born.

Rue took this new character to the set with her the next day — making every single line a hilarious sexual slur — and the entire crew was on the floor laughing. When she came home from work that night, she told me that one director actually doubled over, holding his belly because he was laughing so hard. Rue went on to win an Emmy after she created this deliciously decadent character, Blanche Devereaux, whom drag queens still emulate on Halloween, all over the world.

Who did it? Ahhh did it! I'll take shameless credit for the birth of Blanche, even though I wouldn't realize my own villainous vixen tigress characters for another four years, when I began starring in my series of horror films and landed a lead role on *The Young and the Restless*, where I joined the cast for five months, playing a character that was coincidentally also named Vivian. I've always been typecast as a ravenous man-killer. Call it method acting.

However, I certainly didn't know at the time that shape-shifting my aunt into a wild tigress not only would establish her career — it would one day save her life.

Rue published her memoir, *My First Five Husbands…and the Ones Who Got Away*, just a few years before she died. In the last twenty years I'd seen the men come and go. She married one husband twice. Does that count as one or two? But from my point of view, there was only one true soul mate I ever saw in her life.

His name was Buster — he was a Maine coon cat who never left her bed or her side, no matter what was going wrong. Buster was her companion, her comfort, her love, her strength, her consistency, her oasis of peace and loyalty. He was the only male I saw in her life who loved her unconditionally, never left her, and didn't swindle her out of half her income when they divorced. He slept on her pillow by her right ear every night for the year I lived with my aunt Rue, licking her tears dry when man after man broke her heart. Buster purred her to sleep, proving that there was a man on earth who could handle her every need, surf her emotional turbulence, and adore her while remaining steadfastly in her arms, come rain or come shine.

One day, she rather flippantly mentioned to me that Buster masturbated on her head every night. I was mortified! I asked her how in the world she could let him do that.

She said, "Way-yull, he juss won't let me sleep 'til he's done doin' it in mah ear!"

Rue may not have considered Buster to be her soul mate, but it's obvious that Buster considered Rue to be *his*. Apparently, he had better taste in women than she had in men. *My First Five Husbands*, entertaining as it was, didn't get much critical acclaim. Perhaps she would have had a better shot at the *New York Times* bestseller list with a book called *My First Five Cats*.

Rue may never have manifested her dream marriage in her lifetime, but she sure was good at attracting the world's sexiest and most devoted tomcats. Is it possible that the security and forever love we spend our lives searching for is under our noses all along?

ANIMAL SOUL MATES

I've taught Animal Communication workshops all over the world for the last fifteen years, since my first book, *Straight from the Horse's Mouth: How to Talk to Animals and Get Answers*, was published. I've been privy to the sacred secrets of my students in twenty-nine countries — many more if you count my email fans — and from even the most remote parts of the globe, I hear the same stories: how the one living being who brought comfort, devotion, laughter, wisdom, strength, and consistent love did not arrive wearing a rented tux or an overpriced fluffy wedding gown. The bearers of joy, of hope, of light, shimmied and galloped and pranced and flapped their way into even the most hopeless hearts, bringing the greatest gift a soul mate could ever bring: unconditional love.

They don't need to talk about love. They embody it. They don't need to make empty promises that they will love us through thick and thin. They already do. They don't need to tell us that they'll be by our side through sickness and through death. They already are. These are the ones who are mates for our souls: the ones who can see us hung-over and fat and depressed and still love us; the ones who can see us desperate, broke, and defeated and still cheer us; the ones who lick our tears away even if every human we know has abandoned us; the ones who function as our alarm clocks, work-out coaches, Zen meditation teachers, clowns, spiritual counselors, nurses, dance partners, pillows, footrests, psychiatrists, and confidants — the ones who have paws, hooves, or wings.

Some of my soul mates have stripes and big fangs, and others have trunks, fins, and wide smiles; some have no legs and even spout deadly venom. But to each her own, I guess.

Maybe you don't have access to wild animals as I do, but I'll bet you have a little wild one in your home right now, and although that dog or cat may not be a gorilla or a great white shark (I've known a few Chihuahuas who acted like they were!), that little domestic someone is still your connection with the wild natural world. The essence of the wilderness is in every ounce of your little cat, dog, ferret, or parrot, and certainly in your horses. If you have someone looking up at you with shining eyes, waiting to smother you in furry kisses, always available for a cuddle on the couch or a jaunt in the park, to give you a spanking from a happy tail and a life lesson on how to be fully present and get back into the moment — the moment where we rediscover how to live our lives from our hearts, not our heads — this book is for them. And this book is for you. We're here to explore their wildness and to rekindle the wild side of you.

THE TEMPLE OF LIES

I'm going to take you on a wild ride now, so fasten your seat belt. My initiation into the bowels of third-world corruption stemmed from an Animal Planet documentary I watched en route from London to Los Angeles called *Tiger Temple*, now called *Tiger Temple Part One*, which was filmed in 2004. The film featured a Buddhist monk petting a massive tiger while small prey animals hopped through the frame only a few feet from the tiger's face. When the presenter asked the monk, who turned out to be the head abbot, how he kept the tigers from attacking the prey, the abbot said, "I teach them principles of loving-kindness. I say, 'You tiger no live here without loving-kindness!'"

Now *this* I had to see. The documentary went on to feature almost thirty stunning tigers who had been rescued by the monks or dropped off on their doorstep in Thailand. Or so the abbot said. Who would question that? After all, it came straight from the mouth of the head abbot of a Buddhist monastery. In the Western world, where I'd grown up, I was taught to have respect for such titles. I was instantly under his spell.

Bewitched, I saved my money, hired a camera crew, and enlisted a man I'd always had a crush on to join me for a month at the "Tiger Temple," where I had every good intention of helping the monks with their fund-raising to create "Tiger Island," a spacious dream-come-true sanctuary where the tigers would have their own paradise islands, where the idyllic plan involved housing two tigers on each private island. But while anticipating the trip — the trip of a lifetime, or so I hoped — I started waking up at my apartment in Hollywood with loud SOS calls from the tigers at the temple. As I was bombarded with these urgent requests from the captive tigers that I "hurry up and get over here!" I became even more driven to help the monks create larger enclosures for these tigers. As the tigers blasted through — tired, hurting, upset, infuriated, and running out of patience — I knew this tourist attraction was a time bomb. If one of them lost her temper and went off on a monk or tourist, it would be the end of the Tiger Temple and possibly bring shame on the Buddhist regime in all of Thailand.

At this point, some of the tigers were so enraged, I felt this was a critical moment — a time for me to go on a vision quest. The tigers started transmitting to me morning, noon, and night, waking me with nightmares of their stifling enclosures. I became possessed. I had no inkling of wrongdoing at this point. I was entranced with a romantic notion, fueled by the most irresistible images I've ever seen on the internet, of blissful tourists crouching down to touch and be photographed with surprisingly docile tigers. I was soon to be one of them.

In email contact with the staff before I flew over, I was told that the temple needed a new vet for the tigers. I put out a global plea to all my students, in search of a veterinarian who was qualified to work on exotic wild animals, specifically big cats. This was a bit like finding a needle in a haystack, but I found one. Not one but five of my students qualified and were ready to fly to Thailand to help these monks and their tigers. When the temple upped the ante and made really ambitious requests, demanding that the vet not only have experience medicating wild tigers but also donate six months of his life without pay (That's right — abandon his practice, fly to Thailand on his own dime, and work for free!), I *still* found the right man for the job. And the right man was a woman. One of my students met all their qualifications and was ready to fly in from Hong Kong. This was a miracle and an obvious sign of divine intervention. I was elated. Then, for no reason, her application was denied.

Once I got to the compound outside of Chang Mai with my cameraman, full of adrenaline, ready to interview the abbot, I was told that the abbot was in the hospital in Bangkok and unavailable for an interview. The staff said he'd had a medical emergency the night before I landed and had to be flown to the hospital. I started praying for them. What I didn't know was that what I really needed was for someone to pray for *me*.

The next few days found me swimming in a tidal wave of chaos, drowning in confusing stories, where the staff and volunteers tried to give me interviews but couldn't even get their lies straight. I was there to help them build this new haven for tigers, where the tigers would each have a private Shangri-La but still be visible for viewing by tourists, thereby generating the funding to care for the tigers. It sounded like tiger heaven to me, and I was really excited to help. Unfortunately, when I started interviewing the staff about the projected plans, I discovered that even though seven hundred tourists came through the doors to fondle what the monks advertised as "tame and docile" tigers, the money seemed to disappear, funneled into mysterious random projects, and was not going toward the projects the money was allocated to, such as the building of the islands.

And to my surprise, when I took a tour of the cramped, dark, windowless stone jail cells where the tigers were kept, what I found at the "temple" were tigers who had poor nutrition, being fed nothing but cooked chicken and dog food to make sure they never tasted blood and developed a taste for it; no enrichment to allow them to exercise properly except for when the young tigers were allowed to romp in the river; tigers who were not receiving proper medication; and fishy stories about the births and histories of cubs. The tigers were strangely sluggish. This alone should have been a red flag for anyone, much less a professional animal communicator. But I still had on my rose-colored glasses, hoping that there was a way to improve this unorthodox sanctuary; those glasses were soon to obscure my vision entirely.

At some of the other animal sanctuaries in Thailand, I was already hearing rumors of how the monks had slit the tigers' wrists so that their claws wouldn't work, and how they were secretly herded and made submissive with electric cattle prods and the monks' own urine squirted into the tigers' faces. I didn't want to believe any of this. My rose-colored glasses were firmly in place. Footage had even surfaced of a monk beating a tiger with a stick. Again, I believed what I wanted to believe, in part for purely selfish reasons — I wanted to cuddle the tigers, too, and get to be close to them. But even more important, I didn't want to believe that Buddhist monks were capable of cruel behavior. It seemed to defy everything their religion represents. I'd bought into the fantasy, and I was still holding on for dear life. But when the tigers' distress calls became more than I could ignore, I started talking to them and realizing the ugly truth. I started doubting the "principles of loving-kindness" when the tigers' rumble turned to a roar.

As my rose-colored glasses started to slip off, I turned to the man I'd brought with me for guidance, the one I was infatuated with, and he assured me that I was overreacting and making it all up: the tigers were fine, well cared for, and the monks were wonderful. That's the nature of deceit. Lies are contagious.

It was actually a leopard imprisoned in a monstrous concrete cage who started pounding the truth into my thick head. Located at the front of the temple as a tourist attraction, the furious leopard paced frantically. The volunteers told me that she had attacked the abbot and was being punished because he "didn't like her." Didn't *like* her? What happened to "loving-kindness"?

In one of the most astonishing moments of my life, I persuaded this leopard to hunch down and enter an even smaller cage in the corner of her enclosure so that we could shut the door between the inner and outer cages and drag some tree branches into her enclosure as enrichment. The volunteers told me it was impossible to get her into the tiny cage, even for an instant, but she proved them wrong. Until I got there, she had never entered this small cage, and the volunteers told me that was why she had nothing whatsoever to play with. To their credit, I honestly think most of the volunteers had no idea of the smokescreen that was blinding them to the truth. These cheerful, good-hearted guys dragged huge fallen tree branches into her cage, even though they said, "The abbot would be mad if he caught us." I sang to her, prayed with her, comforted her, and visualized her going into the tiny cage so that we could close the door for only the moments we needed to drag the branches in. She entered the cage not once but six times, while the guys fumbled with the door. Finally, I lured her in once again so that the men could slam the door shut. On cue, we released her back into the larger cage — one that was open on all four sides so that tourists could gawk at her 24/7. She had no privacy and nowhere to hide. But at least now she had some tree branches to climb if she chose to. It was with great sorrow that I left this glamorous leopard, trapped in a concrete cage in solitary confinement, standing in a pool of her own urine.

Losing heart, but on the wings of the success with the leopard, I was shown by the staff to the enclosure of a tigress with an eye infection. They told me that they had drops for her eyes, but no one had the courage to go into her cage and medicate her. When I asked where the vet was, they were vague, claiming that he came around only once or twice a week. Obviously, this ailing tigress wasn't high on his priority list, and yet my fully qualified student had been denied access to these animals. When I asked the volunteers if I could go into her cage and put the drops in her eyes myself, of course they said no. So she was left to suffer in pain alone in her cage. I had lost only my rose-colored glasses. This tigress was losing her sight.

I returned to Los Angeles with ten thousand dollars less in my bank account. I had spent my life savings trying to help these tigers. At this point, I still believed that the building of Tiger Island would get the tigers out of their disgusting dark stone jail cells and into a spacious sanctuary where they could live healthier, happier lives.

And, by the way, nothing ever happened romantically between

me and my dream boy who had guided me away from my own intuition. Of course, now I see what a blessing that was. On this vacation of a lifetime, more romantic than any honeymoon, he ended up in the arms of a Thai hooker instead of me — which was exactly where he belonged. But at the time, when I returned to L.A., my ego was bruised, my savings account was empty, and I was feeling lost, rejected, and heartsore.

And then the other shoe dropped, and when it did, it knocked my rose-colored glasses off and crushed them, along with my dreams about Tiger Island. I got an email from CITES, the Convention on International Trade in Endangered Species of Wild Fauna and Flora, demanding that I take any and all support of the Tiger Temple off my website. They said that the temple was under investigation for illegal tiger trading, smuggling, and animal abuse. I'd already started the fund-raising campaign. Now I had ten thousand dollars' worth of pictures and footage I couldn't use because they would only benefit a scam where tigers would be sold on the black market for body parts. Criminy. No more tiger heaven. Now I was up to my arse in alligators instead.

CITES wrote to say that if I truly wanted to help tigers, I should help them, not the monks. So I am coming forward with this information, embarrassing as it is. I failed the animals I love the most. Now I would like, in some small way, to make it right.

In January 2016, there were still over 150 tigers in the temple in shoddy, questionable conditions. The first attempt to close the temple and surrender the tigers to the government failed. At the same time that I was commissioned to write this book, and I began to emotionally champion the tigers in the Tiger Temple again in the hopes that this book would raise awareness about their plight, one of the tigers attacked the abbot. Fancy that. You'd have to wonder if the tigers could hear me. But finally some justice was done. On May 30, 2016, the Tiger Temple was raided by Thai wildlife officials accusing the monks of trafficking tigers and they discovered

40 dead cub corpses in the freezer. According to a *USA Today* article entitled "Thailand's Tiger Temple Saga Isn't Over Yet," published June 3, 2016,

> On May 30 Thai officials and staff from the Wildlife Friends Foundation Thailand and other NGOs arrived at the temple to start removing its collection of adult tigers, thought to number 137. "International and local NGOs have been calling out this Tiger Temple for citations of animal abuse, of illegal trafficking, illegal selling for years," says Adam Ramsey, a reporter based in Bangkok. "So it's actually more of a question of, why did it take so long?"…
>
> "The veterinarian in charge used to cremate any tiger cubs that died because a lot of tiger cubs die, even in captivity. I think it's about one in three," says Ramsey. "But when the Tiger Temple started being accused of trafficking in tiger cubs the veterinarian changed the policy. They now freeze them, in part to prove that they're not selling tiger cubs on the black market. So it was meant to act as proof that, no, these tigers died naturally and we still have their bodies just in case you thought that we sold them off."
>
> But three days into the operation, that explanation seemed to fall apart. On Thursday, Thai police stopped a truck as it was leaving the Tiger Temple. Inside they found two complete tiger skins, about 700 amulets made from tiger parts and 10 tiger teeth. The two men in the truck were arrested and charged with possession of illegal wildlife. A monk was also detained.
>
> The tigers have all been evacuated from the temple and the monks are finally facing punishment, but I want to make it clear that so many volunteers at the temple over the years, like me, truly loved the tigers and had no idea of the corruption behind the scenes. Many honest true-hearted people

volunteered there because they have a passion for tigers, but now we're learning that passion must revolve around justice.

"Kick That Leg, Aunt Rue!"

And now I'm spilling the next secret: Tiger Soul Secret Number Two. Shortly after I returned from Thailand, I encountered another humiliating man-made smoke screen, when I decided to move to London. This came just on the heels of my disaster at the Tiger Temple and was perhaps a lesson that karma put in my path as payback, or maybe I simply deserved it to learn that the headstrong bulldozer technique I was employing in my life no longer, or never, worked.

For months, I had been emailing the manager of a flat in London that I had found on a beautiful website publicizing properties for rent associated with some of London's most beautiful hotels. When the manager asked for a bank transfer up front to pay for the flat I was renting for five months for myself and my two cats, Doc and Virginia Sue Ann — whom I was flying from Los Angeles to London — I fulfilled the request because B and Bs and safari parks where I'd stayed in Africa often also require bank transfers to secure the reservation. The man on the other end of the email even offered to pick me up at the airport and collect me and my cats to personally give me the keys and drive me to my gorgeous new flat in Mayfair. I moved the money. When there was suddenly something wrong with the transaction and that bank account was closed, I was asked to repeat the transaction (divine intervention trying to get my attention!). I tried to move the money a second time. I had a few doubts about the property manager I was emailing, so I had a student in London call him personally. I was relieved when she called to tell me that he had answered the phone; she also said that he didn't seem to speak good English. At least he answered the phone. And the second-language issue would explain why the emails were filled with misspelled words. My student thought this man might be East Indian.

I hopped through extensive, expensive hoops to get the airplane tickets and meet all the requirements to move the cats. The measures were exhausting, and I admit that I must have moved into a "damned if anybody's going to stop me" mode. I sold my BMW. I sold my piano. I gave up my apartment and gave away everything I owned that didn't fit in two suitcases. Three days before we were to move, I had sold my kitchen table and it was being carried out the front door when I checked the Realtor's site in London and saw the notice, "Phishing site taken down by Scotland Yard." Gulp. The man was not East Indian. He was African, and he was most likely operating out of an "office" in Nairobi where dozens of men sat all day trying to sucker stupid Americans into transferring money into bank accounts for fictitious real estate companies. The bomb had dropped. What a bang! My money was gone! My cats and I had no place to live!

A downward spiral had started when I turned my back on my beloved tigers, and that spiral would continue to plummet hell-bound for years. I somehow muscled through this heartbreak and got myself and my cats on a plane to London, even after my application for a British visa was turned down. Bad move. I'm not telling you this simply to make myself look like an idiot, which I certainly felt like at the time. I'm telling you this story so that we can see what happens when we don't use our intuition, and perhaps why we don't listen to our intuition when we should.

Internet scams were in their infancy when this happened back in 2009, but since then, they have become increasingly rampant, and even now this kind of deceit is commonplace. We must take a look at the ugly truth of what happens when our antennae don't go up — and why. I'm a professional psychic, so this snafu was like having the devil drop in for tea. I had just encountered one of the biggest hoodwinks I'd ever seen — monks smuggling tigers — and my antennae didn't go up when they should have. Now trickery and deceit had knocked on my door, and they cleaned out my bank account. Why did I not act on my instincts when in my heart of hearts I knew that this luscious apartment in the poshest part of London was too good to be true at the price at which it was offered? I wanted my apartment in Mayfair to be real. I wanted to believe that I would undoubtedly get a British visa so that my cats and I could stay for years. I desperately wanted my deluded fantasy to be real, but everything I had was gone. My aspirations had blown up in my face, and the process of getting on that plane was too far along to try to stop it. After a dastardly difficult summer in London juggling flats and B and Bs with my cats, I was finally able to leave them in safe hands in London and fly on down to Africa to teach and visit my lion friends.

My B plan, sans the ability to get the right visa in England, was to move to New York City and spend the rest of my life with my favorite aunt. I'd lived the majority of my life in blistering-hot Hollywood and had always had fantasies about the East Coast. I had romantic visions of wearing stylish boots and coats with matching scarves, of falling in love under flame-colored autumn leaves in Central Park, and of being accepted with open arms into a warm, friendly community of locals who would gather at night in a pub in front of a roaring fire and tell jokes and laugh about their problems. I'd watched too many reruns of *Cheers*.

But most of all, I wanted to take Manhattan by storm under the wing of my favorite auntie, who had been inviting me for years to fly up and join her when she went to parties hosted by Liza Minnelli or lunched with Olivia Newton-John. Tell me there's one of you out there who would say no to that! At this time, Rue had been starring on Broadway in *Wicked* and taking the most punishing pratfalls onstage — hers was an extremely physical role, but even as a septuagenarian she never complained. (We are of hearty Scotch-Irish and Cherokee stock.) And she was in the process of making a deal to star in a new sitcom for the gay channel in Hawaii. She showed no sign of slowing down! In my mind, she was the Unsinkable Molly Brown.

So I flew the cats to New York, where they were graciously taken in by one of my favorite students, awaiting my arrival in the Big Apple. I made it as far as a crummy hotel in New Jersey when I got the news that Rue was in the hospital having open-heart surgery. Five days later she had a stroke.

I arrived at the hospital that night a hysterical wreck. I was so disoriented and grief-stricken that I'd been lost on subways and light rails for three and a half hours. I made every conceivable mistake trying to get from Hoboken, New Jersey, to the hospital in Manhattan — so much so that when I realized I'd picked the fourth subway going in the wrong direction, I finally turned to the person next to me and just broke down, begging, "My aunt's in the hospital. She was on a show called *The Golden Girls*? Can you help me?"

Hours later I finally got there and had with me photos of lions and tigers. Somehow I had summoned the good sense to bring these pictures from my travels. My favorite cousin, Rue's talented son, Mark, was in the air, flying in from Austin, Texas, where he had caught the red-eye with no luggage. He arrived that night, wild-eyed. We sat together praying in the waiting room, where the nurses came in to tell us the horrific news. Rue's entire right side was paralyzed, and if she didn't move it in the next twenty-four hours, she'd never move it again.

When we went into her room in the ICU, we saw that the doctors had knocked out one of her front teeth when they crammed the intubation tube down her windpipe. My beautiful aunt wasn't recognizable when I found her unconscious in the bed that night. She was swollen and white, and not looking human. She was barely alive.

From time to time, a nurse would come in, pick up her limp right hand, and whisper, "Rue, can you squeeze my hand?" There was no response. Then they would say, "Rue, can you move your foot?" Nothing. Her right leg was limp and the nerves were dying. The doctor continued with more bad news: When they removed the tube from her throat the next morning, if she didn't speak immediately, she would never talk again, and they had no way of knowing if she would lose her capacity for speech permanently.

Now, my aunt Rue made her living giving speeches at charity events (most of them for animal charities), and she was a right-handed lady and had used this hand to sign countless autographs for throngs of adoring fans. But first and foremost, she was a talker. She'd taken elocution lessons throughout her life and still did summer stock, starring in theatrical productions even for free. Her love for words and grasp of the English language was her passion. If she lost her capacity to speak — which was unthinkable — her only way to communicate would be through writing notes with her right hand. Losing her ability to speak *and* write was simply out of the question. She'd have no way to communicate, and she'd also be limited to a wheelchair for the rest of her life. This was "not on" with me. She hadn't reacted at all to Mark or me when we said things like "Rue, can you hear me? Squeeze your hand if you can hear me! Blink your eyes if you know we're here!" Nothing was working. We were losing the battle.

Late into the night, after Mark and I had prayed every prayer we could think of and done every meditation we knew to do, and Rue showed no signs of waking up, Mark went back to a friend's apartment to collapse. I persuaded the nurses to leave me alone with her for a while.

Remember that a sweet "Rue, can you squeeze my hand?" spoken in irritating baby talk did not work with my spitfire aunt; nor did "Rue, can you move your foot?" cooed in scared gentle tones by a nurse who didn't know her. I knew her. They didn't. And it was time to take a risk.

I knew she loved tigers. And I knew she was *an actress,* so I had some ammunition these nurses didn't have. I asked for some tape.

I taped eight-by-ten photos of tigers to all the walls, and pictures of me walking tigers and snuggling tigers. I'd carried these photos around with me from country to country ever since I got back from the treacherous Tiger Temple. I also taped up some photos of African lions I know and love, and for good measure, I taped up a photo of Jesus Christ. Rue had always been an atheist, having preferred the company of New York intellectuals most of her life, and she had once said to me, "Mimi, what I admire most about you is your relationship with God. I've never had that."

Well, the time had come to change that, too. Now, I also am an actress and dancer who loves tigers, and my patient was a dying actress who danced and loved tigers, so the course of action simply fell into place. Plus, I'd just been at a lion camp in Africa where I'd been shape-shifting with a local shaman who taught me how to shapeshift into a lion. The velocity and amplitude of your energy expand tenfold when you take on the spirit and physical characteristics of a wild animal, especially a ferocious one, and this disaster called for ferocious measures. It was three AM and the clock was ticking. If she didn't move her right arm and leg in the next few hours, she would never move them again. She was unconscious and not even blinking, no matter what I said. She'd been comatose for hours when my body automatically started to shape-shift into a lion. I felt my throat start to rumble as I repressed a roar. It's not something you want to do in public in America, especially not in a Manhattan hospital where they could easily just move me to the psych ward. But there was no one in the room but us, so I decided to let it roll.

I swallowed the sound and gathered the roaring power that was rising up through my body like a wildfire. Then I took the transformation to an even higher octave, to match the frequency of the most sophisticated design on the planet: the embodiment of grace, power, and beauty; the guardian of the gates between life and death — the tiger. I channeled as much of this power into my human form as I possibly could, using the photos of the tigers to fuel me. I'd taped the photos at eye level for her in case she came out of unconscious-ness and opened her eyes. I remembered my tiger friends and prayed to them to help.

I roared at her, "Rue! You are not human anymore! You are a *tiger*! You're a *tiger*, Rue!" Grabbing her limp hand, I pawed at it and screamed, "That's not an *arm*! It's a *paw*! You're going to reach out and *scratch*! You have *claws* now! You're a *tiger*, Rue! You're going to reach out and scratch! Flex your claws and *scratch*!"

She moved her right hand, suddenly mimicking the movement of a cat flexing her claws. It worked! She could hear me! I decided to keep going and work on her leg. I was in a delirious frenzy, shouting at her and rearing back, arching over her like a tiger about to pounce on its prey.

"Rue, that's not a *leg*! It's a *paw*! We're going to climb a tree! You're going to rear back on your haunches and jump! Climb the tree, Rue! Jump! Squat down, rear back, and *jump*! *Kick that leg, Aunt Rue!*"

She kicked her right leg in the air! Not a little nudge but a fierce high kick! It was the buoyant high kick of a can-can dancer, and this was a moment of triumph I'll never forget. Unfortunately, she was still unconscious, so it was a moment she'd never remember. But I proceeded as if she could hear me, because conscious or not, now I *knew* she could!

I spent the next couple of hours with her, saying repeatedly and with great authority, "Rue, when they take that tube out of your mouth, you're going to *speak perfectly*! You will speak perfectly! Your mouth will move perfectly! Your right side will work perfectly! You'll be able to write and sign autographs, and you'll be able to talk as if nothing had ever happened. God will restore your body to perfect health!"

I stayed up all night talking to her about what to expect when she awoke the next day, even though she gave me no further indication that she could hear me. At six AM I dragged myself home to my depressing apartment in New Jersey, collapsed into bed with my chocolate Persian, Doc, and then fell apart and cried, finally safe in his furry embrace.

When Rue woke up the next morning, the doctors removed the tube from her throat and she could talk. She had no recollection of my being in the room the previous night, but she already had limited mobility in her right hand and foot. We embarked on an ugly period in our lives, where she spent eighty-three days in the hospital and I trekked back and forth, miserable in the snow, rain, and slush, from freezing New Jersey to expensive Manhattan, running up cab fares and praying for some light at the end of the tunnel. But she was alive, so God had heard my prayer.

The highlight of the year was bittersweet. One day I arrived at her hospital room ill. This woman who had been an adamant atheist her entire life shouted at me to get on my knees in front of the photo of Jesus, now a permanent fixture in her hospital room, and pray to Him. A purely sweet celebration followed when she came home to her gorgeous apartment in Manhattan just before Easter, and although she wasn't well enough to join me in church that Sunday, she threw a small party for family and friends, and she herself led the group in prayer before our Easter lunch. I was having a big bowl of gratitude, and she was serving a huge platter of atheist-no-more.

Tiger soul and a newfound belief in God had saved her life and restored her body, but I wonder if she may have died the night I found her in a coma if my saviors hadn't delivered me to her hospital room. A little love goes a long way. And this story opens an entire conversation for doctors, nurses, and concerned family members about the nature of healing. Once again it comes back to my work with nonverbal communication, but this time with a human, not an animal, because I knew how to speak the patient's language. Were that bed occupied by my father, who is an aircraft designer, I would bring in a balsa-wood airplane kit and ask him to build it. Were it my brilliant mother, who is among other things a concert-level pianist, I'd bring in a keyboard and ask her to play Bach's Minuet in C. Were it Dr. Bernie Siegel, I'd hand him a paintbrush, because oil painting is his favorite hobby. If your loved one is a golf lover, you might ask him to demonstrate his winning swing, or if she was a ballroom dancer, you might put on her favorite music and ask her to waltz. For a paralyzed little boy who played basketball, I'd bring a basketball into the room, toss it, and ask him to catch it and throw it back. The concept is to involve the passion of the patient in his or her physical therapy to initiate a turning point in the healing process. Most important, if the patient is an animal lover, short of bringing his or her family pets into the hospital room, the substitute could be the "shape-shift," where we borrow the power and spirit of the animals we love in our times of crisis. We can achieve great things just by pretending to be a dog, a frog, an elephant, or a tiger.

Of course, I'm one of the world's biggest advocates of pet-assisted therapy, and I know for a fact that bringing live animals into hospitals can comfort patients and even save lives. Many studies have been done by maverick doctors like my magnificent friends Dr. Bernie Siegel and Dr. Larry Dossey, proving that when animals are present in the hospital room, the patient experiences less blood loss, recovers more quickly, and is less likely to go into shock. People who have animals at home have been shown to spend less time in the hospital because they want to rush home to their animals. Were their animals allowed in the hospital rooms, I'm certain that recovery times would decrease even more. Hearts would open and bodies would heal. Animals can regulate our blood pressure, heartbeat, and brainwaves. The master healers of these mysterious processes are cats. But because my cat Doc would never be allowed into the ICU, I opted for the photos of the big cats instead. The tigers gave Aunt Rue another nine months with me and the people she loved. But the people she loved couldn't save her. It took her love for tigers to bring her back.

Rue and I shared a magical spring, filled with many warm moments and intimate conversations. She still couldn't walk easily, so we'd meet on the couch, watching National Geographic shows about animals, science, nature, and ancient aliens, and, of course, laughing at a lot of television comedies too, before she finally succumbed to the fates and had yet another stroke. In those final months of her life, she had panic attacks when she tried to lie down, and the only thing that could make her laugh was my impression of a frog. I'd crouch on a footstool in front of her, bulging out my eyes and cheeks, and she'd tease me, "Mimi, *that's* not a frog!" Then she'd bug out her eyes and cheeks in the funniest, most distorted ways, and I'd howl with laughter. I'd stick out my tongue, whipping it around pretending to catch flies. She'd howl back. That's what I remember — peals of laughter, once again shape-shifting into animals to entertain ourselves. The tigers created a lifeline, but the frogs only created more laugh lines. When I ran out of frog impressions, I'd dance around the couch, where she sat bored all day because she could barely stand or walk, and I'd pretend to be an exotic fish. I'd flap my fins and scoot through the water, opening and closing my mouth slowly like a largemouth bass. I think she liked the frog better.

When she finally had the stroke that destroyed her beautiful brain and body, I was still in America about to embark on my annual European tour. My mother had flown in, and so had Rue's best friend, Sue Vacarro. Fortunately, my shrewd mother had power of attorney, but she was faced with the harrowing task of determining — along with Rue's son — when the time would come that Rue would never recover. We three women — my mother, Sue, and I — held hands over Rue's body, weeping, praying, and saying goodbye. I called the archangels, releasing her spirit into the Light and into the arms of her Lord and Savior, Jesus Christ. Do you think He heard me? Do you think she heard me? I think they both did. The king of the jungle had given her new life. The King of the angels gave her eternal life.

And to this day, even visiting Africa, where I'm leading my annual safaris, I have frog jokes and stuffed frogs and even live frogs show up everywhere I go, surprising me, making me squeal with laughter, and reminding me that my favorite aunt is watching me from heaven, guiding my efforts to educate children and rescue endangered species. I had a tree frog pop up out of my suitcase even this morning like a jack-in-the-box as I tried to get dressed for my safari in the darkness before the first morning light.

"Rue, is that you?" I asked. Rue was an animal lover, an animal activist, and a great lover of funny stories. I feel her standing behind my left shoulder, championing me as I write this book. And the naughtiest Golden Girl, the tigress, might even be watching you now as you read it.

Rue proved that tiger medicine is real, and it was tiger medicine that was her salvation. But this is the true brand of tiger medicine, where we connect to their infinite spirits and allow their strength to heal us. We don't need to murder and dissect them, making them into tiny pills that we can eat. And the idea of allowing anyone to slaughter and eat tigers, and the fallacy that there's nothing anyone can do to stop it, is an idea that none of us should continue to swallow.

Eat them? That's right. Eat them. Tigers will be extinct from this planet in the next two to five years if we don't act fast. Why? Some Chinese people are eating them. In traditional Chinese medicine, "tiger medicine" is thought to be the most powerful cure-all, and some Chinese "doctors" have assigned a medicinal value to every inch of God's masterpiece, from their bones to their whiskers to their tails. Every ounce of the tigers, even their internal organs, is thought to have medicinal value. If you go online to search, you will find many heinous pictures of half a tiger with her entire lower body sliced off, or you may find piles of tiger limbs dissected into pieces. Be braced for these atrocities. I was so shocked and horrified at these images that I was immediately reduced to floods of furious tears. There are many images of live tigers being tortured as well.

The very idea that these tigers are being decimated and dissected in order to be *eaten* is a concept so grotesque, it is incomprehensible that this can be happening in our "civilized" world. How can we as inhabitants of the earth allow this to occur? If you're a cat lover, prepare to be devastated and then, hopefully, outraged. If there is a "devil," he is busy at work, but we must no longer let him dominate our world and have the final say on how we treat our planet's animals. I've told you first the fun story about my brand of "tiger medicine." Unfortunately, now we have to address the real issue. Go get a box of tissues.

TIGERS: THE FACTS

Tigers are very difficult to count because of their movements and elusive nature. I reached out to TRAFFIC, in London, where Dr. Richard Thomas, the organization's global communications coordinator, was kind enough to get back to me and help me research the latest facts. He directed me to CITES, the very organization that had contacted me to take any promotion of the Tiger Temple off of my website when I returned from my fiasco in Thailand. I hope in some small way that I can help them now when I failed to do so in the past.

Habitat Loss

Once found across Asia, from Turkey to eastern Russia, tigers over the past century have disappeared from Southwest and Central Asia, from Java and Bali in Indonesia, and from large parts of Southeast and East Asia. Tigers have lost 93 percent of their historic range, and more than 40 percent of their range in the past decade.

Poaching

In the early 1990s, trade in tiger parts was banned worldwide, but tigers remain in serious danger from illegal wildlife trade — poaching — mainly for their bones, used in traditional Asian medicines, and for their pelts and other body parts, such as teeth, skin, and claws, sold as decorative items.

Many tigers are also killed because of human–animal conflicts — when people seek to protect life and livestock. A recent TRAFFIC survey found body parts from an estimated twenty-three tigers on sale in Sumatra, where the critically endangered population of tigers is believed to number fewer than five hundred animals — the last tigers left in Indonesia. In China, several operations are engaged in intensive breeding ("farming") of tigers. The owners of such farms are pressuring the government to allow them to produce tiger products. At the fourteenth Conference of the Parties to CITES, delegates called for an end to tiger farming.

Market surveys by TRAFFIC indicate that medicinal use of tiger bone has decreased since China banned the sale of tiger bone in 1993, but any lifting of the tiger trade ban would spell disaster for wild tigers. It would fuel demand for tiger parts, which would be far cheaper to obtain through poaching than from captive-bred animals. The captive tiger population in China is around five thousand animals; a similar number exists in the United States.

Tigers are listed in Appendix 1 of CITES, which bans all international trade, and all tiger-range states and countries with consumer markets have banned domestic trade, too. However, domestic legislation is weak or nonexistent in some countries, notably the United States, where a 2008 TRAFFIC North America report, *Paper Tigers? The Role of the U.S. Captive Tiger Population in the Trade in Tiger Parts*, found that the government has no way of knowing how many tigers are in captivity, where they are, who owns them, or what happens to their body parts when they die.

TIGER SMUGGLERS BEWARE!

According to an article published on www.traffic.org entitled "CITES Turns Up the Heat on Tiger Smugglers," on March 14, 2013,

> A new international law enforcement initiative to stop the poaching and illegal trade of Tigers and other Asian big cats was signed by the member countries of the Convention on International Trade in Endangered Species of Wild Fauna and Flora (CITES) meeting in Bangkok today.
>
> Agreement was reached to gather information on incidents of poaching and illegal trade in all Asian big cats since the beginning of 2010 and to analyse the information for circulation to relevant enforcement agencies and range States.
>
> The CITES members also agreed to monitor efforts to close down the illegal Tiger trade....
>
> Last week, TRAFFIC, in collaboration with WWF [the World Wildlife Fund], launched *Reduced to Skin and Bones Revisited*, a report analysing Tiger part seizures across 12 of the 13 range States for Tigers. The report found that between 2000 and 2012, there were 654 seizures of tiger parts in Tiger Range States, corresponding to 1,425 animals; an average of 110 tigers killed per year. Crucially, the report illustrates how detailed information on seizures can help pinpoint trade "hotspots," with obvious potential for improved law enforcement efforts.
>
> "Although some countries were frustrated by the brevity of discussions on Asian big cat issues during the agenda,

the meeting nevertheless came up with some important measures to reinforce efforts to close down the underground,
illicit trafficking of tigers," said Natalia Pervushina, TRAF-
FIC and WWF's Tiger Trade Programme Officer.

Let me summarize some of the facts for you: There were origi-
nally nine subspecies of tigers, on the basis of distinctive molecular
markers. Three subspecies have been hunted to extinction and eaten.

That's right. Not soon to be extinct if we don't do something.
They are extinct. The Bali tiger, the Javan tiger, the Caspian tiger,
and most likely the South China tiger have officially left the planet.
They are gone forever. We have failed them.

Tigers are being farmed through extensive overbreeding in captivity so that they can be slaughtered brutally and their body parts
made into "tiger wine." Although the roughly five thousand tigers
in captivity in the United States may be compromised in cramped
cages, they are not going to be eaten. The roughly five thousand tigers being farmed in China are in great peril. I don't need to tell you
that there are tears in my eyes as I write this. And if you love tigers,
there will very likely be tears in your eyes as you read this, but I urge
you to stay with me. Hold my hand. Let's do this together.

The Sumatran, Bengal, Indochinese, Amur, and Malayan tigers
are soon to follow the three extinct subspecies unless we take dras-
tic measures to protect them. We must not fail them. We must regain
some sanctity and sanity in our lives and in our world. Come with me.
I can't do this by myself. I need your help. Take a breath and read on.

The following comes from the "Panthera tigris" page of the
IUCN Red List of Threatened Species:

The Tiger is listed as Endangered under criterion A2abcd.
Comparing a breeding recent range estimate to a 2006 total
range estimate suggests a range decline much greater than
50%.... In 1998, the global Tiger population was estimated

This book belongs to:

oo Tigers (Seidensticker *et al.* 1999). A com-
se population estimates of the 1990s…sug-
of about 50 percent (taking the upper bound
number of mature individuals in 1993, using
ry approach, declining to approximately 3,500
is clear that there have been substantial popu-
s, with Tigers all but eliminated from much of
rest range, particularly in Southeast Asia….
ne has long been considered to hold anti-
properties, with some support from Chinese
rch, but many consider the effect to be more
than pharmacological (Nowell and Xu 2007).
countries have banned use and manufacture
e, illegal production persists in several Asian
pecially in China, Malaysia, and Viet Nam
). In China, there are several operations en-
1sive breeding ("farming" of Tigers), with the
ation reportedly reaching over 6,000. They are
e government to allow them to produce Tiger
1 several have already engaged in illegal pro-
iger bone wine…. Tiger farming perpetuates
s to re-ignite consumer demand (Nowell and
1 2008 the Convention on International Trade
ed Species (CITES) adopted a Decision stating
should not be bred for trade in their parts and
(CITES 2008)….Interdictions represent just
the true level of illegal trade, indicating that
avely imperiled by black market demand.

ENTER THE STARGATE

Are we humans so afraid of the world's most sophisticated killing
machine, but also the world's most gorgeous, adorable magus, that

the presence of the king brings out all the fears and insecurities of the human race? Are we going to massacre the entire species because we devalue them so drastically? On some deep level, humans know that tigers have power and that "tiger medicine" should have a role in human consciousness, but I like my brand of tiger medicine better — one that honors and protects these playful creatures who have the right to be healthy, happy, and free. And I'm sure my aunt Rue would agree.

The challenge remains for humans to help these tigers become independent of human tyranny, stupidity, and destruction. Wracking my brain day and night, I still had a lot of questions that needed to be answered.

So in order to find the right subject to interview, I flew to Johannesburg to visit their zoo. I walked to the Johannesburg Zoo from my nearby B and B this morning to see if the tigers there could shine a light on what they want to convey to the human race. I was dismayed to find no tigers in the enclosure, when suddenly I saw the flash of stripes as a tiger disappeared through a door into a wooden structure. Fortunately, there is an underground viewing station, where I sat patiently looking into a bleak concrete room, sending an invitation for the tiger to come see me. When she appeared, I was thrilled.

I must backtrack here for a moment and admit that I'd been sending the thoughts out in advance of my visit all morning as I made the long trek across my beloved Zoo Lake and Zoo Lake Park to reach the zoo. And I must also admit that something bizarre had already changed in my perception when I entered the zoo.

I work with local African children in my charity, Ark Angel, where I go into schools in the bush in rural communities in Africa to talk to the kids about wildlife and animals' feelings so that the children don't grow up to be poachers. The Chinese illegal tiger trade for Chinese "medicine" is so appallingly out of control and unregulated that now even *lions* — most bottle-fed and bred in captivity so that they'll be docile — are being poached here in Africa and their bones are being passed off as tiger bones. So educating these children about the thoughts, feelings, relationships, and rights of lions and elephants does, in an indirect way, raise awareness about the escalating tiger poaching trade. I love this work in the schools to the exclusion of all else, and being with these impoverished children fulfills me in a way that is beyond words, second only to the rewarding sense of all-encompassing pleasure I feel when I'm alone with the wild animals themselves.

These bright-eyed, bright-minded children have a special place in my heart, so I'm shamelessly partial to them. But as I entered the zoo and was met with a horde of squealing African children in school uniforms, I looked at them and felt something I had never felt before. I was irritated by their presence and cringing at their high-pitched screams. This is not the way I have ever felt about these glowing children before, and I realized the oddness, the strangeness, in the way I was viewing them — as if they were utterly revolting. It was then that I happened upon two lions trying to sleep out in the open, surrounded by three groups of schoolchildren rampaging in the zoo with ear-shattering, high-pitched voices, and I realized that I had left my normal human reality behind and was already shape-shifting into the perspective of the big cats.

Now I'm a big supporter of the Johannesburg Zoo, and I've even taken *Carte Blanche*, Africa's most hard-hitting news program, into this zoo when they filmed a special on my work. In that clip, I brought a few precious African children with me on our telepathing tour of the zoo to allow *Carte Blanche* to film the children as they learned how to "talk" to the animals. I didn't speak to the tigers in the filming of this episode, and I had never even met them yet.

I negotiated a dating problem with a female orangutan who didn't like her new mate; I comforted an aging polar bear who had lost the love of his life; and more tragic still, I worked to try to calm the post-traumatic stress disorder of an orphaned baby rhino who still had open gunshot wounds in her chest. She had witnessed her entire family and community getting murdered by Chinese poachers before the Johannesburg Zoo airlifted her to safety. I tried with all my might to relay feelings of calm, peace, and safety to her, even though she was shell-shocked after the war zone in hell she'd just been through.

On a happier note, the children themselves performed an astonishing communication with an orphaned giraffe. The baby giraffe was standing and cuddling what for all practical purposes looked to be his mother, but despite any appearances or tricks of the logical mind, my troupe of little psychic whiz kids agreed that the big female he was bonded with was *not* his mother, but his aunt! When asked where his mother was, one of the children said, "Loose in the jungle." Another said, "She's dead." And what a perfect description of giraffe heaven "loose in the jungle" must be. The keeper confirmed that the big female was indeed the baby's aunt, not his mother, and that his mother had recently died. The children were not told this information in advance. They tuned in and attained the visions and feelings through their own innate equipment — a clairvoyance that had not been tempered by shame, mockery, and grown-up sensibilities... yet. The children were demonstrating their independence, by showing the world that they could defy socially accepted outgrown belief systems and think for themselves.

So I already knew the giraffes in this zoo, the rhino, the lions, and the orangutans, but I couldn't recall how many tigers were kept at this zoo because I had never worked with them before.

It'd been a couple of years since I'd visited this zoo, so I was honored when the female tiger consented to take this meeting with me. When I asked if she had a mate, she told me that she had a huge male husband and that he was hiding and sleeping. I sat for an hour in front of the glass, but I never saw him. She paraded in and out of the enclosure in front of me, cringing slightly whenever a tourist appeared behind me with a screaming toddler, and I hushed the children and even the howling adults by holding my finger to my mouth and saying, "Shhh! We must be quiet around big cats! If you are noisy, they will run away." It was amazing how well this worked with both the children and also the adults, who were pushing each other out of the way to snap a photo of this tiger with their cell phones.

Somehow, though, the crowds magically subsided, and as if in a dream, she and I were alone for almost an hour, uninterrupted, in silence and peace that couldn't have happened any more completely than if the zoo had been closed and I'd been the only person there. I asked her what she wanted me to tell you in this book. She wouldn't answer and just paced in and out, out and in, in and out of this concrete enclosure as if she had lost her mind. Finally, I started singing her a love song. She stopped pacing and sprayed the wall in front of me. The sound that tigers make when they're happy and they greet another tiger (or human) they love is called a *chuff*. It's not a roar and not a purr, but somewhere in between. I chuffed her. She chuffed me back.

So some sort of relationship was starting between us, but it was in a realm of energy so sublime that there were no words. I kept asking again and again, "What should I write?" I begged her to tell me what she wanted to say to the humans, but she and I were operating in a dimension where words don't exist, perhaps because they aren't necessary. The love is so deep, it transcends the need to name or describe anything. Finally, she climbed a table in front of me, flopped down, and luxuriated right there, licking her paws. I sang to her softly, "I know, baby, I know...I know I could be so...in love...with you..." And she gave me the most delicious flirty eyelash-batting gazes, then turned her head upside down. Something was happening, but there were no answers to my questions. I was about to walk away, totally let down. I said good-bye to her and left the viewing station for the path up the hill. But something told me to stop. I stopped by a guardrail and looked back into the enclosure. There, only a few feet from me, was another female tiger, studying me intently. I started singing my love song to her. "Baby, I know... I know... I could be so in love with you..."

I told her I needed to write this book and didn't know how to present any of the tragedy in an informative light, much less a positive one. I asked her if she knew of the dire straits her fellow tigers were in, and if she knew that tigers are almost extinct from this planet.

"Of course, Amelia," she said! I was pretty amazed that she knew my name. "They can't kill us."

"What do you mean? They *are* killing you!!

"They can kill our bodies but not our souls. We can evacuate the planet. We can have no physical bodies here at all. But there will always be *tigers*. Tigers are indestructible. We are everywhere. Tiger Soul is not destructible."

I had an epiphany that is not easy to describe, and it's very bold of me to present this in the first chapter of this book. But it reminded me of my last conversation of this magnitude with another famous king of the jungle, and I don't mean John Varty, the infamous and controversial big-cat conservationist I'd been following on TV for most of my life. I mean one of his tigers.

Last year, I took a meeting with a tiger named Corbett, who had shredded and almost killed John. I flew up to Tiger Canyons, JV's African tiger sanctuary in the Free State, at his request to "read" Corbett after Corbett had put John in intensive care, where he almost died. John emailed me from the ICU, asking me to speak to Corbett, even though John and I had never even spoken on the phone, much less met. At that time, Corbett's life was in danger, because John was asking the world — challenging the world — whether he should have Corbett euthanized after the brutal attack. I begged JV to spare Corbett's life, and I tuned in to Corbett to hear his side of the story.

What happened when I met with Corbett was something so magical, I couldn't even tell JV. After a global outcry on the tiger's behalf, JV decided to let Corbett live, so I flew up to Tiger Canyons to meet Corbett face-to-furry-face.

In short, Corbett told me he had attacked John because he deserved it, a fact that I don't doubt for a minute. Having spent some time with JV, I know the feeling. He is the kind of man you love to hate, but love nonetheless. This was nothing new to me, but Corbett was about to dish out some fairy-tale wizardry, some metaphysical mastery that was so new, it would change the way I viewed tigers and all earthly reality forever.

High on the hilltop framed by the fiery African sunset, I spotted the wild, angry tiger who had been dismissed as violent and unmanageable. He's a dominant male, and he's very large, so his Sphinx-like profile on a high rock in the distance was so royal, my heart almost stopped. I asked him to come down and see me, and here he came.

There's a feeling I have when a wild tiger is approaching me to talk. It's somewhere between an orgasm and a prayer. I feel an internal symphony of joy mounting up and crashing through every cell in my body. It's as if every atom in my being starts to sing. As the stealthy tiger came down from his throne, high on the rock, I said to him, "I love you, I love everything about you, I love your ferocity, I love your gentleness, I love your wildness, I love your ability to give me tender cheek rubs through the fence."

And boy, did he crave those cheek rubs, too. Did he try to kill me? No. But I gave him something he wasn't getting anywhere else: respect. I honored the God within him, the Holy Spirit that shines through him, his ability and need and even *right* to be an individual who has feelings, including anger, including temper, just like his human father…but that's another story.

I said to this ferocious tiger, "I love you. I honor you. I get it. I dig you. I dig everything about you. I'll side with you no matter what the humans think. John's not going to kill you. He'd have to kill me first. Are you okay?"

His *grrrr* turned to a chuff. The monster disappeared, and in its place was six hundred pounds of purring, smiling, irresistible warm cuddly pumpkin-striped fluff. Suddenly, I entered an altered state of consciousness, and in this trance, we were in motion. The world around me dissolved, and everything I'd ever known imploded. I found myself in a wormhole. A world of spinning sound, of blinding color, where love takes you on a journey that explodes space and time.

The fact that this elusive tiger — furious with the human race — came racing down from his high perch on a mountaintop when I called him and cuddled at my feet was already magical enough, but now looking at him made me so dizzy, I could barely stand up. He seemed to be able to pull me into him in a way that I had never experienced before, and I feared that if I gave in to the seduction, my body would disappear completely. I fought to steady myself and pull myself out of this interdimensional vortex.

We chatted about normal things, about how he wanted a larger enclosure and how much he wanted a mate. When I posed the request to JV, he was nervous that this — his most violent and unpredictable tiger — would kill a mate were she introduced. Corbett insisted that he wouldn't harm her, were he given a wife to love.

I was able to lobby for Corbett's life and dignity, and translate his needs to JV, which was frankly more magical still — not that I could do it, but that JV would listen. The upshot of the visit manifested later in the year when JV got Corbett a girlfriend and a larger enclosure at my request. As of this writing, Corbett is now a very happy cat.

These masters of illusion are the magus spirits of this universe, as I was about to discover. As I stood in front of this tigress, having this otherworldly conversation with her, lost in trance, spinning through a vortex of unspeakable love, dissolved in a matrix of frozen light, suddenly the squawk of a tourist behind me broke our sacred spell.

"Where's the tiger?!" this horrible female voice screeched.

"I don't see one!" a male voice bellowed back.

"But I want to see the tiiii-ger!" the goose voice insisted.

Now, granted I was standing right in front of the tigress, and although I'd been eating too well on this tour and had the muffin tops to prove it, even my muffin tops and me were not wide enough to block a gigantic Siberian tigress from the view of a prying tourist leaning over my shoulder. I sent the thought to the tigress, "Can you make them disappear?"

And then the magic happened. There was a flicker of orange fire, and the tigress and I slipped even deeper into our hypnotic daydream, eyes locked, breathless. We were frozen, in love, outside of space and time. We were together in eternity in a place where nothing and no one else existed. The tigress took me deeper into the void. The obnoxious voice continued, "Where are the tigers? Aren't there any tigers in this enclosure?"

The voice was in my ear. The woman was looking directly at my tiger. The man's voice boomed in my other ear. "I don't see any!" He was looking directly at my tiger from over my other shoulder. After a beat, he concluded, "They must be hiding. I can't see any tigers in here."

Eventually the "Muggles" scuffled off down the hill behind me. I had never broken my gaze from the tigress, who loomed in front of me. We were lost in a wrinkle in time. I felt something shift ever so slightly, and I took a breath. We were back.

"We're the ultimate reality," she said.

"What is the reality? You mean the tiger design? You're the most powerful design in an eternal cosmic library?"

"We are power itself. No human can kill power. They can try to overpower us. But we exist. We will always exist."

"Listen, you! I'm trying to write a book about how to save you guys, and I'm going up against serious scientists who don't believe in any of this tomfoolery! What am I supposed to say? And all of my readers want to save you, and I don't know what to tell them! I already feel stupid enough, and now all you can do is make a fool out of me? I can't tell them that you spout philosophy and play interdimensional peekaboo! I'm trying to write a serious book about conservation, not the next episode of *Star Wars*!"

"See the bigger picture," she said. Suddenly I had a vision of Christ ascending from the tomb. The humans killed His body, but no one had succeeded in killing His spirit. The Christ consciousness cannot be killed. And apparently, tiger consciousness can't, either.

"That's the last thing on earth I can say to the people who love you! We all know you're about to be extinct. What few of you left are already in cages!"

"If I explained it to you, you wouldn't understand. I'm not the one in the cage, Amelia." She showed me a scene of my life back in Los Angeles, struggling through the concrete jungle, braving the freeways in the confines of a little metal car, with all the drivers rushing back to the fortresses they'd built for themselves — their overpriced homes — to protect them from other humans and completely shut out the wild animals.

"The humans are in the cages," she said. "They like to build cages for themselves and everyone else."

Again the vision of smog, steel, pollution, leveled forests, leading to a glimpse of a virtual secondary reality where humans live inside their cell phones and television sets but not out with the animals who need them.

"We won't die, but you will," she said. I then saw a vision of the human race as we know it dying, but a hardworking few would transform into something more beautiful, more evolved. Not all of the humans were going to be able to make the transition from worm to butterfly, but many were well on their way. Tigers, on the other hand, are an absolute truth in the library of creation. They are already perfect in every way, so spiritual evolution for them is unnecessary. We are the little caterpillars struggling toward metamorphosis, who need to turn into butterflies.

I decided to ponder these mysteries on the long walk back to my B and B. I thanked the tigress, sang her one last love song, and slow-blinked her good-bye, but just as I was leaving, she said, "Walk to the other side of the enclosure and look into the window. *He's* waiting for you and wants to say good-bye to you." Following her orders, I walked waaaaaay down the hill to the other side of the enclosure. I stumbled and almost tripped at the sight. What looked like the world's biggest male Siberian tiger was waiting at the window with his nose almost pressed against the glass. In a breathtaking blur of curiosity, his massive head filled the window as he looked for me.

Now, this guy has a totally different personality from the disappearing female, who had held me in a rather menacing gaze. This guy is a six-hundred-pound irresistible beast, and all I wanted to do was get in there with him so that I could hug and kiss his colossal butterscotch mug. Siberian tigers look like Tibetan monks, and some of them have personalities that are suspiciously similar, too. I slow-blinked this gorgeous love machine, and he slow-blinked me back. Then I explained that I was there to take a meeting with him because I was writing this chapter about tigers and now that the humans have killed almost all of the tigers on the planet and they'll be extinct within a couple of years, I needed to get his viewpoint on their endangered status.

He said, "I know!" I braced myself for another magic disappearing act or even some new psychic theatrics, because this tiger looked like he had some serious mojo. This bad boy was one huge cosmic wizard. But he just stood there panting and grinning. He chuffed me. The flirt.

Exasperated, I held my breath.

"Do you have a message for the human race?" I urged him.

"Yes! I do!" he said. Then he turned around and dangled his surprisingly huge furry testicles in my face.

"Tell them to lick my big hairy balls!"

So there it is. Spoken like the true king of the jungle! And I couldn't agree more, I'm afraid. But I have a better idea. Let's begin to educate the children of China so that their generation, then their children, then their children's children can learn to cherish tigers and preserve endangered species in all their glorious forms.

What Do Tigers Represent?

Independence.

What does that mean in your life? For me, independence means mental and emotional sovereignty, especially in affairs of the heart. Achieving true independence means that I don't ever again choose a path that compromises my integrity, and that I never allow corruption to violate my instincts so that I can't hear my own inner voice. My lesson in independence was a harrowing one, where I turned on my own soul, my own "people" (the tigers), in order to try to fit in with the wrong people. Only in the wake of the mistakes I've made can I vow to never step off the path of service and the clarity it brings — even if that is a road I walk alone.

In the Tiger Temple, I had some master teachers try to teach me about independence, to spring me out of the cage. We can't spring the tigers out of their cages until we are freed from our own. Can we be independent thinkers and not listen to the voices of our fathers, mothers, lovers, or peers running in our heads? Can we learn to listen to God's voice instead?

What will I serve when forced to choose between the truth and an inferior set of beliefs? I will choose to leap. I will choose to see through illusions. I will choose faith in myself and all that I have become. I will choose independence.

I know now that the only way to create peace with the world around me and within me is to roar from my authentic true self, a rebellious true self, that must defy the conventions of prior generations even when it is inconvenient. In this spiritual independence, we vow to stay the course steadfastly no matter how desperate situations appear. This kind of independence — this trust in God — is what the almighty tiger represents. My aunt Rue proved this in the last year of her life. Her lessons in independence may have involved independence from paralysis, from the statistics of the patients who had had strokes before her, and even from a possible death sentence. She chose to not trust or fear the doctor's prognosis. She chose to trust God, me, and the tigers instead. That is what I call true independence.

2 | Elephants
Good Vibrations

Dry your tears, Afrika! We have drunk from all the springs of ill fortune and of glory.
And our senses are now opened to the splendor of your beauty. To the smell of your forests.
To the charm of your waters. To the clearness of your skies. To the caress of your sun.
— BERNARD BINLIN DADIE, *Dry Your Tears, Afrika,* 1967

I'M SITTING IN FRONT OF MY TENT in South Luangwa this morning with hippos in my front yard and monkeys all over my desk, stealing my toast. (I'd hoped they would!) I've been totally possessed for the last four days writing the tiger chapter and stories about my frog impressions, while I've found frogs in impossible places every day, including the inside of my toilet paper rolls.

Yesterday, I sat down by the river and started writing just after breakfast. Suddenly, I noticed the sun was going down, I was getting cold, and mosquitoes were biting me. The staff said I'd been writing for over eight hours without a break. I forgot to eat or drink. It was more than any writer could hope for.

But last night, after I'd made the goal of finishing the tiger chapter today, I went for a walk and found my favorite elephant in the world, Princess Naughty Tusk, with four of her family members in a neighboring camp. I told the five elephants that I was in tent number five next door at a nearby camp, and I asked them to meet me here — at my tent — first thing in the morning. It would be quite a distance for them to walk all the way to my tent. Number five is at the far end of the camp.

I woke this morning to the sound of thunder. The entire herd had gathered around my tent! We tourists are forbidden by the management in these camps to approach the elephants, but outlaw that I am, I took my coffee outside and sat down to call them over. All five elephants were within six feet of me, and it was one of the most intoxicating moments of my life. The camp is in a frenzy because the entire staff is talking about how the elephants gathered around tent number five this morning and refused to leave. They brought me a tiny calf and pushed her forward for me to see, and she was all but four feet from me. I was in tears. I'd never been this close to a wild African elephant in my life, much less a tiny baby elephant. I thought my heart would explode!

Even I was a little nervous to have five giants all coming over to talk to me, but I tried to gather my wits and ask them what they wanted to tell me. Princess Naughty Tusk, the mother of the herd, said, "Turn the tiger chapter in today! It's *our* turn now!" Better not keep six tons of fun waiting! So let's start at the very beginning, and I'll tell you how this passion for pachyderms began.

Give God a Peanut

I was four years old. It must have been winter, because I remember the white froth of my breath as I panted expectantly, gazing over the fence, perched frozen on tiptoe. I was at a zoo in New Jersey. I remember arms wrapping around my snug coat from behind and lifting me up — I don't remember whose, father, mother, or grandmother, so intent was I on my mission — to deliver the peanut to the elephant's nose. This was in the early 1970s, long before today's high-security prisonlike enclosures, designed to isolate "dangerous" elephants from innocent children. I'll never forget the feeling — the spontaneous squeal that escaped my lips when the warm, wet sea anemone of a nose reached out and wrapped around my small trembling fingers to take my offering. When that solicitous tube came my way, rough and wrinkled on the outside but muscular and soft on the inside, I popped the peanut in the chute, as if I were feeding a bullet into the barrel of a velvet shotgun.

I have many other memories of being four years old and younger, of tulips, of snow, of jumping naked on my bed, but this memory remains an indelible hologram — a moment frozen in time and space — my first experience of awe, reverence, and unspeakable delight. It was the moment my life began. That was the day I was chosen. The elephant deliberately came to me, over all the other groping sticky crayon-sized fingers in the crowd. In that moment, I was signed, sealed, and delivered into the arms of Ganesha. I had touched the face of God.

I've spent the rest of my life trying to re-create the opportunity to give God another peanut. And my life's work has become an effort to help preserve these glorious animals so that other four-year-olds might share in the splendor and glory of God's most magical wild creations. Will you help me create visions of a future that can sustain that fragile happiness?

Over the course of the last decade, I've had a recurring vision just as I drift off to sleep: I see elephants parading through my mind — not in joyous procession, like the circus animals of my childhood — but grave, glorious, and reverent. Regally kicking up clouds of dust, they disappear over the horizon, allowing me to watch them as they leave this world. They are coming to say good-bye. Why should I be privy to this bittersweet blessing? Elephants have been a lifelong passion for me, but like the gorillas, who also visit as I tumble off to sleep, they have only recently become an obsession. My best guess is that they're visiting me, as the gorillas do, *to have their stories told* before they make their final exodus. I hear their trumpeting in the recesses of my mind, like a call to arms from a Camelot of the misty past; this time, they're searching for a new world where they can live and prosper, whole and complete, unencumbered by human beings.

"Twenty Minutes Up This Road"

My first African elephant miracle occurred when I wanted to drive up to a game park called Pilanesberg Park, about two hours' drive north of Johannesburg. I went on a road trip that resembled an episode of *I Love Lucy* with my wonderful and hilarious workshop coordinator, Sandy, because like Lucy and Ethel, we kept getting into shenanigans. Traversing the most dangerous highway in South Africa, where one just rolls up the windows, locks the doors, and blasts through the traffic lights so that no carjacking is possible, we got lost and pulled off to get directions in a roadside pub, where we found a dozen or so South African men dead drunk in the middle of the afternoon. All I wanted to do was go see some elephants and tell them that I loved them, while Sandy, like the helpful sidekick Ethel, was trying to help me achieve this goal, when we found ourselves in this nightmarish situation. I felt like we'd skipped off the screen from an episode of *I Love Lucy* and ended up in a Quentin Tarantino movie.

Two disgusting gas stations later, we finally got directions and went racing up toward one of the gates of Pilanesberg. We were so late, we'd be lucky to get there before the park closed, and after this hot, exhausting road trip, we were not about to arrive disappointed and have to drive back. Sandy was screaming in her fabulous African accent, "Teell the eel-a-phants weee're coming! Teeell them weee're coming! Teeel them to wait for us!" So here I was, racing up a bumpy road, inhaling dust and dripping sweat, trying to telepath with the elephants and signal to them to come down and meet us. Understand that one can drive through Pilanesberg for hours and never see an elephant. This had been a long shot before we got ourselves lost and were about to arrive three hours late. But I sent out the radar and asked the elephants to walk down to the gate and meet us, not knowing if my efforts would hit their mark. I'd never met any of these elephants, so I was just sending the mental I-love-yous up into the park and letting them spread out throughout the atmosphere, hoping someone with a very big nose and big ears would happen to be "online."

Sandy and I arrived at the wrong gate and were told to go to another gate — something I've learned you can almost bank on here in Africa: you will always be sent somewhere else by an adamant official — so we drove like mad fiends to another gate. When we pulled in, Sandy's jaw hit the steering wheel, and my heart leaped. There, waiting at the front gate, was a bull elephant. The official at this gate said he had never seen this behavior before. He told us, "This teenage bull came down to the gate as if he were waiting for someone." Apparently, he'd picked up the psychic email from me long before we got there and started this trek down to the gate to intercept us. I tuned in to this huge young elephant to thank him, and he said, "Drive twenty minutes up this road and you'll find the herd. They're waiting for you."

I told Sandy, and off we went. The park would close within the hour, so if this bull was leading us astray, we'd drive up and back for no reason. But the herd didn't let us down. Exactly twenty minutes into the trek up this windy road, three elephants danced into view and came up to meet us. Then four, then five, then six appeared, walking out into the road. The hair on the back of my neck stood up. Sandy is a tough cookie, but I looked over at her, trembling with pleasure in the driver's seat, and I'll never forget the awestruck look in her eyes. She was five years old again. She turned the engine off, and we sat in silence as the herd surrounded the car.

Elephants move in a graceful dance when they walk, a blend of strength and ancient beauty that defies analogies in the modern world. Being in their presence is like being in the council of some ancient gods, something so primordial and important, the atmosphere they occupy is charged with tingling magic. This was a moment of awe and reverence, of prayers heard, of promises kept, of magic made manifest, of evidence of interspecies communication that would change my life forever. It was only the first outrageous encounter I've had with these glorious beasts. The elephant miracles had just begun.

Naughty | nô-tē |
ADJECTIVE (naughtier, naughtiest)
1. disobedient; badly behaved: *you've been a really naughty boy.*
2. informal, mildly rude or indecent, *naughty drawings* | *naughty goings-on.*
3. archaic, wicked.
DERIVATIVES
naughtily |-təlē | adverb.
naughtiness
NOUN
4. Amelia's favorite elephant.

SHE'S ON HER WAY TO ME at this very moment, coming to see me off because this is my last night here in the bush in my tent in Zambia. The owners of the camp were not pleased to see the entire herd crossing the river headed directly for my tent, but even the skeptical manager had a twinkle in his eye and a smile forming on his lips as he shouted, "They've come to say good-bye to you!"

So I need to tell you the story of the world's naughtiest elephant while I'm here with her for the last night. I had seen the photos in *National Geographic* magazine years ago of an elephant walking through the lobby of a lodge. I tacked them up to my walls so that I could look at them every day. The photos are very cheeky, and the elephant almost seems to be reaching over people's shoulders to drink their cocktails at the bar. Nothing in the world could have thrilled me more than to have the honor of being touched by a wild elephant, so this became my biggest fantasy — to find this hotel and be there when this goddess of an elephant walked through.

By the time I started leading my safaris, I was told that this infamous elephant, Queen Wonky Tusk, had passed away. She had one crooked tusk, thus the name, but the lodge that she frequented, Mfuwe Lodge, is right here in the same national park where I lead my safaris. Actually, it's just down the road. Rumor has it that there's a mango tree in the lobby that the elephants love, so every November they walk through because this lodge is in the way of their path, but they also like to lunch on the mango, which is an elephant's favorite fruit.

Last year, I was staying at a discount lodge to be closer to the schools where Ark Angel does its work. As I said before, I go into the schools to speak to the kids about elephants so that they don't grow up to be poachers. We dance as elephants, draw elephants, and make up theater games about poachers killing elephants and scouts protecting elephants. I had never stayed in this lodge before, but it was more convenient for me to be nearer the Chipembele offices, where I volunteer. The night I checked in, I had no intention of going out on the five AM game-drive the following morning because I needed to sleep to be fresh for my work in the schools. At dusk, I saw an elephant herd standing across the river, quite a ways from my camp. I waved to them and told them I couldn't go out the following morning on the drive to see them, so would they please come to me instead?

The next day, I was lying in my hut, writing a movie script that had an underlying theme of elephant conservation. The hut was off the beaten path and not even near the river where I had seen them. I heard a soft crashing outside my window and my heart skipped a beat. *They're here! They're here! Oh my Lord! Thank you, God!* I jumped up barely able to breathe, threw on some shoes, and slowly opened the door. I nearly jumped out of my skin when I saw that the mother elephant was standing on my doorstep, waiting for me to open the door! I looked behind one of her massive ears and saw that the entire group had gathered around my hut! I stepped out onto the porch, very gently, very slowly, and spied the guards across the courtyard frozen in place, horrified to see what I might do next. The elephants stepped off, giving me the opportunity to leave the hut if I wished, so I walked over to the open lobby, sat down at the bar, and ordered a Diet Coke. I was virtually alone in the lobby except for the owner of the camp and a few guards. It was midafternoon, after the lunch crowd and before the dinner crowd, so I had the entire bar to myself — well, almost. Fortunately for my uninvited tea party, this lobby had a very high thatched-roof ceiling!

First the mother elephant appeared and brought me her baby. Then her sister appeared and brought me *her* baby. It was the first time my clairaudience kicked in with my elephant conversations. The second mom and calf were shy to come into the lobby, so as the coy mom guided the baby past so that I could meet her, I heard the baby's voice as she peeked curiously at me: "Is that *her?*" she asked. Her mother assured her that I was the one all the elephants had been talking about. I felt a little bit like Marilyn Monroe coming back from the grave — the Marilyn of the elephants.

By now, the owner of the park was about to make a mess in his shorts as the first mother elephant walked into his lobby. He was commanding everyone to freeze, forbidding them to even dare to blink, while she sauntered over to the coffee and tea service and gently turned the table upside down. I imagine she thought it was terribly rude of him not to offer her and her family a cup of coffee, and of course, I totally agree. She looked me over, peacefully eating her fifth doormat, while he was still hissing, "Don't move! Don't move! Don't move, anybody!"

The hissing got louder when a huge male elephant appeared behind the females and poked his enormous head into the bar to see me. I swooned but mentally asked him not to approach me, because the little man who owned the camp was about to have such a tantrum, I thought he'd disintegrate into a puff of smoke like Rumpelstiltskin.

The mother elephant just kept coming despite his repeated, "No, Naughty! No, Naughty! No!" and she strolled through the lobby facing away from me. She stood there for almost forty-five minutes while the rest of us humans were frozen in place. I could only glimpse out of my peripheral vision her mammoth rump, so stiff was I, almost afraid to turn my head to face her. But even then, I could see her rocking gently, her beautiful nose swaying, her huge sensitive ears flapping softly. She was patiently waiting for an invitation. Would I once again let my heart and better judgment be swayed by an ignorant man who was so frightened that he was trying to control me? I finally came to my senses and realized that whether I was scolded to do my impression of a statue or not, I was being rude to not invite her over. Where were my manners?

"Naughty" (I'd gleaned the condescending name), "if you can hear me, come over here and kiss my face," I asked silently, sending the command to her.

My heart was in my throat when her huge head swung toward me. One eye was on me. I felt the heat rush into my reddening cheeks. Her ears flapped like doors opening and closing. She'd been parked there like a 747 in a hangar for almost an hour while I stupidly listened to the little man instead of listening to my heart and to the elephant I loved. Had she heard me? Or had I finally heard *her*? She took a step toward me with her massive foot, and the little man started chirping hysterically, "Don't move, Amelia! Don't move! Don't move!" Of course he had no idea what I did for a living, and he certainly wouldn't have believed that I had called her over. She crossed the expanse of the lobby toward me, as if on a mission. I barely even turned to face her. But I can tell you, as her footsteps came closer, the adrenaline raced throughout my body, and I thought my heart would leap out of my chest. Intoxicated, I looked down, and there were her toes — her beautiful massive toes — planted firmly right next to me.

She stopped just a foot or two from me. I couldn't breathe, enchanted by her presence. I wanted to dive into her chest and put my arms around her, but still obeying the owner, I sat absolutely frozen like a statue. She nudged me with her tusk, gently touching me in the ribcage, as if to say, "Are you okay? What's wrong with you? Are you dead?" Of course my natural reaction would have been to reach up and hug her nose, but I was just sitting there rigid like a stone. I didn't move a finger, and nothing was moving on my body except the tears streaming down my cheeks.

Her nose came closer and closer, and then I felt it. I clenched my eyes tight when I felt the forbidden touch. I dared not look. I could feel a velvet suction cup kissing my face, all over my face, kissing away my stunned tears. I was shaking with joy, exploding with happiness as if all the triple-decker ice cream cones, all the wildflowers, all the jars of golden honey on this earth, were heaped at my feet as we were serenaded by a Bach minuet played on the harp of an angel. Heaven couldn't be closer. Frozen on the barstool, wincing and dissolving in her warm strong kisses, I wept.

She even wrapped her huge nose around me to give me a makeshift hug before she decided she'd done what she'd come to do; then she took her family out of the lobby and they all lumbered off. But if you're wondering what an elephant-nose kiss feels like, well, it would make any vacuum cleaner want to switch off its engine, cast off its dust bag, and throw up its hose in shame. My childhood revisited, here it was again: a loving kiss from a sea anemone, a stickup at gunpoint from a velvet shotgun. I felt like I'd been struck by lightning, the voltage of electricity between us was so high, but the gentleness of her nose as it explored my face was like, well, like a rose petal delivered on the winds of a tornado. Once she left, all of the big African men who'd witnessed the kiss were still frozen like statues, paralyzed with fear. When the elephants were safely out of sight, the men melted into motion and ran up to me to congratulate me.

"Weren't you scared, mama?" they asked. "Of course not," I said. "I love elephants and elephants love me. We don't have problems. It's people I have problems with." This got a few knowing nods and laughs of approval even from locals who barely spoke my language. Maybe they secretly loved her, too, or maybe they just didn't like their boss.

One of the managers told me later that day that Princess Naughty Tusk is the daughter of the superstar Queen Wonky Tusk, and that Naughty has taken her mother's position as the celebrity elephant who makes a scene every November walking through the lobby of Mfuwe Lodge to steal mangos and adoration from the crowd. I guess, being that I couldn't afford to stay at swanky Mfuwe Lodge, Naughty came to see me in my discount camp instead. And with that kiss, my wildest dream came true. I got my wish. Maybe it was the spirit of her mother reaching out to me, or the kiss of all elephants and their ancestors. Ganesha had kissed me on the cheek once again. It's these moments in my life that keep me going: these miracles, these angelic communions, the divine intervention that allows me to be *certain* that the animals can hear me and that God is watching.

Unfortunately, the next day, the manager put an end to all that when he strung up electric fences all around the lobby to keep the "dangerous" elephants away from me. And when Naughty tried to duck under one hot wire and burned her ear very badly, this man had the nerve to brag about what a terrible burn mark he'd made on her ear. He was jubilant that he'd hurt her. I heard later that he'd had a chip on his shoulder about her ever since she'd smashed into his house, broken a window, reached in with his nose, and stolen a bottle of his booze. That's my girl. Always lookin' for a party on a Saturday night!

This first Naughty kiss was how I became entangled and enraged by the human–elephant conflict here in Africa, and by how unimaginative and primitive are the humans' attempts to keep the elephants out of their own homes — not the *humans'* homes, but the *elephants'* homes, because the elephants were here first. The elephants have decided that our camps are their kitchens, and power to them. They don't build houses in the middle of our freeways, but here where I'm staying tonight, it's as if some fool had built a safari camp in the middle of Los Angeles's 405 freeway, the busiest eight-lane highway in America. These tents we've so callously pitched in their way are only causing a bit of road obstacles, and when these gentle giants run out of patience with all these roadblocks stupidly built on their freeways, sometimes they take it upon themselves to remove the obstructions. Wouldn't you? I've lived most of my life in Los Angeles stuck in traffic on the 405. (When you die, if you've been very, very bad and St. Peter doesn't let you go to heaven, he could send you to the southbound 405 on a Friday afternoon.) These safari park owners may be lucky that the remover of obstacles hasn't simply removed all the obstacles and leveled our camps.

Last week, Naughty ransacked a tent to root out some hot-dog buns (sorry, it makes me chuckle, but I guess she and her family wanted an invite to the Saturday afternoon weenie roast happening in her own backyard!), and the furious occupants threatened to sue the management, even though signs are tacked up in every tent instructing visitors not to keep food in their tents. But the humans here are blaming the elephants. An elephant's sense of smell is the strongest in the animal kingdom, so one might consider this when disobeying the camp rules. Not only have the humans built a hotel in the middle of Naughty's highway, but also they've had the audacity to open a bakery there and forbid her to ever have a bite. Who could expect her to not stop in for an occasional doughnut?

Just as I was leaving the camp of the mean little man last year, I had only one night left before flying back to Los Angeles, and I wanted to spend it with my favorite nosy family, but I planned to spend this final night back at Kafunta, the beautiful lodge where I lead my safaris. I told the elephants that I'd be leaving the next day, and would they please meet me at the Kafunta River Lodge instead? Kafunta was a really long walk, even for an elephant, from the discount camp with the electric fence. I took a long, dusty ride in a truck to Kafunta River Lodge, heartsick to be leaving Naughty and her family. I checked into Kafunta and settled in for the night in some staff lodging in the far part of the camp, a place I'd never stayed before, thinking they'd never find me. Then I woke up to the sound of thunder... and a big smile. *Thank you, God!* They'd found me. I ran outside, and there they all were on my doorstep at morning's first light, looking as fantastical as a family of friendly dragons who'd stepped off the pages of a fairy-tale book. Waiting with soft, flirty eyes to see me one last time before I had to fly back to Los Angeles, they let me know with that appearance that they could find me wherever I stayed, that they understood me when I asked them to meet me somewhere new, that they kept their appointments and honored my promises, and that in some mystical, ineffable way, we *meant something* to each other. They could hear me and I could hear them, but something deeper was developing. We weren't just acquaintances anymore. This sensation can't be explained as easily as it can be felt. Kind of like true love.

THE IVORY KEYS TO THE ZERO POINT ENERGY FIELD

Elephants weren't my first love. Once upon a time in a land called Texas, my mother, Melinda Lou, had the good sense to put my two-year-old tuchas on a piano bench. I was barely out of diapers, or maybe still in them, when I fell in love with an instrument so enchanting that its music fascinates me to this day; and although I didn't know as a child that elephants had been sacrificed to make this instrument of pure perfection, I can now estimate their similarities. If a piano were an animal, it would be an elephant; and if an elephant were an instrument, it would be a piano.

And what are they both? Divine designs that reflect this planet's harmonies — sacred harmonies built on mathematics, that simulate patterns and the beauty of cosmic harmonies that are quite frankly outside human comprehension. Let me explain. When my mother put my chubby little derrière on that piano bench, it was with the hope that I would fall in love with her great love, the piano, and be able one day to play two-piano duets with her at the concert level at which she played. Who was I to ruin her dream? I spent my childhood trying, and while I never achieved her concert-level prowess, I enjoyed every second that my little fingers touched the ivory keys.

My love for Bach, Beethoven, Chopin, and Mozart became my obsession — my identity — and by the time I was in the second grade, I had memorized ten classical pieces for competition. But it was not the ego involvement that held me captive; it was the harmonies, the melodies, the feelings behind the minuet, the sonata, the waltz — something so sacred in Mozart's every note that it reflected the harmonies of the spheres, like choirs of angels singing in absolute tireless perfection. And Chopin's channeled music is, I believe, the voice of God himself.

What does music have to do with elephants? Everything and nothing, but everything is more likely.

Similar in structure to the inside of a piano — a piano inside out — is a guitar. The strings are the same, and in the world of masterful guitar players, as activists like the rock god Slash of Guns N' Roses fame would attest and *pro*test (he is one of the world's most outspoken elephant champions), many guitar picks are also made of ivory. Here again is the sad fact that ivory is somehow associated with music. We create music by strumming and plucking with picks made from parts of elephants' dead bodies? It doesn't make sense. But why do we do it? Is there some connection between the mighty Elephant Soul and music?

The title of Don Campbell's *The Mozart Effect* (Avon Books, 1997) refers to a set of research results indicating that listening to Mozart's music may induce a short-term improvement in the performance of certain kinds of mental tasks known as *spatial-temporal reasoning*. This means that well-composed classical music harmonizes the hemispheres of the brain and can be used to help the brain solve concentration problems. The Mozart effect has been the subject of experiments with children who have autism and attention deficit disorder. I can attest that the minute I switch on one of my favorite jams, I instantly feel better, am more motivated, and can think more clearly. The music seems to enter my body itself, give a lift to my step, and help organize my thoughts. It's now a proven fact that when we listen to music, the vibrations resonate in every cell of our bodies and alter our operating frequency. Our bodies are 83 percent water, and although we tend to think of them as dense and crunchy — we pay more attention to the bones than the water — even our bones are full of water. We have fluid inside our *spines*, and that river of fluid houses all the intelligence within the body and constantly circulates it. Every molecule in the body can be charged as the water molecules start to resonate with the music that is introduced to them, working exactly the same as a tuning fork. If a tuning fork is struck, all the molecules around it begin to vibrate on the same frequency. In the language of quantum physics, this phenomenon is called *coherence.* So the ability to cohere, or take charge, is the ability of music to affect everything around it — flying through it, moving inside it, and actually transforming it so that the other beings vibrate on the same wavelength.

I'm a music junkie. I once saw one of my favorite actors, John Cusack, interviewed, and he was asked the secret of his success. He said, "I use music as fuel." I thought that was one of the best tips I'd ever heard, and I realized that I, too, have always used music as fuel. When you dance to it, it is amplified, distributed throughout your body. One of the best dance teachers I've ever worked with in Hollywood said, "When you dance to the music, you *are* the music, the physical interpretation of the music, so if music can never make a mistake, how can your body ever make a mistake? So you see, as a dancer, you'd have to get out of sync with the music to make a mistake."

I've written in previous books about the Realm of Absolutes: As I've dozed off to sleep at night, I've heard Bach's minuets played inside my head perpetually, infinitely, where a note is never out of place and the river modulates to go on and on in a melody of pure perfection for all time. If I had the skill to run to the piano and compose this music I hear, I would be Bach. But I don't. So I have to settle for playing his interpretation of it — not what he manufactured but what he heard. What I overhear may be the music he heard before he channeled it onto the page. I've awakened in a few crashing Beethoven symphonies, too, where the music is hanging heavy in the air as if it is coming from the atmosphere itself. No wonder the genius struggled with madness, being privy to this music that no one else could hear.

Who is to say that other animals don't experience things like this, too? There is something undeniably magical and remarkable about our last living giant land mammal. And housed within her are many secrets of the universe.

You see, they walk ancient ley lines creating sacred geometry, bringing a sense of steadiness and a harmony to this earth that humans don't understand. Some shamans claim that elephants steady the earth and help prevent earthquakes. Is it true? What do you think? Let's pretend that you can see planet Earth from outer space, and you can see the patterns that the elephants walk, creating geometric shapes so ancient, we humans have no idea when the elephants began to trace their sacred ley lines; much less can we comprehend why.

So the idea I propose is that elephants create patterns — they orchestrate harmonies — that, with repetition, like the practice of running daily scales on the piano, create a sense of harmony and order on this earth. They are creatures of habit, and habit could be the servant of order, a divine order in nature that humans crave and seem to have lost. From a mystical perspective, the Hindu elephant god, Ganesha, is always depicted playing a musical instrument. But the latest discoveries of a Stanford biologist suggest that this connection to music is literal. Could it be that elephants not only pick up vibrations, "listening" through their feet, but also can transmit electromagnetic frequencies into the earth through their feet? Are they actually *making music*? Mark Shwartz of the Stanford News Service wrote an article about the research that sent tingles up my spine, but not before it gave me happy feet and made me reach for my salsa-dancing sandals ("Elephants Pick Up Good Vibrations — Through Their Feet," March 5, 2001):

> Few sights in nature are as awesome as a 6-ton elephant guarding her baby from a hungry predator. Rather than retreat, the threatened mother is likely to launch a mock charge — a terrifying display of ground stomping, ear flapping and frantic screaming designed to frighten off lions and hyenas.
>
> But elephant researchers have discovered that there is more to a mock charge than meets the eye, or the ear, for that matter. It turns out that foot stomping and low-frequency

rumbling also generate seismic waves in the ground that can travel nearly 20 miles along the surface of the Earth, according to a new study in the *Journal of the Acoustical Society of America* (*JASA*). More astonishing is the discovery that elephants may be able to sense these vibrations through their feet and interpret them as warning signals of a distant danger.

"Elephants may be able to detect stress from a herd many miles away," says Caitlin O'Connell-Rodwell, an affiliate of the Stanford Center for Conservation Biology and a postdoctoral fellow in the Department of Pediatrics.

"They may be communicating at much farther distances than we thought," adds O'Connell-Rodwell, author of the *JASA* study.

UNDERGROUND TESTS

To test the theory that elephants transmit and receive underground messages, O'Connell-Rodwell and her colleagues previously conducted several novel experiments with pachyderms in Africa, India and at a captive elephant facility in Texas.

"We went to Etosha National Park in Namibia and recorded three acoustic calls commonly made by wild African elephants," she says. "One is a warning call, another is a greeting and the third is the elephant equivalent of 'Let's go!'"

The researchers wanted to find out if elephants would respond to recordings played through the ground, so they installed seismic transmitters at a tourist facility in Zimbabwe where eight trained, young elephants were housed.

The idea was to convert audible "Greetings," "Warning!" and "Let's go!" calls into underground seismic waves that an elephant could feel but not hear directly through the air.

"We used a mix of elephant calls, synthesized low-frequency tones, rock music, and silence for comparison," says O'Connell-Rodwell.

"When the 'Warning!' calls were played, one female got so agitated she bent down and bit the ground," she notes. "That's very unusual behavior for an elephant, but it has been observed in the wild under conditions of extreme agitation."

The young female had the same agitated response each time the experiment was repeated. Researchers also played recorded calls to seven captive males.

"The bulls reacted, too, but their response was much more subtle," notes O'Connell-Rodwell.

"We think they're sensing these underground vibrations through their feet," she adds. "Seismic waves could travel from their toenails to the ear via bone conduction, or through somatosensory receptors in the foot similar to ones found in the trunk. We think it may be a combination of both."

LONG-DISTANCE CALLS

Other creatures produce seismic signals — among them the golden mole, the elephant seal (no relation to terrestrial elephants) and a variety of insects, amphibians, reptiles and fish.

"Many organisms use vibrations in the ground to find mates, locate prey or establish territories," says O'Connell-Rodwell.

The ability of large mammals to communicate long distances also is well established. Fin whales, for example, produce calls that carry hundreds of miles underwater at a frequency of 20 hertz — a range so low that it's barely audible to the human ear.

In the late 1980s, researchers discovered that elephants also produce strong, low-frequency 20 hertz rumbles that can travel up to six miles through the air under ideal weather conditions. Later studies indicated that elephants use these low-frequency vocalizations to coordinate movements with other far-off herds.

In the early '90s, O'Connell-Rodwell began to suspect there was more to long-distance elephant communication than airborne rumblings alone.

"I started working with elephants in Etosha National Park in 1992," she recalls. "I was observing them at a drinking hole when I noticed this strange set of behaviors. They would lean forward, pick up one leg, and freeze for no apparent reason."

She theorized that the elephants were responding to vibrations in the ground from approaching herds.

"When I returned to the University of California at Davis, I teamed up with my Ph.D. adviser, Lynette Hart, and geophysicist Byron Aranson to find out if there really are seismic communications among elephants," she says.

The result was a series of geophysical experiments with captive elephants. The first one in 1997 confirmed O'Connell-Rodwell's suspicion that acoustic rumbles are accompanied by vibrations in the Earth.

"When an elephant transmits airborne low-frequency (20 hertz) vocalizations," she wrote, "a corresponding seismic wave is transmitted in the ground."

To determine how far these seismic waves propagate, O'Connell-Rodwell and her coworkers conducted experiments with two female Asian elephants at a private training facility near Jefferson, Texas.

They placed two microphones outside the elephants' enclosure, one about 30 feet away, the other about 130 feet. The researchers also buried a geophone directly below each microphone to measure underground vibrations, so whenever the elephants vocalized or launched into a mock charge, the geophone/microphone pairs made simultaneous acoustic and seismic recordings of the event.

"Our results show that elephant rumbles travel separately through the air and the ground," writes O'Connell-Rodwell in the December issue of *JASA*.

She points out that mock charges generate airborne and seismic signals with frequencies of about 20 hertz — ideal for long-distance communication.

"Based on our mathematical models, we estimate that seismic signals produced by elephants can travel between 10 and 20 miles in the ground, while acoustic signals have the potential of traveling only about six miles through the air," O'Connell-Rodwell observes....

MOCK CHARGES AND MATES

The implications of O'Connell-Rodwell's research are far-reaching.

In the *JASA* article, O'Connell-Rodwell said something quite amazing: "Elephants may be communicating at much larger ranges than we realized both within and between herds."

The Stanford News Service article continues:

The Texas experiments demonstrated that vibrations produced during low frequency vocalizations and mock charges may have the indirect effect of alerting other elephants of potential predators and other threats.

"Seismic signals may also play a role in elephant reproduction," O'Connell-Rodwell observes. "We know that airborne vocal communication is an important component of mate finding. Perhaps they're also sending out seismic signals to potential mates far away.

"Elephants may be able to sense the environment better than we realize," O'Connell-Rodwell contends.... "When it rains in Angola, elephants 100 miles away in Etosha start to move north in search of water," she says. "It could be that they are sensing underground vibrations generated by thunder."

O'Connell-Rodwell's findings also have implications for the way humans and elephants interact — particularly in countries like South Africa, where declining habitat has led wildlife managers to shoot elephants from helicopters as a way of thinning overpopulated herds.

"There's anecdotal evidence that culling in the northern end of Kruger National Park causes nervousness among elephants in the southern end many miles away," she says. "Helicopter noise is traumatic, so perhaps these animals are picking up low-frequency signals from the rotating blades or from the distress calls and running of the distant herd that's under attack."

Her research also has implications for how we treat captive elephants in urban zoos.

"If elephants are really that sensitive to seismic noise," she argues, "then more could be done to protect them from loud city noises."

O'Connell-Rodwell hopes to return to Namibia's Etosha National Park this year to record and play back more seismically transmitted vocalizations in the wild. Her goal is to determine how far seismic signals actually carry through open grasslands and how wild elephants respond to those underground vibrations.

"If elephants could detect the seismic properties of low frequency vocalizations, movements of other herds, and weather patterns," she concludes, "then seismic signals could expand the range of elephants' long-distance communication capabilities, adding a powerful component to their sensory perception."

NAUGHTY IS AS NAUGHTY DOES

We humans still have much to learn about how elephants communicate. I suspect that their entire bodies function as pianos in the way they pick up, read, and interpret information. And fascinating as these discoveries are about elephants reading signals carried in the earth like big-foot Braille, my own area of expertise would have you contemplating how frequencies may be shot through the earth the way that dolphins, sharks, and whales send their sonar through the water. Add to that an elephant's obvious ability to telepath by sending and receiving quantum information through the Zero Point Energy Field, and this could explain how no matter where I go, they can always find me — unless they can just hear my tummy rumbling after drinking the local water, or maybe they can hear me snoring in my tent.

I'm about to find out. This year I'm in a different place entirely, having finished leading a splendid safari at Kafunta. Now I'm holed up in a different backpacker's camp for the sole reason that I'd heard my elephant family walked through here and the owner didn't insult them with electric fences. Unfortunately, the owner of this camp came to me distraught last week because Naughty had turned over a car and the authorities here were threatening to shoot her. That's right. To murder the very elephants that we tourists fly from all over the world to see. He begged me to ask her to stay out of the camp.

This is a man I believe has a heart. I saw the pain in his eyes, and I heard the frustration in his voice when he told me to ask her to not come here anymore, and this is why he also had to put up electric fences all over the camp.

"It's to save her life," he said. "Tell her I'm trying to save her life. They can't kill her! She has a tiny calf!"

It was going to break my heart to tell her that the brainless humans would kill her if she got into any more mischief, so she and her family needed to stay away even from tent number five. But the next morning, she came again at four AM with the entire family, surrounding my tent, waking me up and waiting to see me. I unzipped the tent, poked my head out, found myself face-to-face with her (or face-to-trunk), and whispered, "The humans are violent idiots! They're going to shoot you if you get into anything else around here! Please stay out of sight for a while and let the little nitwits cool off."

She avoided my camp for all of last week, so I know she heard me, and we've both made this miserable sacrifice. I stayed in this camp only because I'd heard she walked through, and now that I've met her tiny baby calf, it's killed me to not get to visit with her and the baby every day. She's complied and stayed away. It's been a very sad, boring week, spent ducking under electric fences and missing my big-nosed sweethearts. There's a huge hole in your life when you're suddenly missing six tons of fun every day!

Tonight was going to be my last chance to see her until this time the following year. But even as I type these words from my perch on a log bench facing the river, a cloud of dust just swirled from the far bank. *Thank you, God!* They're here! Naughty is as Naughty does, and the elephants are now crossing the river, silhouetted in the setting sun. There are three more added to their party of six, wading and splashing, helping the precious baby cross, keeping her safe from crocodiles. Now nine elephants are headed into the village to pillage the night away, so all hell is about to break loose. I guess the three friends didn't want to miss out on my going-away party!

I've renamed her to give her the distinction equal to that of her mother and the royal respect she deserves. Princess Naughty Tusk will be heading the parade through this tent camp to come kiss me good-bye in the early-morning hours. It'll be nine lanes of elephant highway marching through here tonight, and they'll all be partying in tent number five! Now, they know I don't have food in that tent, and what's so astonishing to me is that the humans never even consider that maybe this is not about food. These animals are friendly. And they're curious about other species and want to interact with us in ways that we don't interact with other species. Could it be that they simply have manners? And that humans don't? And isn't it revealing that all the men in this camp and even the elephant experts somehow know that they're not worthy of being investigated by elephants unless the visit involves hamburger buns? Maybe there's some *friendship* in here somewhere. And maybe even some *love*. Could that be possible? Call me sentimental, but I don't have a peanut in this tent, and the whole herd is on its way over!

Naughty's gathering her forces and so am I, so what a wonderful time we're going to have in years to come.

That tiny baby may be safe from crocodiles, but who will protect her from humans?

If you're wondering what Naughty needed to tell me the morning they waited for me to wake up, surrounding my tent so that they could take a meeting, I've been very quiet about it. What did Naughty say?

"The human design is faulty. They need to be redrawn."

"I know," I said. "But I'm not sure how to do it." I'm going to call on the ghosts of Walt Disney and Leonardo da Vinci to see if there's a way the humans can be redesigned into something more beautiful, something more sensible — something sustainable. It will start with their thoughts, and their emotions, to try to align them with the beautiful, magical, creative God consciousness within them and the angelic Christ consciousness they could become. I will try my very best to "redraw" the humans. This book is my humble attempt to redraw our world. The next chapter will be about lions and their spectral connections to the Lion of Judah. We'll talk about the kind of humans that God intended us to be: loving, caring, respectful, devoted, protective, growing, passionate, and free. But first let's have some fun with that abalone appendage that makes me ask, "It's a finger? It's a trumpet? It's a fire hose? And she can kiss me with it?!" Well, you know the old joke, "You can pick your friends. You can pick your nose. But you can't pick your friend's nose." That may be true, until *my* friends drop in for tea.

Fun Facts about Naughty's Kisser

The trunk is a modification of the upper lip and the nose combined. At the end of the trunk are two fingerlike projections that are used to pinch and grip both small and large food items and objects. The trunk is composed of over one hundred thousand individual muscles that make it a very strong appendage. It is an especially amazing adaptation when you consider that the entire human body has fewer than eight hundred individual muscles total and that there is no other appendage in the entire animal world known to be as specialized as an elephant's trunk.

An elephant uses its trunk to suck up water and blow the water into its mouth or onto its body for bathing and cooling purposes. However, an elephant cannot drink water through its trunk.

In addition to food gathering, drinking, and bathing, the trunk is used for social interactions among herd mates. Elephants make regular contact with one another using their trunks. Such social interactions may include greeting, caressing, and demonstrations of dominance or submission through subtle positioning of the trunk and different trunk postures. The trunk can also act as a resonating tube, producing the classic sounds of an elephant trumpet or the sounds of a subtle, reverberating communication rumble.

Perhaps one of the most interesting and yet lesser known facts about an elephant's trunk is that it is able to detect and distinguish smells several hundred times better than any dog! An elephant's sense of smell is one of its greatest senses, and it is all located in the trunk.

MAGICAL MAP MAKERS

Elephants are pathfinders and path makers. When we are guided by our own North Star, steadfast on our proper path, something unprecedented can happen. We can enter a synthesis with creation where the time-space gap closes, and all you have to do is think about what you want — provided it is in service of people, of the animals, of the planet — and then there is no lag in your ability to manifest. You might call it synchronicity, but I believe that, to paraphrase Einstein's statement, "Coincidence is God's way of staying anonymous." Jesus called it "grace." In an act of grace, I just boarded an airplane and picked up the current copy of *Sawubona*, the South African Airways in-flight magazine. The subject of the article on the page I flipped open? Queen Wonky Tusk.

This tribute gives me more insight into the family I just met, because although the piece didn't mention Naughty by name, it did say that Wonky's daughter took over the red-carpet affairs leading to the mango tree in Mfuwe Lodge, and I was privy for the first time to the names that the loving people at this lodge have bestowed on my favorite elephant family, the Tusks. The bull who poked his head into my lobby and almost gave the little twit of an owner a heart attack is Naughty's uncle, Wonky's brother, Wilber — whose full name would be Wilber Tusk. Also in the congregation that gathered at tent number five has been Naughty's bro, Wellington Tusk. But according to this article, the baby presented to me in the lobby bar, the one who asked "Is that her?" was Wonky's grandson, Naughty's older son, Wilkenson, born in 2013. The teeny tiny baby, the most irresistible pint-sized pachyderm brought to tent number five last night, is such a new recruit, he doesn't even have a name yet. I'm not going to tell you he isn't the cutest thing that ever lived. He is.

Baby elephants remind us that there is innocence and goodness in the world, as so many of our baby clothes would indicate by sporting pictures of baby elephants on infant onesies and toddlers' tiny dresses, as if our human children would encounter elephants in the street every day of their adult lives. Elephants are used as emblems on our infants' clothing, perhaps as protection, as unconscious as this choice seems to be, because we are stamping our babies with a sign that elephants will be an important part of their lives, and certainly with the dream that elephants will still be on the planet when these children grow up. It is my mission to make this dream a reality.

As I write this, at this very moment here in Africa, the authorities and safari park owners are threatening to kill my favorite elephant in her own home — but Africa is *her house,* and we have moved into it, demanding that she and her family move out.

I'm proposing that elephants are the masters of sacred harmonies, of geometry, of patterns, of design, and no matter how often or feverishly the humans chase them out of the villages and safari camps, at the end of day, there is only one "authority" in charge here in Africa. It is the elephant.

I am of Cherokee and Choctaw descent, and in the belief systems of my ancestors, humans do not own land. The land owns us, and I'm sure the elephants would agree.

A Heartbreaking Postscript about Naughty

Upon returning to South Luangwa a year later, I was given news that broke my heart into a million pieces. I'm afraid the postscript of Naughty's story is a tragic one. When I arrived at the airport in Mfuwe after I'd spent the day mid-air praying to Naughty's family to "meet me at tent number five," I was greeted by a taxi driver who grabbed me in an excited hug and told me the elephants had come into the camp (which is rather unusual) and they'd been waiting for me all day. We arrived after dark, and when my truck pulled up, Naughty's family was indeed waiting in a grove of trees just in front of my tent. I recognized the tiny calf, who a year later is not so tiny at all, and I identified the youngster Wilkenson, who is now a year older, but I was surprised to greet a young female caretaking the kids. I felt Naughty's presence but could not find her.

From that night on, the elephant family disappeared and did not visit me again. I spent the week sad and Naughty-less. I found myself surprised at my levels of anxiety, waves of depression, and nightmares as I wondered where she was and why the elephants were no longer gathering at tent number five. When visions of Naughty, insistent and furious, kept me awake at night, I dreaded the news my ears had not yet heard but that my heart already knew. The owner of the camp flew in at the end of my miserable elephant-less week with very bad tidings but also the answer to why I had hit such rough emotional waters. In the autumn of 2016, just after I left her, Naughty broke into the homes of the three top wildlife officials who govern the park. They shot her and killed her.

She didn't hurt anyone. She clearly had something to say to them, and they obviously couldn't understand her. This news left me devastated. I was told this deadly visit came at the end of a mad destructive spree in which she had broken into numerous homes. She never harmed a human but was simply in search of food (so the people say) — or, from my point of view, in search of understanding.

I visited the Mfuwe Lodge, where her mother left her famous tea-time legacy and taught Naughty that humans wouldn't harm her. I'm sure Wonky indicated to her daughter that they were in fact celebrities whom the humans adored and lavished with attention. When they came into human homes, the excited tourists, who had flown across the world to see them, would be snapping their cameras at them. Imagine Naughty's surprise when she found herself not in front of a camera, but the wrong end of a rifle.

I met with Amy, the manager of Mfuwe Lodge, who told me Naughty had broken into seventeen homes after I left and had actually even broken into Amy's home, stealing sugar and gourmet Italian salad dressing, and was intercepted before she made off with a case of expensive champagne. That's my girl.

Natalie, the owner of the luxurious spa at Mfuwe Lodge told me that Naughty had broken into her home also, stealing eggs, butter, and flour. Natalie joked that Naughty had dropped in at her house for breakfast and stole the ingredients to make her morning pancakes, then gone on to Amy's for her evening cocktails. Honestly, if Naughty missed me a fraction as much as I missed her, she could have been going house to house looking for me or hoping to find someone who could call me to tell me she needed me back. But the way the humans viewed it, she was simply binging on gourmet food. They didn't realize the violent bender could have been an attempt to qualm some heartache or frustration. Across the globe, I did the same, drowning my sorrows in culinary delights, but no attempt to pacify my sugar cravings could compete with her sweet kisses on my face.

Whatever her interest in fine dining and alcohol, I feel that her visits to all three wildlife officials was more important to her than stealing their bottles of beer. Don't you think it's odd that she demanded the attention of the top three officials who control the management of wildlife in the entire park — the very men who make all the final decisions?

A hippo cull was called in South Luangwa last year just before Naughty's rampage, proposing that two thousand hippos be shot and murdered under the guise of preventing the spread of Anthrax. Were this done in a humane manner by professional game wardens, I would ruefully understand the necessity of protecting the rest of the hippo population. Unfortunately, the Born Free Foundation, run by wonderful Virginia McKenna, posted a link protesting the advertising of "big game safaris" where "hunters" can fly in from all over the world and murder their very own hippo. A ludicrous photo pictured a hunter standing proudly over his freshly murdered hippopotamus. Were a necessary cull performed correctly, the meat could feed many hungry locals in the village, which I would also understand. But more rumors reached me about hunters selling the meat of the hippos to villagers at prices they could not afford. Rather than having game wardens perform the cull quietly and respectfully, the officials charged tourists big money to come shoot the hippos instead. Corruption abounds.

On the way to South Luangwa last month, I wrote a desperate letter to the president of Zambia and the head of tourism pleading to stop this carnage. South Luangwa has a reputation for forbidding hunting, and these bloody horrors (in which the hippos are skinned) would certainly impact tourism at the park. Auspiciously, at the time I wrote this appeal — before I had any knowledge of Naughty's murder — I wagered that the shooting of two thousand hippos would upset the other animals in the park, being that they have never been exposed to guns and, therefore, cluster to the side of the road to pose for tourists.

How could anyone think the animals would not react when the humans they've always trusted suddenly appear armed with rifles and open fire in their territory? I suggested that this shocking assault might even make the elephants become violent toward humans. Could this have been the message Naughty so ardently wanted to relay to the wildlife officials? Was she trying to be a voice for all the elephants, or even all the species of animals, about the betrayal of trust and violation of their peace treaty with humans?

I sent out a Facebook request in need of two thousand signatures to stop the cull, and the next day it was halted because of "public outrage." While we succeeded this time, hippo culling is an ongoing battle. I later found out that the head of tourism who opposed big game hunting was fired last year and replaced by an official who has legalized lion hunting in Zambia. Only animals outside the park are at risk, but these are numerous. On this most recent trip to a camp outside the park, my favorite lion, Ginger (Doc's dad from chapter 3), set up camp right next to my chalet and brought several of his lionesses to patrol my camp every night. But now with this new ruling, Ginger, and any of his lioness girlfriends, could be slaughtered and decapitated. Naughty's family are also at risk because they like the pathways they have established outside the park. I spent my final week in Zambia trying to relay the message to my lion and elephant friends not to stray outside the park.

In the end, I was comforted to hear that another young female adopted Naughty's young calf and other child. It was she who greeted me when I arrived at the camp. And I was heartened to hear that Naughty's little brother Wellington and the other members of Queen Wonky Tusk's family still parade through the foyer of Mfuwe Lodge every autumn on their pilgrimage to their favorite mango tree. Mfuwe Lodge is within the park and so they are sheltered from hunters. I had a meeting with the lodge owner, Andy, a true elephant lover who has no electric fences around the lodge and never allows anyone to chase the elephants away. The elephants are welcome no matter how much that may inconvenience the staff or slow them in their duties. They even come into the spa! Natalie's accounts of wild-eyed masseuses hiding in the bathrooms waiting for the ellies to leave made me chuckle.

Out of respect for Naughty and her mother, I will now be leading safaris at Mfuwe Lodge, where Wonky left her legacy, and I will do my best to time it right every October or November so that you can meet Naughty's brother Wellington, her Uncle Wilber, and the rest of Naughty's family, including hopefully her son little Wilkenson and his new stepmom — all when their mango tree bears fruit and my favorite family of elephants join us for tea, or mango daiquiris.

WHAT'S HIDDEN IN *MY* TRUNK?

You're learning my life story in a very roundabout way, but now I'm going to elaborate on one of the most important concepts I learned — or tried to learn — from my art training with the American Animation Institute. You may wonder, and I have always wondered, why I seem to have such a different perspective on most things in this life than "normal" people do. For instance, where my students may see a "dog," I see a matrix of frozen light. Where the furious park owners here may see an "elephant," I see a matrix of frozen light. Where normal people may be viewing the outside edges of things and bringing to the table only their own opinions, prior experience, and emotional reactions, I leave those things at home. I connect to the animal on a bridge of unconditional love from my heart to theirs and try to incorporate as much mobility of consciousness around the problem that I can muster. It's this mobility of consciousness that makes clairvoyance possible. If I were stuck in a perspective of seeing elephants only as two-dimensional objects, with no emotional content, I certainly could not overhear their thoughts and feel their feelings, much less see inside their bodies. Psychic ability is an art, so I'm going to tell you a story about my most memorable art class.

DRAWING WALLACE

When I first started taking art classes in Los Angeles, I signed up for life drawing, which I knew very little about, and nothing could prepare me for what I was going to learn there. I knew that models stand in front of you for hours, stark naked, and you try to keep your wits about you and sketch them. As if drawing classes weren't intimidating enough for young green artists, I was being asked to draw every intimate curve and fold of a naked person. In the beginning, young waifish wannabe actresses and fashion models would come pose for the class, and their nymphlike, curveless bodies were pretty easy to quick-sketch.

But one night, a man appeared who had to be at least seventy-five years old. He was introduced to us as Wallace. I could draw the pencil-thin actresses' angular bodies in about fifteen minutes. But when Wallace disrobed and stood buck naked in front of me, I thought, "Uh-oh. This is going to take a while." I mention Wallace here in the elephant chapter because there were obvious similarities. The complicated tapestry of wrinkles and folds, this plethora of dark and light shading exercises, could have kept me busy for weeks! Drawing the young twiggy models was as complicated as drawing a drinking straw, whereas drawing Wallace was most certainly as complex and time-consuming as drawing a baby elephant, or at least a large bulldog.

In pen and ink, I was learning a technique called *cross-hatching* where you make hundreds of little lines, and then cross the lines in a waffle pattern, to create depth and shadow in dark, not-easy-to-see areas obscured by folds. Wallace was quick to become my king of the crosshatch.

It was in the course of my feverish attempt at drawing Wallace that my brilliant art teacher, Karl Gnass, who trains the animators at Disney, DreamWorks, and Warner Bros., raised the stakes and taught a lesson in perspective drawing that I will never forget. I have found over the years that this idea applies beautifully to Animal Communication and actually to all the relationship problems in our lives, including the human–elephant conflict.

How Do We Gain Another Perspective?

Karl once proposed that there are three ways to change our point of view, thereby completely changing the picture we see. What are they?

1. The Model Moves

Now, if you could imagine, to make matters even more challenging, every thirty minutes or so, Wallace would rotate ninety degrees to face another wall, spinning in slow motion in the course of a four-hour art class, like an overcooked rotisserie chicken left too long on the spit. In this way, we would get to investigate every single crack and crevice of Wallace from every possible angle. If the left side of the model is lit up, he only needs to rotate his body to make the light hit the opposite side of his body, thereby changing the entire view of what the artist sees. A moving model is not something that you, as the artist, have any control over. The teacher will simply ask you to draw what is presented to you, and as the model moves, the artists must adjust, and therefore they have no choices. If you perceive only what is in front of your eyes without any mobility, you will see life at face value but not be able to view anything — including wild animals — from another point of view.

If the "model moves," then perhaps something extraordinary happens with one of your animals, and in a moment of epiphany it makes you change the way you see the animal. Say your dog saves your life, or even just leaves the room and comes back with his leash in his mouth before you showed any sign of taking him for a walk, except for the thoughts you were entertaining about walking him. Maybe your animal has done something that makes you realize that she is more intelligent, loving, observant, intuitive, and able to reason than you ever realized before. Most people don't ever have the luxury of watching the "model move." Their perceptions stay stuck unless an animal does something uncanny to prove that he can actually think, feel, intuit, and communicate. But this is not the norm. How do we look at the same thing but see an entirely different picture?

2. Move the Light

Here we get the same results as when the model moves. What was dark is now light, and you can use the light to illuminate and investigate what was in darkness, thereby achieving an entirely different picture when viewing the model from another perspective. If we replace the word *light* with the word *consciousness*, then you can imagine that the light of consciousness shines from within you, so with this new flashlight inside your being, you can make choices in how you perceive the world and light up what was always in darkness. I "light up" the insides of the animals, so that I can see and feel inside their hearts, minds, and bodies. Using your consciousness in this way is a *choice*, and with this new tool in your toolbox, you now have two ways to view animals: not just from the outside in, as we have all been taught, but from the *inside out*. You now have two colors in your crayon box. But there are more shades of awareness to be collected. And this is where it gets even better. How else can we look at the same thing and get a totally different perspective?

3. You Move

At this point, clever Karl did not request that the model turn around. He demanded — and this is why he is so darned brilliant — that we "move" around to the back of the model and draw his backside in our minds.

Interestingly enough, this instruction produced a huge groan from the magnificent professional animators in the guild class. Until this time, four years into my art training, most of my sketches looked as if I were drawing them with my feet. I was still squeaking along with my cartoon training, drawing crude stick figures, trying to get my skills up to par so that I could birth my Woozels, Electrolynx, Clamshankers, Gronkeydoddles, and Squirrelicorns here on Earth. If I couldn't get my skills up, the stars of my children's novel would never be brought to this world, so the stakes were high, but my crude drawing left much to be desired. In short, I stank.

When asked to draw the model from the perspective on number one (the model moves), I couldn't do it. I choked on fear, and every "I can't draw" mental pygmy from my childhood danced around in my head, poking me in the head. When asked to draw from perspective number two (move the light), I still couldn't do it. The pygmies were having a party in my gray matter, because the learning curve in this point of view was still too similar to that of the first fear-producing exercise. It was the same idea but from another direction. So I was still stuck: fear from the left, fear from the right. But when asked to use our imagination and "fly" behind the model to sketch him from the opposite side, employing imaginative speculation about something that *no one could see,* I was the only person in the room who could do it. I discovered that I actually *can* draw, or at least a little bit, but only when asked to employ my imagination and use my own initiative. For the first time in my life, drawing was not a terrifying chore. It actually became *fun.* So what I propose is to use these elements in the human–animal conflicts.

THE LATEST BUZZ

In the midst of this park now strewn with electric fences to keep my favorite elephant out, as God would have it, an elephant expert, a PhD researcher for Elephants for Africa, just booked into the tent next to mine, and as a conservationist who manages nothing but the elephant–human conflict in Botswana, he's explained that while electric fences and even chili fences don't and will never work to deter elephants, even when the chili is burned or used as a spray to burn elephants' eyes and noses, what does work is one of God's smallest and most magical creations. There is only one thing that elephants dislike so much that they will avoid camps full of hot-dog buns and other good-smelling food, and abandon human camps and

farms to go back to their own savannas. What is the dangerous de-
terrent, powerful enough to terrify the earth's largest land mammal?
Bees. Elephants don't like bees.

Being that beehives create honey and therefore are a great way
to bring income to farmers, nothing could be more perfect than
keeping bees on properties where elephants are not welcome for
dinner. And although one might assume that elephants don't like
swarms of bees (when they knock the hive with their noses, the bees
swarm out) because they don't like bee stings, what smart conservationists have discovered is that elephants don't like the sound that
bees make. In even smarter efforts, the buzz of bees has been recorded and is played from the trees where elephants are unwelcome.
Now perhaps it's the pitch that irritates an animal who has some of
the largest ears in the world, and thus the best sense of hearing, but
just imagine, and I am only speculating, that perhaps there is something here more sublime than not liking the buzz or sting of bees. As
nature would have it, our largest, most intimidating giant is afraid
of one of our smallest beings. Maybe these tiny intelligent beings
are placed in the elephants' paths when elephants are in danger of
being harmed by humans, and the bees know this, so they may say
to the marauding elephants, "Knock it off or the humans are going
to kill you."

More than likely, the ellies probably just don't like the sound
that bees make. I love all animals, and my reputation would be ru-
ined if I didn't, but when I have a big buzzing bee dive-bombing me,
even I tend to run the other way.

But this bee solution is so innovative that it shows what can happen when one dares to think outside the box (or hive). So the buzz
is, a creative mind found a peaceful solution and solved a problem in
a night that farmers have struggled with for years. Our commitment
to change our perspective and thus come up with new solutions must
be rigorous, but if we view problems the way we always have —
from everyone's perspective except the animals' — we will always

have the same old problems and we will never get any new positive results. For years to come, I'll be presenting the notion that it is up to you, all of you out there with your wisdom and creativity, to experiment in new ways to help solve human–animal conflicts. And I suggest that you start right away. I'll still be right here drawing Wallace, and it's going to take me a while.

Elephants: The Facts

Ginette Hemley, vice president for species conservation at the World Widlife Fund, shared with me these facts from the Wildlife Conservation Network about the noble work of the Elephant Crisis Fund:

> A renewed and virulent wave of poaching is threatening Africa's elephants by taking their lives to get to their tusks. Every year at least 33,000 elephants are illegally poached. This equates to one elephant every twenty minutes.... A world without elephants would be a tragic failure of our humanity. The Elephant Crisis Fund addresses this crisis....
>
> The ivory trade is primarily driven by a burgeoning demand [for] ivory in China. Ivory has played a centuries-old role in Chinese culture and is seen as an important medium in art and as a symbol of wealth.... The rapidly growing middle class in China is fueling demand and escalating the price of ivory ever higher.... Sophisticated criminal elements — the same groups that smuggle arms, people, and drugs — orchestrate the poaching and smuggling of ivory. On-the-ground antipoaching efforts are outsmarted and outgunned. Borders are too porous and unenforced to stop the flow of ivory. The demand in China seems insatiable....
>
> The elephant crisis is now too big for any one organization or government to solve. It requires a multifaceted response from a coalition of effective leaders, NGOs,

institutions, scientists, media, and governments. Work must be done by the coalition on all aspects of the crisis. To save elephants, we must identify and fund effective partners that address the supply, trafficking, and demand for ivory....

Antipoaching efforts are crucial to stop[ping] the killing of elephants in Africa. Demand for ivory products has to be stopped in China and elsewhere to lower the price of ivory and remove the incentive to kill elephants. This approach requires a coalition of effective organizations that can rapidly implement projects on the ground to save elephants.

The following facts are part of an eloquent appeal to the U.S. Senate made by Ginette Hemley, vice president for species conservation at the World Wildlife Fund, to honor the African and Asian Elephant Conservation Acts of 1997.

With a total wild population of only 35,000 to 50,000, the Asian elephant now numbers less than one-tenth of the African elephant.... The conservation needs of the Asian elephant are urgent if humans are to make a significant difference in ensuring their survival....

Perhaps no other wild animal has had such a close relationship with people. In Asia, the unique relationship between people and elephants runs deep and dates back as far as 4,000 years, when elephants were first captured and trained as draft animals and for use in religious ceremonies and warfare. Its cultural contributions are especially noteworthy. Ancient Hindu scriptures frequently refer to elephants, the elephant-headed god Ganesha is revered throughout India, and the white elephant has special religious significance for Buddhists throughout Asia....

Beyond this unique relationship with human beings, the

Asian elephant is a flagship for the conservation of the tropical forest habitats in which it is found. Elephants range over long distances and across a variety of habitats that are home to numerous other wildlife species. As they need very large areas to survive, effective conservation and management of elephants can deliver widespread benefits for other endangered species such as the tiger, rhinoceros, kouprey, clouded leopard, Asiatic wild dog, gaur, Malayan sun bear, Hoolock gibbon, and countless other wildlife sharing its home....

Poaching of Asian elephants for ivory, although far less significant than with African elephants, is still a problem in parts of South India, Cambodia, Vietnam, Burma, and Laos.... Hide is turned into bags and shoes in Thailand and China, and bones, teeth, and other body parts are used in traditional Chinese medicine to cure various ailments. In Vietnam, such poaching is a threat even to the remaining domestic elephants that are allowed to roam freely in forests.

Ivory. Imagine it. There are still parts of this world where useless doohickies made of ivory wield such value that elephants are heinously slaughtered in order to divorce them from their tusks. Piano keys, gun barrels, guitar picks, perfume bottles, and, most wretched of all, religious icons are often made from ivory. The Vatican is a major importer of ivory, and the shocking truth is that murdered elephants' tusks are carved into little statues of Jesus and St. Francis, which I'm sure couldn't be further from what they would have wished for themselves. Chinatowns around America, especially the one in San Francisco, have been so stocked with ivory for purchase that elephant lovers have conducted protest marches through the streets, yet America remains one of the largest importers of ivory. But wait. There is a glimmer of hope. Many groups are working tirelessly to save the elephants from extinction and conserve their habitats.

The Asian Elephant Conservation Fund provides support for protection of the remaining elephant populations and their habitat against further loss and degradation. The World Wildlife Fund and other international conservation organizations, such as the International Union for Conservation of Nature and the Wildlife Conservation Society, have been working to identify priority elephant habitats throughout the species' remaining range and to promote establishment and management of corridors and special protected areas.

I heard Jane Goodall say that the only way conservation will ever work is if it is made profitable for the indigenous people. As with the plight of chimpanzees, the survival of elephants is dependent on the almighty dollar. As long as starving humans can murder animals to make a buck, they will. Paying them to *stop poaching* by teaching other means of survival seems to be the only viable solution.

If you have internet access, go online and take a look at the photos of elephant keepers and baby elephants starving on the streets of Bangkok, and see if you can keep your heart from exploding into smithereens. Try to keep your heart in one piece, but don't keep your wallet in your pocket. Take that two hundred clams you were going to spend on a Kate Spade handbag *and tithe.*

Here's my challenge. If every well-fed person in America, Canada, Europe, Australia, and so on — who is not even affluent but just middle class — forfeited the purchase of one car wash, one weekly manicure, or one tube of designer lipstick and sent that fifteen bucks to a conservation organization instead, there might still be wild animals on this planet when our children grow up. Your Kate Spade handbag wouldn't last that long, anyway, but maybe the elephants will.

ARE YOU AN ARK ANGEL?

I'll be in Africa doing charity work for the rest of my life. My non-profit charity, Ark Angel, came into being when I meditated, prayed, and cried over the plight of the elephants. There are already wonderful conservation organizations working to rescue elephants from extinction. What could I possibly do to make a difference? It took years of soul-searching before I broke down and admitted that the work to be done to rescue animals and this entire planet cannot start with animals. It must start with children — human children. So I pulled out my credit card and decided to fly up into the wilds of Zambia, stay on after my safari, and do some charity work in the schools. But what could I do to reach these kids? For these kids, being a poacher is the financial equivalent of being an American drug dealer. A man could feed his family for a year from the proceeds he gets from one dead elephant and the sale of her tusks. And these are not just any families. These are families in dire straits, living together in huts with mud floors, where 50 percent of the villagers are HIV-positive and have or will die of AIDS, where babies are dying from malnutrition, and where grandparents are in the same house, often ill and also needing to be fed.

Where does the money come from for these people? I'm not arrogant enough to believe that wealthy people have the right to judge these native people and take their resources away. But I am confident enough to believe that there are new job opportunities opening up, especially in the modern world, that would allow these men and, most of all, women to entertain the thought of new careers in the worlds of conservation, working as scouts or guides; or even reformed poachers could work as protectors of our beloved elephants. New careers are also available in the service industry with the advent of safari parks hiring beautiful young hostesses and dashing African barmen and waiters, of which I've seen a few, as well as extremely qualified guides operating as experts on guided tours of

Africa and her animals. The future is ripe with possibilities for the African people to enjoy employment that doesn't require them to shoot an elephant and watch her die slowly.

Most people don't know that poached elephants die slowly. We have it in our heads that a poacher puts a gun to an elephant's head, pulls the trigger, and presto, the elephant dies on the spot. Poof! But that is not how it works. Three years ago, I took a seven-hour car ride across Africa from Nairobi, where I'd flown to meet with Daphne Sheldrick and to meet Kuki Gallmann, the bestselling author of *I Dreamed of Africa* (Penguin Books), which was adapted into a movie in which Kim Basinger played Kuki. One of my students had suggested I reach out to this famous writer and icon, and I did so with no pretense. I never thought she'd get back to me. But when that email was shining in my inbox one morning, inviting me up to her elephant sanctuary, I heard the angels sing and wrote her back immediately with an emphatic "YES!" Over the three days that I spent with her in Kenya, huddled in the gazebo watching the torrential rain, Kuki revealed to me some stories that were close to her heart. She told me about finding one of her elephants with a gunshot wound in her leg. This is how poachers do it, you see. They don't kill the elephants quickly. They shoot them anywhere they can and wait for the infection to build. Kuki followed the elephant for three days and three nights, sleeping with her, until the abscessed leg became so swollen that the elephant could walk no more. Kuki lay with her on that third night when she thankfully finally died and was free from suffering at human hands.

Kuki now hires reformed poachers to be her scouts. And who better to know the ins and outs of what a poacher will do than an ex-poacher?

But my strategy, here in Mfuwe, was to reach the children young, before any damage had been done to their hearts and psyches, to their families and wallets, and most of all to the elephants.

The first program I gave in the schools was very successful. I had the children dance as elephants, draw elephants who had relationships with each other, and even make up plays to act out the poaching. This was the most incredible. When I asked the kids if they thought a baby elephant would miss his mother if she got killed, they all said, "No!"

Then I had a girl play the mommy elephant, another girl play the auntie, and a boy play the baby elephant. We had one boy volunteer to be the big bad poacher. He shot the mommy and the auntie and killed them both. Both girls fell to the floor. The little African boy went up to his dead aunt and mother and just gently nudged them with his hand, pretending it was his nose. He mourned their loss so beautifully, and he made it look so sad even without words.

Then I asked the class, "*Now* do you think a baby elephant would miss his mother if she got poached?" and they all said, "Yes!" I had them yell at the top of their lungs, "Poacher—*no*! Protector—*yes*! Poacher—*no*! Protector—*yes*!"

It was a huge success, and I can't wait to do more of this in schools all over the world — and get you involved, too. As you can imagine, elephants are not easy to count. But I wanted to give you the latest numbers so that we'd have an idea of how much their population has decreased in the past century due to the poaching crisis.

WHAT DO ELEPHANTS REPRESENT?

Perseverance. As the Remover of Obstacles, Ganesha knows no bounds in his ability to achieve his goals. Their message? "Stay on the path," and "Keep your feet on the ground!" Find the path that God and nature have intended you to walk in this lifetime, and stay the course at all costs. Keep moving forward, remove all obstacles, and stick together. An elephant's sense of community demonstrates to us that we are far more powerful in groups — marching sure-footedly, flanked by others on the same spiritual path. Elephants show us consistency, level-headed good habits unswayed by any distractions in the world around us, and a joyous sense of stability and belonging to God's world and this earth. They also show us that there's strength in numbers.

What else do they teach us? The importance of family and the power of strong women. If one elephant falls ill, a "nursemaid" is assigned to take care of that elephant so that he will not suffer alone. Elephants have much to teach us about successful community, well-run political systems, and how to establish order in our lives. And at all costs, they encourage us to be nosy! They teach us to maintain friendliness with each other and other species, to reach out to one another, and to cultivate curiosity about the world around us.

3 | Lions
Kings and Queens

My God's not dead, He's surely alive
He's living on the inside, roaring like a lion...
— Daniel Bashta, from "Like a Lion"

One of my most memorable lion encounters happened several years ago when a South African student of mine, Wynter, wanted help with a difficult case. She emailed me a picture of a baby white lion cub named Zintle who had just died mysteriously. One minute the cub was fine, and within a matter of hours, baby Zintle was dead. Paul Hart, the owner of the Drakenstein Lion Park in Cape Town, was very worried that Zintle's sister, Ziyanda, would also die of this sudden unpredictable illness. He was out of his mind with worry and grief. I'll never forget opening that attachment, looking at the heart-melting ivory fur face, and dropping everything right before Christmas so that I could help this poor man figure out why his precious baby lion cub had died.

I read about the cubs' background in the brief email from Wynter: Zintle and Ziyanda were both born on December 10, 2008, and they had arrived at Paul's sanctuary on March 11, three months later. Zintle had suddenly become ill in the early hours of August 12, and despite emergency veterinary intervention, passed away later that day. No one knew why. She was only nine months old. I spent a few moments praying to God and gazing at the creampuff face. Then I ran a body scan and performed medical Gestalt on the photo, where I went into trance to have a chat with the baby lion angel in heaven. Like lightning, I connected with the spirit of the lioness and launched into motion, typing answers on my keyboard without thinking — before my analytical mind could try to deny what my intuition was telling me. Even as an established psychic, I still battle my own internal critic after all these years; but when I felt pain in my right side and put my hand over my liver, I knew she had had distress there. I forced myself to go on mental autopilot and look further while I channeled these words:

> My take on this is that her internal organs had not developed properly. When I "look," I see a problem with her intestines. Zintle's body was not prepared to house her mighty energy. Her problems were birth defects in her colon and intestinal structure. The intestinal wall was too thin, and I feel the distress was in her lower right abdomen at the point where the colon and small intestine meet. There's a twist and turn there where food has to go up against gravity. Her intestine twisted, swelled, and ruptured.

Wynter wrote back to say that an autopsy was about to be performed on baby Zintle, so the results would be confirmed scientifically one way or another within two weeks of my intuitive reading. She said my email had been forwarded to the owner of the park, Paul Hart, who was a huge skeptic.

I forwarded the photo of Zintle's precious face to one of my American students, Heidi. Knowing that the vet in South Africa was going to do an autopsy gave me butterflies in my tummy — I was a little nervous but awfully excited to have this scientific validation, so I capitalized on the opportunity to do a double-blind experiment with one of my most talented clairvoyant students, who happens to be an ex-police officer. I sent Heidi the photo and asked her why baby Zintle had died. I did not utter a word of my own opinion. This is what Heidi wrote back: "The very first thing I got was an image of an intestine that had a wall that is too thin. This looked to me like an intestinal bubble, or aneurysm, or embolism, I'm not sure of the medical term. I'm not sure if her intestine ruptured, but it was bound to."

Now, the awesome challenge of this quest for us both was that we were not asked to perform a body scan on a living animal, but rather we were to do a psychic autopsy on an animal in heaven. I was comforted to hear that Heidi and I were in perfect agreement, even though I had been careful not to breathe a word of my impressions to her to sway her intuitive reading. I was even more impressed with Heidi now than I'd ever been, and I was proud to be her mentor.

Two weeks later, Wynter sent the official report from the vet who performed the autopsy on Zintle in South Africa: "Post Mortem and Laboratory results have determined that Zintle suffered from an intestinal congenital defect that resulted in degenerative liver failure. Her condition was untreatable."

One of the greatest rewards of my life was flying to South Africa to visit the lion park and meet the gruff, controversial, wonderful Paul Hart — whose last name is a tribute to his shining heart of gold. I got to listen in person to his story as he shared with me the tragedy of losing his treasured lion cub, Zintle. He told me he had stayed up countless nights, worrying that Ziyanda would also die of this mysterious illness. He said he had received the emails from me in Los Angeles assuring him that Zintle's health problem was congenital — she'd had it from birth — and that her sister Ziyanda did not share the illness and would live out her life as a strong, healthy lioness.

Paul — this big, butch South African man — was near tears telling me how amazed he was when the vets found that my intuition was correct. Ziyanda was not in danger, and Zintle's death was no fault of his. I'll never forget the look in his eyes when I said that Zintle had insisted I tell him the problem was a birth defect and not a result of the treatment she had received in his loving care. Despite the twinge of awe, confusion, and disbelief in his eyes, a wave of relief washed over his face. It's in these tender moments of confronting skeptics and overcoming my fear that I find I can comfort even some of the most skeptical animal lovers on earth. These are scary moments for me. I have feelings, too, and I don't want to be wrong. But when I can help comfort a man like this — an animal champion and hero — no matter how skeptical he is of psychics, I realize that courage, not talent, is the key ingredient of my controversial work and its value.

Of course, my career has other infinite perks. During a private tour of Paul's park, I got to meet baby Ziyanda in person and speak to her. She is the cutest, spunkiest white lion cub in Cape Town, so if you live nearby, please go out and support Paul with his rescue work. My next story is even more mysterious, because it's about a lion who isn't really a lion...yet.

Dream On, Hayley

"Zees cat! Zees giant cat! You've got to see zees cat. He is the biggest cat you've ever seen! Zees cat is impossibly big! And he only limps when you are looking! You need to come take zees cat!"

These words were delivered by Albert, my masseur in Los Angeles, my healer, an Argentinean medicine man I trusted so completely, I would do absolutely anything he said...except this. I didn't want another cat. And even the idea of taking the world's biggest house cat, who limped only when you were looking, wasn't enough to make me want to adopt a cat when I traveled for a living.

"You come see. You will fall in love with zees cat." I had no intention of doing so.

"You must take him. He will be killed if you don't."

Yikes.

The story was that my masseur managed an apartment building in North Hollywood where the tenants were not allowed to have cats. Someone took in this cat and saved his life. Now the forbidden cat had been passed on to the manager of this cat-free zone, who was technically also not supposed to have cats. But my secret was that Albert had been the cat sitter of the infamous Flo (Ol' Aunt Flo), the star of my second book, *The Language of Miracles*, and he kept the ten-pound can of whoop-ass, Florabelle, while I traveled the world teaching Animal Communication. Even when the ancient old broad was on her ninth-and-a-half life, he loved her as I did and could mimic the difference in her raspy voice when she yowled that she wanted to use her litter box ("I am now entering my litter box to pee!") as opposed to the yowl afterward as if to say, "I have now completed peeing and have successfully exited my litter box." He mimicked the beseeching "before" (*mrow-ree-rowh!*) and proud "after" (*mraaayuh!*) declarations to me with utter glee, with sincere caring; he not only noticed Flo's needs but delighted in her ability to vocalize her most delicate moments.

This man wasn't just my most trusted confidant when it came to healing and medicine; he was also an authority in my life when it came to cats. And he was quite certain that I needed to meet the world's largest house cat. Gosh, I'd never told him my private preferences, so how did he know I was a sucker for big, fat male cats?

The day I drove to this ramshackle apartment in North Hollywood, I had absolutely no intention of adopting another cat. But then God dropped in for a cup of tea. I took one look at the biggest chocolate Persian I'd ever seen on this earth, and he gave me the "big-eye," like an amused rock star. Having been a backup dancer for Smokey Robinson and Ray Charles, I've known a few. He looked me up and down, chuckled, and then said, "I'll come see you after I eat." Then he left the room for the kitchen. I laughed out loud at his attitude. What gall he had to make his rescuer wait even though his life was at stake! So certain was he that I would take him that he decided to polish off the remnants in his food bowl before he packed his bags. After his snack (maybe he'd been partying all night and had the munchies — who knows?), he strolled back into the room and looked me up and down again with a wide, contagious grin of approval on his massive mug — it's true, I'd never seen a larger house cat in my life — and he said, "Okay, baby doll...let's roll."

I hoisted him up into my arms, almost slipping a disc in the process, and he put his arms and legs around me, bunny-hugging me like a gigantic koala bear, then snuggled his face into my neck, licked my chin, and tried to put his tongue up my nose. I roared with laughter and told him, "You're a very funky cat. The kind I don't take home to mother." I didn't feel like I was adopting a cat. I felt like George Clinton had just landed in his spaceship. (If you are too young — or too old — to know who George Clinton is, the Commander of the Intergalactic Parliament of the Nations of Funk, I highly suggest you look him up and get acquainted with the grand master of funkadelic grooves that will make you laugh out loud and want to jump up and dance no matter how un-groovy you may feel at the moment. The funkiest of all rock stars began every concert with his mother ship landing on the stage in a thick cloud of smoke — the kind of smoke you don't smoke in front of your mother. Then he'd emerge, sporting a mane of dreadlocks perched akimbo on his head like antennae connecting him to his home planet, high-heeled wedgie boots, a huggy-bear hat, and an outlandish pimp outfit — an ensemble apropos to fulfill his divine mission to deliver extraterrestrial funkmanship to our boring, rhythmless, and humorless planet.)

I gave this mammoth cat a jiggle to test my theory and discovered how he loved to dance — to be bobbed up and down like a gargantuan baby. Yes, he was indeed twenty-six pounds of furry, funkalicious fun. The more I bounced him up and down, making him hip-hop, the louder he purred. His ham-hock legs bobbed one way and his front paws twisted another, reaching like a DJ mixing a record in a midnight house party. Apparently, the Feline Emperor of Funk had found his way into the arms of his new attendant and dance partner. I found myself addicted in our first paw de deux — he'd instantly made a funkaholic out of me.

"I'll take him!" I said to Al. And to the Rastafarian feline, I said, "Okay, baby doll...let's roll." And that was that. I was his. And I was in for a wild ride.

I can't say that I rescued this cat. I can say in retrospect that he rescued me. And I was never to become his "owner." I was happy just to be one of his "bit-chez." But back on the first day we met, I knew only that I was taking in a house cat the size of a bulldog. Little did I know that his ferocity would make any real bulldog cower. At this point, you may be wondering why I'm including a story about a house cat in a chapter about lions. Well, there's a method to my madness. Come along for the ride. Okay, baby doll...let's roll.

I took this colossal cat back to my apartment in North Hollywood, which fortunately was a fairly cat-friendly place, having been the home of Flo and Hopkins before they joined the angels. Aside from some pesky traffic out front, the apartment was safe for cats. As I mentioned, the first thing I noticed was that this was the first house cat I'd ever met who loved to dance. If I put on dance music — and it had to be a song he liked, and these were only certain old-school funk jams — he'd head-butt my shins and shout, "*Rah! Rah!*" until I picked him up and let him dance in my arms. I heard him demand, "Dance! Dance!" I'd hoist him onto my hip like a sack of Chinese dumplings, and then the love-fest would begin with this chocolate

Persian hip-hopping and doing the Running Man in my arms. We'd dance for literally hours every night and never leave out his favorite tune, "Comin' to you directly from the mother ship, top of the chocolate Milky Way, home of the extraterrestrial brothers...Make my funk to P. Funk, I wantsta get funked up..."

The second thing I noticed was that he had no name. All animals' souls have names, but when I tuned in to find it, no name ever surfaced. No matter what I came up with, it never felt right, and he would not respond when I tried to call him with one of the new nonsense names. (Michael Jackson? Luther Vandross? Barry White? Ice T? Kanye? Chris Brown?) My healer said that he would come only when you made a clicking sound with your tongue, which sounded like, "Xcl! Xcl!" No matter how I struggled to find his soul's name, he would only answer, "Xcl! Xcl!" Of course, I called him "P. Funk" for a while, because what's a girl to do?

The third thing I noticed was that this very funkadelic cat never said "Meow," like a cat. He only said, "*Rah!*" unless he was dreaming and talking in his sleep, which he did loudly every night, in which case he would say, "*Rahah-ra-bad-ababah-rar-rah-reee-rah!*" Another odd thing I noticed was that when spooning in my arms every night (he would wrap his big arms around me and spoon my back from behind), sometimes he would shape-shift into a Zulu king. I'd wake up with a large rotund man snoring next to me, feather headdress and all, and a belt of medicine pouches around his chubby waist. There's never a dull moment in a psychic's life, I know. Fortunately for me, I'm very comfortable around chubby Zulu kings, or cats who involuntarily shape-shift into them, so all this was A-OK by me. But I can't say it wasn't a bit of a shock the first time my Persian shape-shifted into a Zulu king. Chances are we were together in a previous life where I was one of his many wives, and he'd found his way back to me because we were still in love, even though I was then, as now, just one of his "bit-chez." Nonetheless, I was thankful to discover why he was so bizarre, so when I discovered the truth, I breathed a sigh of relief and said, "Oh, now I see who you are. But could you keep the snoring and talking in tribal languages down to a whisper, please?"

Thus began our epic, groovalicious love affair. A love affair that took this house cat from Los Angeles to London to New Jersey to New York City — and perhaps, just perhaps, even "home" eventually to Africa.

But shape-shifting was just the beginning. This scandalous cat was a washroom attendant who would follow me into the bathroom every night and lick my toes as I perched on the throne, so convinced was he that I simply wasn't safe in the bathroom on my own. When I asked him about this, he said, "There's water in there," as if I were a fool who didn't understand the dangers. Over the years, I've met countless cats and dogs — especially Chihuahuas — who are bathroom attendants to their humans. I stayed with a student last year whose two Chihuahuas would faithfully follow me to the ladies', push the door open once I was indisposed, and stare intently at me as I did my business, like little bug-eyed gargoyles frozen at my feet. Intimidated by their stares, I asked why I wasn't allowed to use the toilet by myself, and then I heard them begging to lick my butt, convinced that toilet paper was a sad substitute. When I protested, the more insistent of the two said, "But I can do a better job than you can! And it will feel *good*!" I actually found his reasoning hard to refute. But I decided to do it the old-fashioned way with Charmin, not Chihuahuas. Doc would never stoop to such crass behavior. Doc would wait for me to mount the throne so that he could lick my *toes*. (He may have been funky, but he wasn't a freak!)

There are many other four-legged bathroom attendants out there without such ambitious motives. When I question them about their obsession with their self-appointed jobs, they show me the dangers of our toilets. How the water is connected to an underground sewer, where at worst we could fall in, but honestly, at best, we are subject to an energetic field that our animals don't approve of — they sense our homes' vulnerability in having energetic leaks that connect clean-looking houses to underground contaminated cesspools. These were cesspools my Doc would never let me face alone. He'd wake from a loud snore to follow me, stumbling along half-asleep, into the bathroom, behavior he displayed even in his later years when he could barely walk. I'd hear him rumble awake and labor heavily down his stairs (he was a full-figured gentleman in his later years and needed his own set of baby stairs to get on and off the bed) if he heard me making my way alone to the bathroom — a wicked place where I was simply not safe without him. Many of you know this feeling and have these protective animals following you to the loo every night even as you read this. Now, that's real love. But there was more to his obsession with the porcelain library.

Every morning, when I was in the bathtub, Doc would push his way through the cracked door and he'd head-butt the tub, yelling, "*Rah! Rah! Rah!*" I'd say to him, "You can't be serious." And he'd continue, "*Rah! Rah!*" One day I got tired of his roaring through my bubble baths and smashing his head against the tub, and I said, "Good grief! Okay." I reached down and hoisted his gargantuan self into the bathtub and rested him between my knees. He kicked back in the bubble bath with hot soapy water up to his neck, and he just said, "*Prrrrr!*" That's right. He started *purring*! I scratched his big fat wet belly and let the water-loving beast soak in the bath with me. Ol' Doc would lie in my arms purring like a motorboat as I scrubbed him and cuddled him in the hot bath. Doc was a *kook*.

There was something else very un-house-cat-like about this cat. Once he moved in with me, he retired completely from ever going outside alone. I'd walk him like a little dog around the neighborhood, and he'd trot along beside my ankle, answering only to "Xcl, xcl." But he had big issues with dogs. One day he rushed into the bedroom looking very upset. I asked him what was wrong and followed him into the living room, where he showed me that the front door had blown open in the wind. He roared at me until I shut it. Not only would this cat never ever run away, or ever leave my side, but he was horrified when the front door accidentally blew open.

"Why does that bother you so much?" I asked him.

"Some other animal could run in here and eat my food," he said. And I'll never forget the day one tried to. The latch on my apartment's front door was not very sturdy, and the Santa Ana winds in California are fierce. So one day when the door flew open, a big dog — I mean a really big dog — ran into my apartment. She was a large poodle mix that the neighbor was dog-sitting. God bless this poor dog.

Doc was just polishing off his second breakfast, or maybe it was his snack before lunch, when he turned around and found her in my living room. To my dismay, he transformed into some sort of ferocious beast I'd never seen before. He froze. Every long hair on his body stood on end as he blew himself up to the size of a porcupine (*porcupussing* is what I call it), and he started stalking this big dog, trying to roar like a lion and doing a darned good impression of it, and chasing her all over the house. I admit, once I got over the shock, I couldn't stop laughing, but I also couldn't back him off. She ran frantically into the bedroom, looking for shelter from the onslaught, then into the bathroom, but he was hot on her trail, and his claws had turned into a wheat-thresher.

He was so terrifying, I was actually scared to separate them as he kept attacking her, but I finally shooed the tornado of hissing and flying fur back into the living room, where he porcupussed her right out the front door. I ran out to comfort her, being that she was, after all, a *canine*, and she had just gotten her tail whupped not by a wild alley cat but by a house cat, and a *Persian* house cat at that! How embarrassing! I promised not to tell any of her dog friends. When

I found her cowering on the balcony, she was shook up, and he was so shook up that I had to take him for a long drive on the freeway to calm him down.

His favorite pastime was sitting on my lap in the car as we cruised down the freeway, low-riding. He loved to ride in the car, and whenever other motorists looked over and saw this colossal chocolate Persian sitting on my lap with his paws on the steering wheel, stuck in traffic on a Los Angeles freeway, they'd roll down the window and howl with joy. He'd mug out the open window, greeting his fans like the mayor of the town, the way I've seen Jay Leno do on Coldwater Canyon in one of his classic cars. Doc was a rock star. Now you may be wondering why I named him Doc.

How Doc Got His Name

I'd accepted the coveted invitation to be a bridesmaid in a wedding...again. Now, if there's one way I'd like to spend my weekend, attending a wedding is not it. Wakeboarding with walruses? Yes. Wandering after warthogs and wildebeest? Absolutely. Cartooning Woozels? Most definitely. Whispering with a one-eyed weasel named Wanda? Certainly. (I wish I'd had that appointment to use as an excuse.) But attending a wedding? Not on your life.

But once again, someone I loved was getting married, and I couldn't say no to the bride, so I'd been forced to spend a small fortune on a hideous bridesmaid's dress. You know the dress. The ensemble comes with a cropped matching sequined jacket, so from the waist up you look like one of Liberace's doormen, and from the waist down you look like you're attending a Muslim funeral. The bride assures you that you can take this dress (that she *adores* and chose with *you* in mind) to a tailor after the wedding and have it hacked off above the knee to wear on special occasions. (In case you spend New Year's Eve in Las Vegas or one of your friends throws a Bollywood-themed party and you find yourself with nothing to wear.) And of course, you will want to keep it forever to commemorate her big day and wear it in memory of her. (In another life… in the distant future… on another planet.) Naturally, it will be up to the bridesmaid to find a pair of matching shoes.

After wheezing at your credit card bill to pay off that painful purchase, you'll go out to buy an overpriced, unnecessary gift. I got to Robinsons-May too late to tick off the plum items at the top of her wish list, so I ended up purchasing a dishwater-gray shower mat and his-and-hers toothbrush-holder cups shaped like little tuxedos (made in China). Of course, the wrapping cost more than the gifts.

To add insult to injury, the wedding was being held outside the country, and I was stuck with the honor of buying my airfare to a wedding I couldn't afford and didn't want to go to, to see people I didn't want to see.

And in this upcoming weekend of festivities, I had no partners in crime to riff with. No one in this wedding party was funny, and I knew that the bride and groom were going to repeat vows and read poems and such, sniveling and blubbering with tears, too choked with everlasting love to squeak out the words. This alone was going to take *hours*. As you have gleaned by now, I'd rather have a Pap smear than be in a wedding.

But I'd stupidly accepted, which tipped off my passive-aggressive pity party, which helped me contract my signature illness, which I only get when I agree to do something I don't want to do: strep throat and laryngitis at the same time. The strep manifested as a reward for my stifling my anger, and the laryngitis for my inability to confront the situation and be honest about my feelings, much less express them out loud. (*Not* gonna happen!) So the week before the wedding, I got sicker than any human should ever get and still be alive. I didn't break down and go to the doctor, so convinced was I that I could get myself on the mend with vitamins alone. Silly me. I had enough bacteria in me to kill a rhinoceros.

The night before the flight, half my face fell, so I looked like I'd had a stroke, even though I hadn't, and the congestion in my head was so agonizing that I couldn't open my left eye. Now, I had to get on a plane at the crack of dawn the next morning and not only fly to a foreign country but also be camera-ready for *pictures*. I was so miserable, I couldn't sit up in bed, so I lay in the quagmire of my own negativity, knowing that no amount of NyQuil was going to get me through this night. My head was killing me. I tried to sleep. I started to cry.

And that's when it happened. This new Persian cat of mine clambered up onto the bed and thumped up my right side. Then he did something he'd never done before — something I'll never forget. He kept walking until he reached the top of my head. I felt him turn around on the pillow above my pounding skull and plant himself on my head like a Russian hat. I felt one paw reach down and a big soft pad land on my aching left eyelid. Then I felt the other strong furry arm wrap down around my right ear to absorb some of the tears rolling down my right cheek. A few minutes later, he took his paw off my left eye and reached down with both arms. He cradled my head tightly, holding both paws under my trembling jaw as I cried. Then he rested his chin on my forehead and started to purr.

Even in my delirium, I could still tune in. "What are you doing?" I mentally asked him. I heard his thought: "I'm balancing the two hemispheres of your brain." He went on to explain something about recalibrating brain waves and other healing modalities too complicated for me to understand. I wish I could recall it all for you, but I dare not even try. All I can tell you is that the next morning, I woke up well. Not kinda-sorta feeling better, but *well*.

I boarded the plane and survived the debacle, and when I returned, the circus tent of a dress made a nice nest for a family of rats living behind a recycle bin out back, where the rodent youngsters could pretend that every day was a day at the big top. But whatever cure Doc had performed on me that night was some wizardry that my wise old Jewish ear, nose, and throat specialist in Beverly Hills couldn't have performed on me, even if he'd brought me home-made matzo ball soup from his own kitchen. And, by the way, this head-squeezing hemisphere-balancing act never happened again, because it never needed to. Once I acquired this cat, I never got that sick again. This cat was a *doctor*. And this miraculous healing he'd conducted was just more proof of his interplanetary funkmanship.

This shaman-healer cat was also soon to become my therapist, as well as my alarm clock, workout coach, meditation teacher, spiritual guru, and personal clown. But most of all, he was my psychiatrist, so I named him Doc (short for Doctor Funkenstein). And that was only because he didn't have a name or couldn't tell me his name other than this clicking sound, "Xcl."

A year later, one winter night, I put on a new jam called "Dream On Hayley," by James Morrison. It's a bittersweet love song, with the kind of melancholy that cuts right through my soul. I started to sing him this song softly to see if he liked it before I picked him up to dance:

Some people sleep easy. Some people don't.
Keep the light on because you start to feel so alone.
Somebody's disappointment over the years.
Willing to love completely, but it always ends in tears....
Dream on Hayley...

It's the kind of song I understand. And much to my surprise, he looked up at me with the most startled knowing look in his eyes. Apparently, he understood it, too. He looked away for a moment, pensive. I had struck a raw chord. This cat knew a thing or two about abandonment, betrayal, and all the pain that humans can cause. His limp was actually caused by his own claws, which had been neglected for so long that they had formed loops and were cutting into his beautiful paw pads, driving themselves deeper into his flesh with every step, like nails in the hands of my other favorite "Lion." I had had to have them surgically removed, they were so bloody and embedded in the soles of his feet. A shadow fell over his face as I kissed his aching feet, but as I sang the poignant song, every time I said "Hayley," he'd look up at me with a sparkle in his eyes and raise his chin with a sideways grin! I'd never seen him do anything like this before, so I hoisted him up into my arms and we danced to this song for the first time, spinning gently around the living room as I sang in his ear: "If you don't feel loved, dreaming is the way to go. Dream on Hayley…" From that night on, he answered to "Hayley" as well as "Xcl." This became our nightly ritual, ending every day with a slow dance as I sang "Dream on Hayley." And at long last, he had an English name and a nickname I could pronounce.

Don't think I've strayed too far off the path. This little lion in my apartment was only leading me to real lions in Africa, so stay with me. There's a method to my madness. At this time, I was trying to live in New Jersey, which you may recall was not going well. Doc was losing his sight, and the day he memorized every inch of my apartment, rubbing his whiskers three inches from every object, I knew that it was no longer fair to juggle him between the two apartments when I was so often out of the country. I left Doc in Manhattan with his cat sitters, a wonderful tattoo artist and his lovely wife, while I embarked on a trek to Africa to enjoy my first safari — and I would have, if it hadn't been for Peter.

Peter's an Asshole

There's a well-known legend about safaris that I had heard for years but never really believed. And that is that when you go on your first safari — and pay a pretty penny for it, too — be it for your mother's birthday or your silver wedding anniversary, or whatever event in your life calls for a celebration of this magnitude, your entire safari will be spoiled by one of the guests because the biggest asshole you've ever met in your life will be on your truck. Being that you are usually grouped with the same people for every ride, you will find it virtually impossible to escape the asshole, and he will ruin every single game drive you go on, being loud and obnoxious and claiming to know more about the animals than even your African guide does. He will boast that he's been everywhere you want to go and already has the best pictures of everything you want to see. I'd heard about this legend but wasn't convinced that it would happen to me, divinely guided as I am. Wrong!

I was still in Victoria Falls, where I had landed first to white-water-raft the Zambezi. (That's twenty-four death-defying Class III to V rapids, where you get tossed out of the raft like a handful of confetti on New Year's Eve and tumble head over heels in endless waterfalls, gasping for your life in a river full of crocodiles. Good times. But that's a story I'll elaborate on a bit later.)

I was lying in bed in Victoria Falls the night after I risked my life in the Zambezi, when a young lioness blasted into my mind and demanded, "Where are you?!" I said, "I'm in Zimbabwe. Where are you?" She said, "We're in the Luangwa National Park. We're waiting for you! Hurry up!"

"How many are you?" I asked.

She said, "There's me and my boyfriends, and then there's a pride of a mother and father and three babies. But they are separate from us. I need you to come quickly."

"Why?" I asked.

"I have two boyfriends, but I need you to help me pick the right one." I saw a vision of a very golden male lion and a darker, more chocolate-colored young lion.

"Why do you need my help?" I asked.

"He may have to fight the other male someday." She showed me a huge dominant male who was the head of the other pride.

"Okay," I said. "Hang on. I'm coming."

Next, as I was dozing off to sleep — or trying to — a leopard blasted into my mind.

"Where are you?!" she asked.

"I'm in Vic Falls. Where are you?"

"We're in the park! We're waiting for you!"

"How many are you?"

"There's me and my mate." I saw a vision of this female leopard in the road, and far above her in a tree was her mate, looking down at me, peering between branches as only sneaky leopards do.

"Okay, I'm coming. I'm sorry to keep you waiting. I fly out tomorrow. Please wait for me." It was clear to me that both the lioness and the leopard thought it was utterly ridiculous that I was keeping them waiting because I'd chosen to spend the weekend in Zimbabwe, where I was risking my life in a *boat*, of all things. And I got a mental glimpse of my daring act from their perspective — a bunch of screaming monkeys going down waterfalls in a boat. What could be stupider than that? I'd come to Africa to meet *them*, for heaven's sake, not to die along the way doing something silly.

I told both girls that I'd be there as soon as I could, and if they'd wait for me, they could meet me the next day after I flew into Mfuwe, got settled into the park, and went out on my first game drive the following night.

I was traveling incognito on this trip. I had not yet begun leading my annual Sacred Harmony Safaris, which evolved out of this first trip, and although I had used a travel agent, no one at the Kafunta River Lodge to my knowledge knew who I was or what I did for a living.

So I joyously boarded the truck the next day with a bunch of tourists, and I kept quiet about my career. I think I told everyone that I was a salsa dance teacher. I wanted to quietly meet my lion and leopard friends and not let anyone know who I was. But my anonymity was about to be shattered.

I was sitting in the back of the group, minding my own business, when the big African guide, Josephat, who was about to drive us into the bush, turned to the group and said, "There is a la-dee on this truck…who has a very special gift…for being able to talk to the animals."

Uh-oh. I didn't know these parks did web searches on their guests. Surprise!

"And I would like to know what she has to say. Amelia, what do you need in order to hear the animals speak?" Gulp. Deep breath. The spotlight was on me. I said in my sweetest, quietest voice, "Well, thank you, Josephat. I need to go out in a state of silence and prayer, so I'd like to ask the group to be quiet and only think about the love they have for these animals. We'll need to connect to them with love and thanks before we take pictures, and we'll need to remember not to talk about ourselves too much in the presence of the animals. Lions aren't terribly concerned with human problems."

Suddenly the man next to me roared, "I don't believe in any of this and I don't want this woman on my truck!"

Ahh. The asshole. There he was.

Josephat ignored the asshole — whom I quickly found out was named "Peter-the-asshole" — and revved the engine to drive straight down a riverbank as we went off-roading on our first safari. Josephat pulled up in front of a group of small rodentlike animals that I had never seen before. The group of little creatures was traversing the savanna at high speed and disappearing into the woods.

"Amelia, what do these animals say?" Josephat demanded. I reached out with my radar to this group of odd little beings, who looked a bit like striped ferrets. Come to find out, they are called banded mongooses.

"Who's in charge here?" I telepathically asked them.

A female matriarch came up on my radar. "What's going on?" I asked her.

"I have to move my family into the woods!" she said, terribly upset.

"Why?" I asked.

"Yesterday morning, my husband got eaten by a hawk!" she said.

A bit nervous to reveal this conversation in front of my comrade Peter, I took a breath, summoned some courage, and just blurted it out anyway.

"Josephat, it's a female matriarch, and she says her husband got taken by a hawk yesterday, so she has to move the entire community into the woods."

"I saw the hawk take her husband yesterday morning," Josephat said.

I sighed a breath of relief until Peter-the-asshole drowned us out: "I don't believe in any of this bullshit and this is not what I paid for! I paid a lot of money for this safari, and I'm not going to stand for this! You need to stop asking this woman what she thinks! This is all nonsense!"

Peter's asshole wife nodded her agreement in her very expensive Tilley hat. I can tell you that that was the end of the magic for that night. My lioness did not appear, and my leopard did not appear. Nor did they appear on the game drive the next morning or the next night; nor the next morning or the next night. Getting worried, I reached out to the big cats and asked them where they were. I heard my lioness say, "We're waiting for Peter to leave!"

The next morning, Peter-the-asshole and his asshole wife got packed up and were finally ready to disembark for the airport. He was grumbling, "I don't care about lions. I didn't come to see lions. We've seen lions before. I got the best pictures anyone could ever take of lions years ago back at...yada, yada, yada." He was clearly upset that the lions wouldn't manifest for him. I hugged him good-bye and told him how much I'd miss him. Caught off guard, he clearly didn't know how to respond to my compassion when he obviously didn't have any himself. Not to mention, my years of working as an actress on shows like *The Young and the Restless* had done me good. So I waved him off. When we left for our first evening game drive, Peter-the-asshole was safely on a plane back to Assholeville or wherever he came from.

Josephat, the remaining kindhearted tourists on my truck, and I were not fifteen minutes into our drive, bumping along on a sandy beach, when I looked up the riverbank and let out a gasp. Josephat cut the engine and triumphantly pointed up. There she was! Perched on the cliff-side just above my head was the lioness waiting for my truck! Her front paw and back leg were dangling down in a flirty pose as she casually waited to surprise me. She was no more than thirty feet from me, almost straight up. She batted her long eyelashes at me. I slow-blinked her back.

"Is he gone?" she asked.

"He's gone," I said.

"Good. There's someone I want you to meet." She gestured into the bush behind her, and out came the most dashing teenage male lion, tossing his short blond mane, only a few feet above my head. She was introducing me to one of her boyfriends.

I asked them to shinny down the cliff into the sand in front of our truck, and she did what most cats do when you call them. She sashayed back and forth on the cliff, giving me attitude as if to say, "I don't take my orders from humans." And then she conceded, as if to say, "Well...all right!"

She climbed down the cliff with him right in her wake, and the two stood in front of my truck only a few feet from my astonished eyes. Then they gave me one of the greatest honors of my life. They started mating right in front of my truck. Fortunately, the only people left in my party were being won over by the idea that we should greet the animals with reverence and respect, so I was not the only person on the truck holding my breath, fighting back tears. Within a matter of minutes, there was not a dry eye in the group. But another tourist truck roared up next to us, and they did what many other tourists do — never on my safaris, but on your run-of-the-mill "Muggle" safari — they started catcalling, popping off pictures, and making sneering jokes about the mating they were witnessing.

These lions are *wild*! They don't have to show themselves to humans — ever! Much less display their most intimate moments in front of a bunch of noisy tourists. My lioness walked off with her blond boyfriend, but she told me that she would meet me later when we had a more private place to commune without other tourists gawking at her.

We drove off, and I was still shaken and spellbound by what I'd seen, when we happened on a leopard standing in front of a tree waiting for me.

"Is he gone?" she asked.

"He's gone," I said.

"Good," she said. She sauntered out into the middle of the road in plain view, so of course everyone on my truck went crazy. Then she indicated for me to look up in the tree. There was her mate, peering down, just as he had in my vision. Leopards are so elusive and hard to spot in the trees that you can drive a week and never see one, or even fly home totally disappointed when the leopards refuse to show themselves, which happens all the time. So these two exquisite cats' keeping their appointment with me so that we could meet not one but two leopards in plain view was such a treasured moment, I didn't think it could be topped that night.

Later, after our sundowners, Josephat and I returned to the river to see if we could take a private meeting with the lioness. This time, she brought me both of her handsome teenaged suitors, and for our eyes only she mated with the other one, a chocolate-colored big handsome boy who looked suspiciously funkadelic.

"Why are you showing me this?" I asked her.

"I want you to bless our union," she said.

For all the world, I wondered, "What the funk?" Why would she want me there to witness this, as if I were the minister performing a marriage ceremony for two wild lions? Then it became a little clearer when she said, "I want you to bless the conception of my first child." I didn't get it right away. I had to sleep on it, putting my mind-blown head on a pillow for the night to let the information sink into my subconscious. The next morning, when I woke, I understood what was happening. Doc was dying. My own extraordinary roaring little house cat was going to die in Manhattan. There's a myth down here in Africa that the African kings can reincarnate as lions and lions can come back as human African kings. I didn't know this back when I started waking up with a Zulu warrior in my bed, who sported a big feather headdress and chased dogs for fun. Could I have just met his new mom? Shortly after this safari, I took a trip up to a lion camp where I met an African man named Xolani. The "X" is pronounced as a click. In the Corsa language, Xolani means "the wise one." I was informed that while the Corsa language is most famous for these tongue-clicks, the Zulus also click. And in church, I found out that Nkozi YamaKhozi, also pronounced with a little click at the beginning, means "the King of Kings." Now the mystery was solved.

It wasn't until I got back to Seattle, where I was living at the time, that I got a loud SOS from Doc. If you recall, I'd left him with Scott, the cat sitter in New York, because Doc was going blind. When Scott and his wife, Mona, told me, "It's okay. We love him just the way he is, even if he goes blind. We don't care if he can see or not," I knew I had to leave him with them permanently. It was the toughest decision I've ever made in my life, but sometimes we must think of what is best for our animals, not for ourselves, whether we like it or not. And when I heard that he licked their noses, followed them into the bathroom to lick their toes when they were on the toilet, and even spooned in Mona's arms every night, cuddling her from behind, I knew that he could stay there happily and that they did indeed love him the way I did. They'd fallen in love with the snot-eating, toe-licking funkasaurus and even called him P. Funk and acknowledged that he was the feline version of George Clinton landing in his spaceship.

The night the SOS arrived from Doc, the premonition came as a feeling of dread, of panic, of grief, but also of lightness, like an exhalation from the angels. I'd been doing this work for years. It was an unmistakable feeling. I took a deep breath and emailed Scott in New York to say, "Doc is going to die tonight. He wants to die alone in your arms, undisturbed. He doesn't want the assistance of a vet. A big blast of poison in his arm is not what he needs to make his ascension. This will be the hardest thing you've ever done in your life, to let him go through his process, do what he needs to do, and let him die in your arms. I'm begging you to do it."

It took two days for him to make his ascension, but I got a call from New York forty-eight hours later to say that Doc had died in his daddy's arms and that he did it exactly the way he wanted — no vets, no poison. And agonizing as it was for the human standing by, Scott let Doc make his ascension with dignity, not like a little house cat, but with all the majesty of who this little house cat really was — a Lion King. I'll never forget the amazement in Scott's voice as he told me, choked with tears, that when Doc took his last breath and his spirit left his body, he let out a mighty roar! This work I do always takes me on a wild ride.

The grief of losing my best friend is an anguish that doesn't diminish with time. Years have gone by, but it feels like just yesterday that Doc was dancing in my arms. So when the tears start coming again, I put on his theme song by Parliament, "P Funk Wants to Get Funked Up," and I can't help but smile when George Clinton starts to purr:

> If you've got faults, defects, lay them on the radio.
> Let the vibes flow through.
> Funk not only *moves*. It can *re-move*.

Even with his hope of reincarnating as a wild lion, when Doc left the planet, he said to me, "As long as you are on earth, I will be with you. I will never leave you down there alone." He proved this in the most astonishing way, in a phenomenon I never dreamed possible. The first time a big fat fuzzy angel arrived in my bed with a loud thump and waddled up into my arms, I thought I was going to have a cardiac arrest. But now it's a pretty common occurrence. Even from beyond the grave, Doc is still, as his theme song states, "coming atcha in 3-D!" And these new physics-defying miracles are as "chocolate freakin' habit-forming" as his nightly visits were when he was technically alive. Evidently Doc hasn't noticed that he has no physical body. He was never one for details. But Doc doesn't visit me every night. Sometimes I guess he's busy flying his mother ship around the galaxy and hooking up with his other bit-chez. But at least once a week, a miracle manifests on my bed no matter what hotel I'm staying at in different parts of the world. The visitations occur reliably at times when I'm stressed, anxious, or feeling especially vulnerable. But sometimes I'll have a night of the Thumpasaurus for no reason.

Even last night, something invisible shook the bed, and I heard the familiar thunderclap of his paws landing on the duvet. I realized that the Funkapuss had landed. With every step, his paws rustled the covers as he thumped across the bedspread. I dozed off feeling his presence beside me, an arm's length away, but woke in the early hours of the morning to feel a warm heavy weight between my shoulder blades wrapping me in a shroud of celestial velvet. He was spooning my back! I felt his baritone purr vibrate in my heart and radiate out into every cell of my body, sending chocolate Persian vibes flowing through me. But this time, he pinned me to the bed, clutching me in his arms, holding me tighter than he ever had before. I got a very strong sensation that my grief is not a one-way street. Even from heaven, he misses me, too. Doc has proved that love is not the slave of space and time, and he's answered the question to my favorite line in our silly song, "Is there funk after death?" Apparently so.

Doc's future mom had three cubs the following year, but I never got to see them. When I arrived at the park to lead my first official Sacred Harmony Safari, which I now conduct every year in South Luangwa, I heard that all three cubs had unfortunately died. Africa can be rough. But every year she comes out to see me, waiting for my truck, and if you get online, you'll see many photos of her on my website, because she is my favorite lioness. I named her Anastasia. She wears a tracking collar, so she's very easy to identify. Last week I went out to see her and found that she had added yet *another* two new boyfriends to her pride. So while the other pride is now a pride of nine lions, Doc's mom has her own pride with her *four* handsome boyfriends. Party on, Anastasia! Now she has four times the chance that Doc could be born here again soon. I'll go see her again tomorrow, and who knows? By the time you come to South Luangwa, Doc may be back, and I can personally take you to meet his mother. And I can assure you, there will be no Peter-the-assholes allowed on your truck.

LIONS AND THE LION OF JUDAH

I admit that I had lived most of my life thinking our Lord Jesus Christ was vacationing on Alpha Centauri and wanted nothing more to do with planet Earth, nor should He have to after the way He was treated here. To my knowledge, He had never answered my prayers in my life, and I'd actually altered the Corinthian prayer in my first book, *Straight from the Horse's Mouth*, to address it to the lion-headed goddess, Sekhmet, from ancient Egypt, because she has always come when I've called her. Rather than praying "Lord Jesus," I wrote "Goddess Sekhmet." I addressed my second book, *The Language of Miracles*, to Archangel Raphael, but now I've come full circle. It's time to bring it home. And let me tell you why.

After Doc died, I tried to live in Seattle for a while. It would have been a very good idea...if I'd been a duck. It had rained every day for five months and I was down in the dumps when I found a framed picture of Jesus at a roadside gas station. And yes, it was sitting on the floor right alongside paintings of Elvis on black velvet. But something about this image caught my imagination. In this painting, He had a rainbow of pink, blue, and gold beams of light blasting out of His heart. Intrigued, I bought it and took it home, not knowing any of the history of the painting. I put a candle in front of the framed picture that night, and as I dozed off to sleep, I kept the candle lit, with the photo of Christ facing me — something I now do in every hotel room and even every tent I sleep in all over the world. But this first night, I just thought it would be comforting to keep Him lit up. As I gazed at the image, I thought I saw His hands move. Hooked on the feeling, I brought the little framed painting to Africa and put it in my tent in Zimbabwe, where I was preparing to white-water-raft the Zambezi. Now, I've mentioned that I got tossed out of my boat like a handful of beans, but what I haven't told you is that I almost died that day. You're supposed to do this, you see. That's part of the fun.

When you're preparing to white-water-raft the most dangerous river in the world, and you ask the cabbie in Victoria Falls, "Did you white-water-raft the Zambezi?" he'll shout, "I white-water-raft

Zambezi!" Then if you ask, "Did you almost die?" he'll reply with zeal, "I almost die! I almost die!" And if you ask the waitress at your lodge, "Did you white-water-raft the Zambezi?" she'll grin and nod: "Yes! I white-water-raft Zambezi!" And if you ask, "Did you almost die?" she'll squeal proudly, "I almost die! I almost die!"

So I was as prepared as anyone could be to almost die, but I didn't know the extent of the word "almost." With rapids named cheerful things like the Devil's Toilet, you try to prepare for what's to come. Strapped into a life jacket and assured that it will float, thus I will float, and I will pop up to the surface no matter what, being that the river isn't really that deep, and also assured that the crocodiles stick to the edges of the river (they wait until you take one step past "almost" before they roll you to the bottom of the river to snack on your fresh carcass for lunch), and that expert kayakers will be trailing our boat to come rescue stupid Americans who pop out of the boat like toast out of a toaster, and that our rescuers will allow us to latch on to their kayaks and float on our backs like waterlogged sloths as they paddle us back to safety and throw us back in our rafts...

Okay, get the picture? We were on the fifth rapid, and I was paddling furiously at a mountain of water coming at me like a tsunami, when I became airborne. When I went under, I had a sensation I've never had before. The terror totally consumed me. I'm a land mammal, so this life jacket was the only comfort I had, being that I don't swim very well. I found myself tumbling head over heels underwater, watching white froth churn in front of my face as I started hurtling in somersaults down a waterfall. So I tumbled head over heels, and heels over head, and then head over heels, and heels over head, until I thought, "Hmm. I haven't had a breath in a really long time." And then, I tumbled some more and then some more, and I thought, "Gosh, maybe I need to breathe some air soon," and I held my breath some more, and tumbled head over heels, and it finally occurred to me: *I'm going to die now*. So I waited for my life to flash in front of my eyes. When it didn't, I thought, "Hmm. I thought my life was supposed to..."

I surrendered to my imminent death, and then it happened. I popped up. The boat was nowhere in sight. I was gasping frantically, zooming down the river, still caught in the current, when I spied my savior, a little wizened African local paddling toward me in a kayak. After what seemed like hours, he reached me and demanded that I lie on my back and clasp onto the front of his kayak even though my lungs were full of water, so I did. He couldn't make it back to my raft upstream, so he hoisted me like a half-dead porpoise into the raft of a bunch of Portuguese tourists who didn't speak any English. Eventually, they threw me back into my own raft, and as I sat horrified and breathless, the guide turned to me with a big smile and said, "Only *nineteen* more rapids to go!"

I had white-water-rafted only one river in Washington to prepare me for this trip. The pale-faced girl sitting next to me in the raft had never rafted before in her life. She had just broken her finger in the crash, and she spent the rest of the trip in tears. I didn't break anything, and I didn't realize at the time how truly close I had come to death.

It wasn't immediately, either, but maybe a week later that I was lying in bed, meditating, when I saw a figure crouched in front of me. He was on his knees holding something. He was hunched over some small object, fixed on it, as if it were very precious to him. As I came closer, I saw that he had beautiful shaggy brown hair and he looked suspiciously familiar. But the locks were obscuring his face. I saw that he was wearing white robes, but I still didn't recognize the spirit. I came closer to see what he was holding in his hands. It was so small compared with him that it fit in the palm of his hand. He held it to his chest, sheltering it. When I finally got close enough to see what it was, I gasped. It was my boat!

"You?! *You* saved my life?!" I asked Him. "I thought you were off the job!"

We had a private conversation that I won't go into here, but I can tell you that the rumors about his big blue eyes are real, and in short, I discovered that He has always been watching over me, saving my life on multiple occasions, and He was always secretly saving me, standing silently in the wings, never center stage. But that has changed now. I am now allowing the King of the Angels to take His rightful place in my life, not on a cross, but on a throne, and this throne has moved center stage in my life and will remain there forever. I did not know that I belonged to Him and was one of His charges. Now I know better.

I've seen Him many, many times since, and He always beams through this one image that I call Rainbow Jesus in order to contact me. I've found that the image is a portal that He uses like a window into this world. I personally have never experienced this channeling with other images of Him. But there's a magic spell on this one specific image. For years, I've carried it around with me, always insisting that Rainbow Jesus face me whenever I go to sleep, no matter where I am in the world. I've always been prone to nightmares, but never when Rainbow Jesus is facing me, lit up by a candle. I've started collecting the images in religious stores from Italy to Ireland to Portugal, so now I have quite a collection, and I never teach without Him facing my students; and now most of my students also want their own pictures of Rainbow Jesus so that He can beam into their lives, too. And now He is.

What does this have to do with Animal Communication? Everything. It is the rainbow of God's unconditional love streaming from my heart that the animals see, smell, and respond to. When I ask wild animals like lions why they come to my safari truck, they say, "You smell good." Or, even more mysteriously, dolphins and whales tell me, "We smelled the Light." When I ask feral cats what they see when they look at me, they say, "Rainbows of color beaming out of your heart" and "You smell like flowers."

If you don't stream the compassion of Rainbow Jesus out of your heart, you are not creating the good smell. I throw it out into the world around me like a strand of a web, and the animals catch the end of the strand as if they were catching a lifeboat on a rope. It's this bridge of Lumensilta, a word I coined that means "bridge of light" in Latin combined with Finnish, that makes interspecies communication possible (see chapter 4 for a more detailed discussion of this idea). You have to give lions a reason to speak to you. You have to give them a reason to trust you. You have to give them a reason to want to love you. You have to smell good.

I only just taught for the first time in Portugal, where I met a very wise new friend, Jorge, who is also a lion-man. When he took me shopping in religious stores in Portugal, searching for Rainbow Jesus, he explained the history of the image, which I had never heard before. In the latest noted appearance of Jesus Christ on earth, He appeared as an apparition to a Polish nun, Faustina, and projected this image to her with the rainbows of pastel color streaming out of His heart. He told her in this vision that if she would paint this picture, He would use it as a portal into this world. He asked her to tell everyone to put this particular picture of Him in their homes so that He could protect them and their families.

No wonder. It was all beginning to make sense. I just turned over a copy of my Rainbow Jesus, and on the back is written, "the Enthronement of the Miraculous Divine Mercy Image. Jesus said to Faustina: 'I am offering people a vessel to which they are to keep coming for graces.'" The vessel is this image with the inscription "Jesus I Trust in You," and on the back it goes on to say, "This image is a source of endless grace for all the family. Place it in your home and let it be a means to re-Christianize and protect your family. The image should be placed where it can be seen by all who dwell in the house as they go about their daily lives."

This image is for those who believe in divine mercy, and I don't think there could ever be a better description for the psychic communication we are learning to use with animals than to call it an act of divine mercy. And it is only through an act of grace, where there is no emotion, no ego, no ulterior motives, in a love that transcends all space and time, that the communication becomes possible. I believe that this space outside karma is what Jesus called "grace," and it was through this grace that He healed the sick and overcame death. It is through this grace that we learn how to heal ourselves and those we love — and to listen and assist when other children of God are in trouble. Remember that many of God's children have paws, hooves, scales, fins, and wings.

Keeping My Promise

I didn't set out to become an expert on the apocalypse, but from audiences in Switzerland to audiences in Mexico, someone will inevitably raise his hand and ask me if the animals know that it's the end of the world. Even Shirley MacLaine, whom I respect from the bottom of her tap shoes to the top of her brilliant curly head, put me on her radio show on Mother's Day and wanted to talk about the end of the world. Do they know? Of course they know. How could they not have noticed? But this book is not a jaded opinion but an open conversation, and despite the horrors that the human race has inflicted on this world, the animals are surprisingly upbeat about it all. Maybe they know something we don't?

More recently, everywhere I go, even on the most skeptical host's talk shows, someone will ask me what's "wrong" with the human race. "What's wrong with us?" is the question I hear most often around the globe, and it's always asked by someone choked with tears. When encountering questions like "Why are humans here?" "Where did we come from?" "What am I supposed to do with my life?" and "How could it all have gone so terribly wrong?" I have to venture inward, into the psyche of the human animal, because we are just that, another animal, and I investigate daily what it means to be human — not a violent, selfish human stuck in a perspective, but the kind of human that God intended us to be.

I find that this is a human who is compassionate toward other species; one who laughs, dances, makes music and art; one who nurtures plants and animals, who shepherds the earth; one who is generous toward other people; one who is grateful and praises God and life, not only with her words but also with her actions. When we become the true human animal that we were created to be, only then can we relate to the other animals from an authentic place where harmony reigns. "Love one another," He said. I interpret that not to mean "Sit in quiet meditation and let the animals suffer." I think it means, "Get up off your duff and help make this world a better place!"

And to tell you honestly, I don't sugarcoat any of this apocalypse business anymore because it's too late in the game to gloss over the dire straits we're in and the jeopardy in which we've put our animals. When people ask me what's wrong with the human race and if we got genetically altered along the way, I tell the truth: "I think the human race is the science project of a fourth grader in the constellation Orion, and if I were his teacher, I'd give him a big fat F." If you could imagine the human race like a bunch of newly created insects whose ecosystem fits in a jar, but the humans kill everything in sight, including each other, eat everything, and poison the entire hive for everyone else — well, if it were an insect colony he'd invented, I'd tell the fourth grader to flush the whole lot down the toilet and start again. And so we must, in a way. And we start by flushing out mental virus programs we are all running. (I call counterproductive belief systems "virus programs" because they are harmful to ourselves, each other, and our world.)

Finding the Path Back Home

There's a lot of evidence that suggests the human species is becoming more and more disassociated from the natural world. Our inability to fit into the harmonies of nature and coexist peacefully with Earth's other inhabitants, the animals, makes some people wonder what went "wrong" with the human race somewhere along the road. But I take the most heartening advice from the psychic I trust most, Edgar Cayce, who in the 1930s made history in America, acquiring the title "The Sleeping Prophet." Fourth-grade science experiment aside, Cayce in *Edgar Cayce on Angels, Archangels, and the Unseen Forces*, by Robert J. Grant (A.R.E. Press, 2005), gives us the most optimistic way to look at the mixed bag of genetics we're all walking around in. He doesn't feel that the human body and mind are flawed. Quite the contrary, he believes they were created as the ultimate vehicle for divine excavation and the ability to achieve ascension on our journey back to God, and he uses my Lion of Judah, Jesus, as an example that the human form is a vehicle through which we regain our spiritual perfection and realign with the God within. Here is a ray of glorious sunshine. Edgar Cayce's opinion is one of the most uplifting points of view I've ever read about the mess we humans are in:

> For many centuries Christ has been viewed in the light that he is in an unattainable status. He has been depicted as a supernatural being which should be worshipped but not as something which we can become. There is a hesitancy, even among the faithful, to see Jesus as a human being. All along, however, Jesus's primary teaching was that we would eventually be able to do many of the miracles He performed. He is a picture of our future, our spiritual potential realized on earth. This was a promise, a promise that each individual

soul contains all the spiritual elements of God, the angels, the Archangels and the very powers of heaven. The powers of the Universe could be unleashed through proper attunement.

Jesus's promise was that the things He did were not merely a possibility, but an eventuality. His role as the Messiah was to show us our future. The readings indicate that the entire Universe changed when Jesus was resurrected. The whole vibratory pattern of creation was altered because the first man had finally overcome the world and returned to God. Jesus's status after the ascension was in the planes of consciousness higher than the angels. Why? The angels and Archangels never left the presence of God. Jesus embodied the Prodigal son — one who went his way and returned willfully to his father's house. His position, then, became as one who rules with God because he has fulfilled what was promised. There is a much larger truth embodied in a verse in the Gospel of John than has been previously realized: "And there are also many other things that Jesus did, the which, if they should be written every one, I suppose that even the world itself could not contain the books that could be written." (John 21:25)

In my opinion, His mission and presence on earth did not end with the resurrection and ascension. The Cayce readings explain that because Jesus overcame birth and death and resurrected the body, He can now once again appear in the three-dimensional world as he did two thousand years ago. Suddenly, remarkable stories are emerging around the world from people who are now not only experiencing Christ in dreams and meditations, but seeing Him — like I do — in three-dimensional form.

The author tells us more about this inspiring phenomenon:

In G. Scott's book, *I Am With You Always* (Bantam), one is left with the conviction that the Christ is present in many people's lives as he was 2,000 years ago. This is why this particular time in the earth's history is vitally important. The Second Coming represents God coming into the spiritual consciousness of the masses. This is an inner as well as an outer experience. People are not only experiencing the Christ Consciousness through dedicated spiritual disciplines, such as meditation and prayer, but are having experiences where the Man Jesus comes to them and performs healings. In this sense, the so-called Second Coming is happening right here in our time. This is one of the major reasons the angels are active throughout the world at an accelerated rate. At the same time of Jesus's appearances in the twentieth century, the manifestations of his mother, Mary, are also occurring all over the world — Medjugorje, Lourdes, Fatima, Garabandal — and the message from both Jesus and Mary seems to be: "Lo, I am with you always, even unto the end of the world." (Matthew 28:20) Now, more than ever, do we need that reassurance in these days of change.

So I propose that both philosophies may be true. We humans may have been designed as God's pride and joy, but later we got mangled and genetically contaminated by an off-planet intelligence that has made most humans go bat-shit crazy and act like a bunch of kooks. In my own humble opinion, free will was a very bad idea. But according to Cayce, free will was essential in our journey so that we might actively choose to ignite the Christ consciousness within us, and some new alchemy is now kicking in like a time capsule in our evolution, trying to help the human race self-correct. That is the promise of Christ. That we can self-correct and find our North Star, to steer us all back on course.

KINGS AND QUEENS

How do we find our way back to the Garden now after having been away for so long? The transformation starts in each and every one of us, when the calling of maturity makes itself heard and we realize that we are truly good enough, worthy enough, important enough, and trustworthy enough to shepherd other beings from harm. How do we find enough comfort within our own skins to even want to comfort others? There is no road to happiness but service, and it's amazing how hard we avoid taking the service road! But it's the only road that leads us back to Eden and ultimately through the gates of heaven. How do we find this new lion-heart who is so calm, confident, and in charge that we can be beings of light who bring comfort and shine hope?

If we work with the idea of an Antichrist, it's an abstraction that's set sometime in the future, and even then it requires speculation; but maybe a more available idea for a right-here, right-now solution is the creation of the Anti-lion, the Cowardly Lion, which is everything that a true lion is *not*. The Anti-lion would reflect the aspects of our ego that rule when we allow ourselves to be consumed by the demons of doubt that prevent us from acting like kings and queens. These feelings of self-doubt, fear, or inadequacy, or of being an outsider or an alien to this world, are negative feelings we can no longer allow to rule our lives. They are the very same feelings that keep us from making efforts to invoke meaningful change in our world. It's this self-esteem problem, this feeling of "I don't matter, so what's the difference? It's gone too far and I can't change the world" that keeps us from feeling like powerful lions — like kings and queens with kingdoms to rule on this earth. Lions don't do this. They know they belong here.

We humans are in a territorial battle now, an angelic territorial battle, and the outcome of ownership of this planet depends on you. Your starting point may be something very small: you go comfort cats in the animal shelter this weekend or help with their medication; you contribute a small amount of your income to an animal charity or shelter; you volunteer a tidbit of your time every week to help rescue animals, feed animals, clean rivers and streams, plant trees, visit a children's hospital or a home for the elderly, so that you in some small way act as a steward in your own little patch of the world.

Aside from my work with animals, I've gone Christmas caroling through children's hospitals in Los Angeles on Christmas Eve and choreographed versions of *The Nutcracker Suite* that my classes performed at the Motion Picture Home in Los Angeles where many elderly actors, singers, and dancers finish out their final years. I don't sing well, so God bless the kids who put up with my singing, but they smiled even through all my flat notes; and maybe my little dance troupe wasn't American Ballet Theatre, but my little students toddling around on their pointe shoes gave it their all, and it seemed to be the end-all to the elderly people in their wheelchairs who were spending Christmas alone. And on a higher level, it brought me joy. It brought the singers and dancers joy, and it brought the sick kids and elderly people some comfort and joy.

I may not be Mother Teresa, but that was all I could accomplish in my own little patch of town that Christmas, and it made me feel like a queen — a lion queen. Money can't buy that feeling. Anything that I could buy or that could be bought for me that holiday season could not have replaced the smile on a dying child's face, or the smile sweeping over the face of a regal elderly lady who clapped and sang along in her wheelchair when we did a very makeshift, low-budget modern version of *The Nutcracker* before her eyes. For a moment that old actress was the Sugar Plum Fairy, recalling her youth and beauty in Hollywood's heyday. My dancers reminded her of what it felt like to be young, flexible, beautiful, and alive. Money can't buy these things. We have to reach out to the animals and over to each other with gestures of kindness, no matter how small.

If we all did what we could and seeded our gardens with little acts of service, our patches would green up quickly. Maybe there's a way you can start or contribute to a project in your own personal field — in your own hometown. I believe this is what the holy Shepherd was trying to teach us — how to shepherd the world around us, even if we can cultivate only a few flowers and keep them safe from the storm.

You will begin to feel like the king or queen of your pride, and there's a reason they call it a "pride," because that's the emotion these little triumphs bring. This is the opposite feeling of what the Anti-lion brings. His breeding ground is regret and guilt, and his knockout punch is self-pity. Remember how the Cowardly Lion in *The Wizard of Oz* burst into tears and threw a tantrum when Dorothy gave him a pop on the nose? It's the sense of martyrdom — and the addiction to playing the martyr — that is the dark demon that fuels the Anti-lion. It's these feelings of being betrayed, abused, lied to, innocent, and mistreated that breathe life into the creation of the Anti-lion. We carry our burdens around, we carry our crosses, and we are unable to forgive the past and move forward, so convinced are we that we have been dealt a bad hand, that we didn't deserve the mess that we ourselves made out of our lives: we married that woman or man, started dating someone whose challenges were apparent from the beginning, took a job that was out of our depth, bought a house that we couldn't afford; we started drinking, doing drugs, running up credit cards, abusing our bodies, working ourselves into states that could escalate high blood pressure or heart problems or even cause cancer; most of all, we stumbled into toxic situations, taking no responsibility for the problems we created for ourselves, then self-medicated with more toxins, then acted martyred and surprised when karma took its toll and there was an equal reaction to our actions…

This is the kingdom of the Anti-lion, where we propagate

negativity; spew it onto the people, the animals, and all of nature around us; and then act like martyrs about what we've done to ourselves and our world.

The story of the undeserving martyr ended on a cross. But the glory began three days later with an empty tomb when the King of Kings rose to show that we are not martyrs and victims, we are not powerless pawns in a maze of happenstance, but we are in essence kings and queens, each and every one of us.

Maybe your kingdom is the computer, or the hospital or office where you work. Maybe your kingdom is the horse arena or even just the park where you take your dog for a walk. Maybe your kingdom is in your kitchen where you cook, or the nursery where you put your child to sleep every night. Lion queens, Mother Mary is there with you as you do these things, even as you shop for groceries for your family or wash the clothes. She's there as you rule companies, start charities, and run businesses. She's there for you as you help others as an administrative assistant, and certainly as a teacher, nurse, or doctor. And lion kings, the archangels mingle with you even as you play golf or basketball, watch movies, work for companies, drive your family down freeways. Because you see, the kings and queens are within you. And it's a feeling you have even when you do the dishes. A feeling of gratitude and pride at what you've accomplished that day when you helped someone or cleaned something or made someone smile. That feeling does not just bring power. That feeling is power itself.

We must feed ourselves with selfless acts and use this feeling of accomplishment as fuel. And we must teach our children how to generate this feeling so that they will know how to self-comfort. To chop up some herbs for supper, to plant a few vegetables in the garden, to strum a few notes on a guitar. Some small contribution to this world that brings joy to ourselves, our animals, and others. Soon these moments will grow until they fill our lives, become all that we are and all that our lives are truly about. No one can teach us this better that our own little miniature lions — our house cats — who luxuriate at the mere thought of being alive. They revel in their own magnificence and — sorry, but I've got to make up some words here — their own spectacularity and Godaliciousness, no matter what is happening in their lives.

Even when my Doc was going blind and his hips were failing, I'd catch him luxuriating on the bed, reveling in his own spectacularity. Humming a funky feline tune to himself, sometimes he'd purr so hard, he'd knock himself down and simply roll off the bed like a sea lion flopping off a bouncing buoy into the sea. Then he'd hoist his rotundity onto his stairs, climb back up, and purr himself back to sleep...grinning. Doc knew the meaning of satisfaction. And he knew something about gratitude. If I were losing my sight and ability to walk, I wouldn't be purring myself to sleep, so caught up in my own magnificence that I rolled off the bed onto the floor and woke up chuckling. That's why I called him Doc. He was an effective psychiatrist. Doc had class.

Our little house cats teach us to have some dignity, but also some gratitude, to own our own territory with peace and pleasure; and when, God forbid, we make a mistake that everyone sees, like slamming into a closed sliding glass door, we must jump to our feet, compose ourselves, and look over our shoulder as if to say, "I meant to do that!" Our little lions teach us how to act like lions with grace and humor and to own our own world, not to be strangers in it and roll over to evil forces as if we were skittish prey animals scampering for the shadows — to hold our heads high like kings and queens, knowing that we belong on this earth and we came to help it. Lions don't go through life stressed and worrying like little prey animals. They revel in the sunshine, sleeping like babies all day, but when they go into action, they do so with no hesitation, no self-esteem problems, and no remorse. Those of you with the biggest, warmest hearts feel the most like impala running for cover from the big-fanged predators of corporate monsters who rule with guilt, shame, and greed. And it's you pure-hearted ones who must find the lion within you and learn to roar, so that we don't just exist on this earth. We rule. The you-do-not-know-yet-what you are becoming is a king or queen. The time for justice and transformation has come. I personally think this deserves a good roar.

Lions: The Facts

The tragic fact is that one lion every day is murdered in a "canned hunt." This is a sterile name for what we now call "cage-slaughter," where a hand-reared lion cub who has been born and bred in captivity, who has been bottle-fed by humans and come to trust them, is shot multiple times inside a cage or fenced area where she has nowhere to run. She is murdered in front of her family and friends, sometimes drugged, but often not. The hunters are rarely good shots, and it takes many bullets and multiple attempts to murder the lion or lioness, whose body flies up into the air again and again with every shot. The lion is then beheaded, and his or her head is flown back to the "hunter's" hometown, where he is likely to hang it on the wall over his pool table.

This is how humans treat the feline kings and queens of this planet. Not only is there no law to protect lions in South Africa, but they are now falling under the same laws as factory-farmed chickens, so that factory-farmed lions can be killed as easily. For the sum of about $60,000, some sadistic freak can fly to Africa and murder his very own (tame, trusting, totally innocent) lion. What is it in humans that makes us so insecure that we must murder powerful beings in order to feel powerful ourselves? Do we think we can steal their power? Where is the balance between our self-loathing insecurity and our overinflated sense of entitlement? And why do the other humans on this planet allow these atrocities to continue while they look the other way?

The Humane Society of the United States (HSUS) website contains a statement criticizing "captive hunts": "Captive hunts, also known as 'canned hunts,' are the very opposite of fair chase. Shooters at captive hunts pay to kill animals — even endangered species — trapped behind fences." The HSUS calls canned hunts "cruel and brutal activities" in which the hunted animal has "absolutely no chance of escape." It goes on to say that animals have been "psychologically conditioned to behave as a target by life in captivity," among other objections.

Even some hunting groups that focus on hunters' ethics also object to canned hunting on the grounds of "fair chase," the idea that an animal has a fair chance of escaping the hunter. These hunters believe that canned hunts remove these elements, but unfortunately the Safari Club International accepts animals killed in canned hunts for inclusion in its record books as well as in its award categories.

The following article, by Taku Dzimwasha, from the August 15, 2015, *International Business Times* in South Africa, reports on the global outcry over the murder of Cecil, a perfectly tame hand-reared lion who was minding his own business when he was heinously murdered by an American dentist, an act that thankfully has caused outrage toward a practice that has gone on unnoticed for decades.

THOUSANDS OF LIONS BRED IN CAPTIVITY FOR SOUTH AFRICA'S CANNED HUNTING INDUSTRY

The killing of Cecil, the popular Zimbabwean lion, has brought the debate on "canned hunting" to global attention. In canned hunts, tourists kill lions, which were bred in captivity in enclosures....

Tourists select the lion which they want to kill by picking it out of a brochure, then travel to South Africa where they kill the animal with a bow and arrow or a rifle after it is released from a pen. The lions are usually tame, because they have been raised by humans.

A hunter can pay as much as £20,000 to shoot a lion in a canned hunt, and it is thought that the trophy hunts generate around £10m per year, the *Times* reported. Canned hunting is legal in South Africa, where environmental groups argue that the regulations controlling the activity are nonexistent.

"They're like lambs to the slaughter," Paul Stones, who has been conducting hunting safaris for 25 years, said to the *Times*. "It's not a hunt of any description. These animals are hand-raised. They're fed before they're shot. I refuse to say that they are 'hunted' because they're not."

Fortunately, the article goes on to give us some hope:

However, hunters attempting to transport their trophies back home will face difficulties from the end of 2015. Two major airlines which serve South Africa — South African Airways and Emirates Airlines — have banned the transport of elephant, rhino, lion, and tiger trophies.

In March 2015, Australia also outlawed the import of lion trophies.

I believe Cecil did not die in vain. I am confident that public outcry can have a positive impact even on the biggest challenges that wild animals face. Progress has been made since Cecil's death, thanks to lion lovers like my fearless friend Wayne Pacelle, president of the Humane Society of the United States. In an article on that organization's website published December 30, 2015, titled "New U.S.

Protections for African Lions Should Doom South Africa's Canned Lion Industry," the Humane Society International gives us encouraging news:

> According to international trade data, American hunters comprise the vast majority of the clientele for South Africa's notorious canned hunting operations for African lions. Of the 429 trophies from captive lions traded internationally in 2014, Americans took the lives of 363 lions and imported their body parts into the United States — about 85 percent of the total.
>
> Wayne Pacelle, president and CEO of The Humane Society of the United States said: "The federal action to place African lions on the list of threatened and endangered species could and should cripple the canned lion hunting industry in South Africa, given that Americans account for nearly nine of every 10 kills at these despicable, deplorable facilities."

What Can We Do for Lions?

What is it in the human psyche that makes us want to crucify our kings? Can we find enough self-esteem to cohabitate with nature's royalty and protect them instead of playing Judas and delivering our most majestic cats into the custody of the devil for a handful of coins? You can sign petitions, discourage your coworkers from engaging in canned hunts, be mindful not to pet lion cubs in Africa who are being secretly groomed for an exploitative end in a cage slaughter, and, most of all, support your local lion sanctuary! I support many lion rescues around the world, but Drakenstein Lion Park is at the top of my list, because I've visited the fearless owner several times and I know his acts of selfless bravery and generosity when he flies in abused lions from French circuses and takes in tiger cubs bought as pets for the teenage sons of sheiks. Paul flies in big cats from all over the world on his own dime and lovingly cares for them at his spacious sanctuary in the countryside outside Cape Town. The description of his park informs us:

> Drakenstein Lion Park was established in 1998 to provide lions in distress with sanctuary, where they could live in safety, free from abuse and persecution, and be treated with the compassion and respect they deserved.
>
> The Park is situated in the scenic Cape Winelands and comprises 50 acres of sprawling lion habitat.
>
> The Park is actively involved in improving the quality of life of lions in captivity, locally as well as internationally, either by offering these animals a lifetime home or working in conjunction with other animal welfare organizations to secure a safe future for individual animals in dire need.
>
> The Park is not involved in commercial breeding or trade and offers lifetime care to all of its animals. All the animals brought to the Park are captive bred / hand reared and cannot be rehabilitated to the wild. The animals at the Park are assured a chance of living out their natural lives in an enriched and safe environment.

Support your local lion rescue or help contribute to Drakenstein Lion Park to ensure a long, happy future for Ziyanda and her friends. You will feel like a king or queen when you reach out to help the feline royals of this planet regain their dignity.

What Do Lions Represent?

A sense of belonging. They belong to this earth and they know it. They came to reign supreme, and they do so with an uncompromising sense of clarity. What if you could be the king or queen of your own life and rule with absolute authority? Wouldn't you, as the alpha lion or lioness, bring a sense of being alpha — calm, confident, and in charge — not only to yourself but to the world around you?

Lionesses cooperate. They know there's strength in numbers. They agree on a plan of attack. They work together. They hunt together, they eat together, they share, they sleep together, loving each other in a state of perfect cooperation and bliss. They do not compete for food or rank in the pride, and they do not fight among themselves. Male lions rule diligently and protect the females in their pride. They do not fight with the females, pick on them, harm them, or make them feel outcast. They are the shepherds of their own pride, overseeing the group and making important choices for the good of all, when to take risks and when to wait for the next opportunity to come along. The lions and lionesses, no matter their rank in the pride, can each hunt and be self-sufficient, but they all know that they work better as a group because they belong together. What do lionesses embody? Cooperation and teamwork.

In the cosmic sense, the lions are the militia of the archangels and the Lion of Judah. They are invincible and at the top of the food chain wherever they go, but they rely on each other. They are raw power, pure sunshine, but they travel in groups, unlike tigers. They are a social group of protectors, a particular kind of angelic warrior that is sent into a foul system to clean energy. Here on earth they have been sent to terminate corruption, clear pollution, and bring a world spinning out of control back into order. They are on this earth to anchor us back to our own Christ consciousness, our own God selves, so that we can realign with our own inner confidence and power.

Until we see this beauty within us, we will not see it in our world and feel we have the power to protect it. When we find our inner lions, we will know that this is our earth to cherish and nurture and protect. Only then will we as a species have a sense of place within nature's world. When we evolve to this level, we will "belong" here, because only then will we be worthy of this world and its animals. The lions will walk through the Garden once again. And when there are enough of us, we will form a pride, a royal family that answers to God and is ruled by the proper King, one who rules with compassion and love.

4 | Great White Sharks
Joy with Jaws

Ah, Beauty! You are not so unfortunate as you suppose. Here you will be rewarded for all you have suffered elsewhere. Your every wish shall be gratified. Only try to find me out, no matter how I might be disguised, as I love you dearly, and in making me happy, you will find your own happiness. Be as true-hearted as you are beautiful, and we shall have nothing left to wish for. . . . Only do not let yourself be deceived by appearances.

— The Beast, in *Beauty and the Beast*

"SHE'S COMING! The reason they didn't show up this morning is that their appointment with me is in the afternoon! The matriarch of the pod is the biggest white female you've ever seen in your life, and she's bringing me a dark-colored adolescent boy!"

The team awaiting me on the boat was made up of half a dozen hot young African extreme-sports-type dudes, equipped with cameras, a wetsuit for me, and lots of scary instructions for the little blonde American kook. But even after I tried to explain to them what an animal communicator does, they did *not* believe in what I do. The mood on the boat was decidedly grim. I'd arrived in South Africa in February, the wrong time of year for shark sightings. The morning had produced nothing but one disappointment after another. Six shark boats had gone out that morning, and they'd come up cold, with no shark appearances whatsoever, so these proud dudes had to escort six boats full of unhappy tourists back to the dock and humbly promise them all discounts should they ever want to try to go cage diving again in the future. These guys were bummed. I loudly assured them that I had "called" the sharks and that this female *would* show up as an ambassador of her species to take a meeting with me, from one female ambassador to another. And that she was indeed bringing me an adolescent boy shark as well.

To heighten the stakes, I had Lesley Rochat, the world's most beautiful and fearless shark specialist, telling me on camera that the females do not stay with the children once they've been delivered, and to her knowledge, sharks are solitary predators. They don't even team up to hunt.

But in my mind's eye, I had seen an entire family pod of sharks and blurted into the camera that at least the huge matriarch and her little teenage boy were coming to see me. When I tuned in intuitively, I saw that these great whites were living in a huge community and the ones who answered my psychic sonar appeared to be a family group, even though this was not what the scientists know to be true. And I had perceived all this not from a boat in the ocean in South Africa but from Hollywood, several months before.

Here's how the great white conversation began. I had received an email from a female icon, a woman as brilliant as she is gorgeous, as gorgeous as she is fearless, as loving as she is unstoppable. The breathtakingly beautiful Lesley Rochat had sent me a fan-letter email from South Africa, appealing on behalf of her loved ones, the sharks. She sent me a YouTube special she'd filmed herself on her own dime that catches a sacred glimpse of her swimming underwater, holding the fin of an enormous great white shark. It is one of the most magnificent and touching pieces of film I've ever seen in my life.

But in some hard-to-stomach footage, Lesley's self-made documentary goes on to show hundreds of sharks being hunted by fishermen who cut off their fins and throw the sharks back into the ocean still alive so that they drown, bleed to death, or at worst are attacked by other sharks. Although humans would like to attribute these latter attacks to the viciousness of sharks, for all we know, the attacks may be mercy killings that these wise creatures perform on their own kind. As I watched the clip, I burst into tears, not only at the cruelty of the fishermen but at the beauty of this iconoclastic woman who is desperately trying to create legislation to help ban the torture of these graceful and majestic beings. Lesley Rochat's work is landmark, and she needs all the support she can get. This petite woman has devoted her life to stopping the hideous ways that sharks are being tortured. The torture is heartbreaking, and her courage is astounding.

I emailed Lesley to tell her that I'd do anything in my power to help and that I'd save my money to fly to Africa to meet her and dive for the first time into the ocean to meet her big-nosed, smiling misunderstood pals. (News flash: You're more likely to be killed by a falling tree branch than you are by a shark attack. All the hype about how dangerous they are is just that: Hollywood hype. This is yet another arena where human beings have misplaced their fear in order to rationalize inexplicable cruelty. Sharks rarely attack human beings. Human apes don't taste good.)

Even before I left Los Angeles for London and London for Johannesburg, I intuitively tuned in and explained to the sharks that I was flying all the way across the world to see them, on my own dime, and that I'm a land mammal — I do *not* swim and I do *not* like the water. I've never scuba dived or even snorkeled — and I can barely swim to save my life. But my long period of neglect needed to come to an end, and I ached to overcome my fears in order to meet them in person, learn from them, and bask in their beauty. In my meditative trance, the sharks told me in advance which huge old female was coming, and she showed me which adolescent boy she was bringing to see me. I told her that I was willing to go into the sea and pay my respects to the plethora of creatures under the water, and I was especially willing to take a meeting nose-to-nose with the queen of the most powerful predators on earth, but I was terrified of the water and I needed to ask her help.

I'm not afraid of sharks. I'm afraid of the *water*. Who better than great white sharks to give me my first swimming lessons? On land, I treasure my ability to work with tigers, Mother Nature's most sophisticated killing machine and God's most elegant design. I'm not afraid of beauty, wildness, and raw power. But the time had come for me to greet and give love to the most dangerous predators in the ocean, so that I could tell them I'm here for them and personally apologize for the deplorable behavior of the human race — up close and in person.

At great expense, I flew all the way across the world to look into the eye of the queen of the great white sharks. Lesley attended my workshop in Johannesburg and then took me on a road trip north of Cape Town to a lovely seaside landing where our boat was waiting. But on the way to the launch, Lesley got a distressing call: there had been no shark sightings all day, and six tourist boats had been sent back disappointed. A dark cloud fell over Lesley's face when she got the bad news. Had I flown all the way to Africa to fail? Lesley had a camera pointed in my face as I kept yelling, "She's coming! She's the biggest white female you've ever seen in your life, and she's bringing me a dark teenaged boy!" I couldn't get the images out of my mind. I knew this vision couldn't be just wishful thinking.

Well, when the first three adolescent females showed up, there was pandemonium on the boat! My South African skeptic dudes went wild. And then when the teenage boy showed up, it was mayhem. But this was followed by a tense, dismal period of silence, and after almost an hour, Kim, the remarkable "Shark Lady" who ran the expedition, wondered if we should give up, turn the boat around, and go home, because nothing was happening. We seemed to be getting radio silence from the sharks. But I kept screaming into the camera, "We can't leave yet! She's coming! She's coming!"

And then, suddenly, out of the stillness of the ocean came the *biggest, oldest* female great white you could ever imagine! The skeptic dudes went nuts and it was chaos again on the boat. The shark specialists identify the sharks by the nicks in their fins, and they knew this old matriarch but hadn't seen her for over a year. I dunked my head underwater in the cage so that I could get a look at her on her own turf. She swam past me several times, and the thrill was beyond my wildest imaginings.

She had come to see me and assure me of the fact that nonlocal communication is real, that these phenomenally regal beings need our help and are willing to connect with humans telepathically. And her appearance secured me in the knowledge that the spirit of God within me could contact and commune with her even from across the globe. This was a first. I had never tried to talk to a shark before. What struck me most about all the sharks was their effortless grace. They simply floated through the water, and the minute they were near, they infused me with the most incredible sense of peace and calm I'd ever experienced. I found this beautiful quote in Donald Epstein's *The 12 Stages of Healing* (New World Library, 1994), where he's talking about a more advanced stage of integration, but this passage describes exactly how I felt when I was underwater:

With the energy I have released, I somehow feel vulnerable and tender. I sense an internal rhythm very loudly and the rest of my body is actually having a talk with that rhythm. I can sense my heart and my lungs communicating with me. In Stage Eight, we can sense communication taking place between the new vulnerable areas and the strong, supportive rest of us. We know that something deep within us "knows." We may not yet know what it is, but we know that we know and that we will become aware of it soon. Somehow this newness is exciting, yet scary. We may say to ourselves, "Can I be quiet? Can I be still? I experience, I hear, I sense. Am I paying attention to myself?"

I was paying attention to my inner processes, and all I could find there was love for this magnificent matriarch. These misunderstood animals so need our help and our love, not our fear. Their playfulness is no different from that of dolphins...if you can get smiled at with teeth the size of a *T. rex*'s without wetting your wetsuit!

That famous footage is on my website, but ever since it went up, people have emailed from all over the world to ask me what the queen of the great white sharks had to say to me. And I wish I had said this in the video clip. Our conversation was about the future of our species. This is what she said: "If you could tell humans to teach *their* children how to talk to *our* children, there might be some hope for the future of this world. Our children can already talk to *you*. Can you teach *your* children how to talk to *us*?"

Well, I'm pedaling as fast as I can! I've been on a world tour since 2001, when my first book came out. I've been lecturing on Animal Communication and teaching seminars in ten to fifteen countries a year for the past fifteen years. I don't know that I'm making a dent in the problem yet, but I intend to keep my promise to the king of the tigers and the queen of the great white sharks. The greatest success I've had in my life was just after I got published in Korea. I started receiving a flurry of tender, loving emails written in broken English from Korean children telling me that they no longer wanted to eat dogs and cats. My focus with my new charity, Ark Angel, is to educate the children of the world, not only about wildlife conservation but also about consciousness. I'm starting with Africa, going into schools to teach that animals can think and feel, and even have conversations with us when we humans stop thinking only with our heads and learn how to think with our hearts, too.

I made that promise to the queen of the great white sharks, and I intend to keep it. Sometimes I feel like I'm trying to bail out the *Titanic* with a paper cup, but Mother Teresa once said, "We can do no great things. Only small things with great love." Her daily life attending to small things added up to a great thing, indeed. So it's with great love that I try to do small things every day to help animals, because I believe that if we were all empowered to do small things, we could change this world. Here is a small lesson in learning how to talk to animals like sharks, or, more important, how to listen.

DIVE DEEP

Let's talk about how Animal Communication works. With the shark, I could pick up her sonar. And she could pick up mine. What does that mean? What is this psychic sonar?

There is a still, small voice within you that is your spiritual intuition. It is the most loving friend you will ever have throughout your life. I do not do this work alone. It is the "Father within me" that does the work, and the only reason I can hear animals "speak" is that when the soft quiet voice of God within me speaks, *I listen*. We can't ask that still, small voice to compete with our chattering thoughts and turbulent feelings. We have to make space for it, and get quiet in order to hear it. We're moved away from the Divine Presence when we are guided only by our analytical minds. God's desire for us is always for our highest good. What causes us to go against our divine guidance? To answer this question, I'm going to quote one of my favorite ministers, the eloquent Dr. Charles Rose, of Ahiah Center for Spiritual Living in Pasadena, California:

> Hanging on to security blankets that are externally defined offers only a false sense of security. This false sense of security may disguise our need to develop our spiritual resources and so we remain insecure. To be secure, we cannot depend on external things. We can understand them, respond to them, enjoy them, and love them, but we cannot be controlled by them.
>
> Being secure is not so much a thing, a person, or a place. It is an inner attitude of confidence, trust, and faith not only in ourselves but in a Power Greater than ourselves. It is a hard one — faith in one's own powers to cope and survive. It is the confidence to be alone with nothing but one's own internal wisdom and strength and the Presence of God. It is the security that comes from knowing you have resources no one else can take away. It is the freedom from needing external security blankets. So the question becomes: How do we find this internal security? How do we develop this strength and independence?
>
> 1. We need to own our own strength. We do that by accessing that divine dimension of our being which allows us to give in and let that divine presence be a current flowing through us as our lives.
> 2. Congratulate and reward yourself when you have made a faith-based decision that allows you to take all the stops out and stop living your life on the layaway plan.
> 3. Listen more often to your *inner voice* and less to the

conflicting demands of others. That way you begin to use the spiritual coin of surrender.

4. View outside supports as bonuses, not as things you need. That takes you to a realization that the good of God is intangible substance and is everywhere present at all times.

5. Realize you're the only authority on what's good for you. That allows you to open the floodgates of your heart and access what needs to be accessed in order to give you a sense of peace and knowingness.

The force of your personal evolution speaks to you through your *spirit*, and it will move you toward your dream. Your role is to move with the strongest energy you feel. If out of fear and insecurity you try to hold on to something such as those emotional security blankets that no longer serve you, you will feel constricted and you will continue to feel unfulfilled.

If, on the other hand, you give more power and attention to your destiny rather than your history, doors will open in amazing ways. Do you have a strong intention to follow your dreams? Is your fear throwing up a smoke-screen? Tap into your faith and your fear will dissipate. Fear and faith can't coexist in the same mind and same place. The antidote to fear is to tap into a deeper knowing, and we all have it — a deeper knowing that is at a deeper level than the level where the fear is speaking to you from. That deep place always exists inside of you. Our role is to relax into it and summon courage. Courage simply means to feel the fear and do the thing anyway in order to move ahead.

The answer to fear is not force. It is heart. You can consider the universe a loving parent that is more than happy to support you to live the life that you would sincerely choose because it was the power and presence that imprinted that desire in the first place.

Because I'm trained as a practitioner in the church of Science of Mind and deliver the ministry around the world, these are the philosophies I live by and preach. But I also extend these principles to the other inhabitants of this earth who have paws, hooves, and wings — and yes, also fins and jumbo-sized smiles. We could learn to smile back, you know. They are God's children, too. The queen of the great whites showed up for me because I acknowledged this, and I kept my appointment with her to make sure she knew that the SOS sonar she was sending across the sea and even the dry land was not sent in vain. I wanted to assure her that the spirit of God in some human somewhere would pick up her distress signal and show up for her. If we are going to find our own souls and, in so doing, find some compassion for animals we humans fear, we're going to have to learn to dive deep.

That's my story, but I'm not the only one shining light on the lies and prejudice that sharks are drowning in. Lesley Rochat literally dives deep with them on a regular basis, so now I need to share with you Lesley's most famous victory, one you may have read about in the newspapers because it made global headlines a few years back. Maybe it's not easy for you to find compassion for these large, smiley-faced beings, but it may be easier if I introduce you to this little woman who fell in love with a shark.

THE SHARK AND ME

"Mighty Maxine, contributes to research!" This was the headline of an article just prior to the release of Maxine, the special raggedtooth shark. Soon after it was published, Maxine was back in the ocean after spending nine years in captivity at the Two Oceans Aquarium in Cape Town, South Africa. Her release made many headlines: "Famous Maxine, the shark ambassador," "Maxine free at last!" "Why I'm a very lucky fish, says Maxine," "Satellites track Maxine's return," "Raggy Maxine's living to tell her tale," and endless more. If one did a Google search, one would get over 140 links to Maxine. I had managed to make Maxine, a shark, world famous!

And that's exactly what I had planned when I found out about Maxine's extraordinary past and decided to use her as the icon for a shark conservation and scientific research programme I designed. Maxine's true story goes like this: In 1995 Maxine was caught in the shark nets in KwaZulu Natal. Fortunately she was found alive, promptly tagged and released by members of the Natal Sharks Board. Maxine was indeed lucky to be alive, since only 40% of raggedtooth sharks, or raggies, as they are affectionately called in South Africa, survive the shark nets, and fishermen kill many more annually. Badly wounded by the nets that had cut deeply into her flesh, but lucky to be alive, she continued along her breeding migratory path. Ninety-one days later, and 1369 km farther down the coast, she was caught at Struisbaai during a fishing tournament. It seemed that her luck had come to an abrupt end. But again she was fortunate. The anglers knew that the Two Oceans Aquarium in Cape Town was looking for a shark her size. Maxine was transported on the back of a van to a tidal pool at Cape Agulhas, nearly 20 km away. By the time she got there, she was close to death. Again she was saved, this time by a man named Mackie, who revived her by moving her around in the pool until she was strong enough to swim alone again. Eleven hours later the aquarium staff collected her and transported her back to the aquarium.

She was successfully introduced to the largest display there and named Mackie, after the man who had revived her, until the staff realised she was female and changed her name to Maxine. Once Maxine was in the exhibit, and for three months, it appeared that she was sulking, as she refused to eat even the tastiest morsel offered to her. It was only when a much-prized shoal of longfin tuna was placed in the tank with her that she proceeded to feed, feasting on them over the weeks that followed. Maxine became a perfect star; she grew handsomely in the exhibit and enthralled visitors from around the world.

While Maxine was swimming around in circles in the aquarium and not free, I was feeling the same: I was caught up in the rat race of the corporate world and very unhappy. For sanity I travelled a lot and became a freelance travel journalist and underwater photographer and also began video productions. Often I returned to the same destinations and witnessed the deterioration of the areas. This perturbed me greatly, and the more I researched and became aware of the plights of our oceans, how "improved" fishing practices were raping our oceans of all life, the more concerned I became.

I was learning about sharks, animals that play such a critical role in maintaining the delicate balance of the fragile marine ecosystems, how as other fish stocks decline worldwide, sharks are being targeted. Most are caught by longline vessels that trail up to 140 km lines with over 2,500 hooks attached. The demand for shark parts, in particular their fins, the most expensive fish product in the world, is increasing to satisfy the palate of the elite of the East in a broth called shark fin soup. How their fins are obtained is one of the most cruel, barbaric and wasteful practices, compared to the illegal ivory trade, whereby sharks are finned alive and then thrown overboard, to die a slow and cruel death. I felt the need to do something about it, and being a freelance environmental writer just didn't seem enough, but I didn't know what else I could do to help.

But destiny was at work, and six years after Maxine arrived at the aquarium, I met her: As a freelance environmental writer and underwater photographer, I had gone to the aquarium to dive in the shark exhibit and photograph the sharks for an article I was writing about the plight of sharks worldwide. Maxine stood out for me from the other four sharks she shared the tank with, and I noticed the scar left around her gills by her ordeal with the shark net. After investigating how she got the scar, I realised Maxine's potential to play a pivotal role in shark conservation.

Over the next three years, I set a course of events in motion that changed both of our lives dramatically: I took a leap of faith and packed up my corporate job, and founded a nonprofit organization, AfriOceans Conservation Alliance. AfriOceans pioneered shark conservation in South Africa in 2003, at a time when people told me I was crazy to want to conserve sharks because people viewed them as monsters of the sea, and plentiful monsters at that. I then designed a high-profile shark conservation programme, for which Maxine was the icon, called *The Maxine, Science, Education and Awareness Programme,* and I influenced a decision for Maxine to be released back into the ocean.

Three years since our first meeting on 18 March 2004, as a bright, amber sun rose over the Two Oceans Aquarium, my production crew buzzed about on the roof of the aquarium. Months of planning had gone into this, and the day had finally arrived — Maxine was going home. News crews cornered us for interviews while famous Maxine nonchalantly swam around in the quarantine pool, having been tranquilized two weeks earlier. Now ten sets of hands worked swiftly to lift her out of the pool and lower her down the two-storey building — within less than 10 minutes she was in the tank on the back of the truck that would take her back to Struisbaai, her original capture point. In true celebrity style, against the backdrop of Table Mountain, she was escorted out of the city of Cape Town by two traffic officers on motorbikes with flashing blue lights.

Four hours later, a crowd of Maxine's fans jostled for the best position to watch her being transferred into the tank on the back of the boat that would take her out to sea. By the time we got to the reef, the weather had taken a turn for the worse – a strong wind and choppy swell had us stumbling awkwardly on the boats. Maxine was promptly tagged with two satellite pop-up archival transmitting tags. With great effort, she was lowered in a stretcher between two boats. While we struggled to keep the boats from crushing her, a small buoy on a thin line was tied to her tail, necessary for tracking her from the surface for the first few crucial minutes. Then finally it was time for her to go...gently she was pushed out on the stretcher and into the waiting ocean.

Six months later in January 2005 we unexpectedly heard from the first tag. I was relieved. Maxine was alive and well and doing what raggies do, following her annual migration up the coast. We were successful!

Maxine, and all the sharks we later tagged and released who joined her in the shark hall of fame, were fantastic ambassadors for sharks, and for Africa's marine environment in general. Due to overfishing, up to 100 million sharks are being slaughtered every year — populations are plummeting around the world, and many will become extinct within our lifetimes. For all their perceived menace, sharks are extremely fragile and in deep trouble.

To find out more about Lesley's work, see www.lesleyrochat.com or www.aoca.org.za.

How Do I Survive the Pain?

How do we summon the courage to look at animal abuse that makes us all want to look the other way? If we don't look, we're certain to never help the animals. I explored some of these concepts in my second book, *The Language of Miracles*, but in keeping with my promise to the shark queen, I'm going to offer a little lesson here for those of you who are not yet familiar with my work — or as a refresher for those of you who are. Most of my students these days don't ask me, "How do I learn to talk to animals?" They're already doing it. The most common question is "How do I survive the pain?" Here's an interesting way of looking at it. This wisdom comes from one of the sermons of Dr. Raymond Charles Barker, one of the keystone ministers in the Science of Mind, in his book *The Power of Decision*:

You project yourself onto the screen of life. You are the cause of your own experience. Situations, events, and things proceed from your consciousness to appear on the screen of life. The screen of life is as impersonal as the motion picture screen in a theater. One week a tragedy may appear on the screen and the next week a comedy may be shown. The screen does not know what it is showing to the audience. It only knows how to show it. A motion picture scene wherein a man is shot puts no hole in the screen. It remains what it is. In your own life, you are the projector of your consciousness on the screen of experience.

I'm going to translate this passage to include the idea that every animal's pain is also being projected onto the screen of life. The pain isn't you. Dr. Barker takes it so far as to infer that not only is the animal's pain not your own, but your *own* pain is not your own. When we can differentiate between the screen (our outer experience) and the film rolling through the projector (our intentionality) and even the light pouring through the film (our consciousness), we are no longer a slave to space and time.

Dr. Deepak Chopra uses a couple of terms that serve us really well: "silent witness" defines the "other you" in your mind when you are arguing with yourself, the "you" that knows better. This is the aspect of you that houses your soul and intuition. Within this inner sanctum, we can stand back — detached from our emotions — and identify that we are not our thoughts.

Dr. Chopra speaks of the "space between the thoughts" and refers to this realm of meditative mastery as "virtual domain." It is here in this space where we can remove our thoughts and emotions from our mind in order to hear the thoughts of animals. If you can't attain this distance from your own physical machinery, when you tune in to animals you're going to be a hysterical basket case. If you think you *are* your thoughts and feelings, you aren't going to be able to rescue one furry little head, much less tackle huge issues like bloody shark-finning.

Meditation and emotional distance require a huge amount of discipline; I don't mean to be glib about any of this. My trigger that tells me I'm tuned in to an animal is the fact that my eyes fill up with tears. I cry through almost every contact I make with an animal. You can't learn to feel their pain without feeling their pain. We're ripping the fabric off the universe as you know it. It may be thrilling, it may be life changing, it may be searingly painful, but it will not let you exist in your current comfort zone. Our goals here are to focus on content and meaning instead of form, on motion and process instead of stasis. I can't tell you it's not going to hurt, but I can tell you that it will be worth it! How can we send waves of comfort if we can't also feel pain? We must identify with the pain in order to locate it, share it, disperse it, and transform it into joy.

SLOW DOWN!

If you want a piece of information from an animal, send them a wave of love together with a sense of patience that they've never felt from a human being before. Human beings are in a terrible rush. Most of us are a bunch of clumsy fusspots racing around like chickens with our heads cut off. Our animals tell us something over and over and over, and we're so busy being flusterbudgets and filling our lives with nonsense that we can't hear them, so they eventually give up. When you're having trouble downloading a piece of information, or when you're calling your cat to come in for the evening, send this thought: "I will wait here forever. You don't think I'm that stubborn, but I am. I will wait right here for hours and stand in silence until you answer me or come home." Then expect to get what you want. I'm not saying it will always work, but you'll be amazed at how often it does.

I don't give up easily. That may be one of the primary reasons that I've succeeded with Animal Communication. One of the most remarkable art teachers in the world, Glenn Vilppu, said, "I'm not more talented than anyone else. I'm just more patient." He'd spend hours or even days on a drawing that the rest of us would abandon and crumple up in five minutes. So it is with animal rights. The world is not changing quickly, but it is changing. We just have to out-stubborn the animal abusers. There's a saying, "The longest journey you'll ever take is from your head to your heart." Well, if we've got a long walk ahead of us, let's get going, okay?

THE HEART OF THE MATTER

Resogenesis, a word I've coined from the word *resonance*, means to resonate (or vibrate) on the same frequency as an animal. You may achieve resogenesis and feel as if your body is a radio and the transmissions from the animals or other humans are a radio program you're listening in on. This is what happened to me when the sharks sent a tune my way from the oceans of Africa both through the sea and across the land. I happened to have my extrasensory radio on. Or an even better analogy might be that the sharks "emailed" me and I happened to be "online." The email analogy is more accurate because the communication is a two-way street. I could email the shark queen back to say, "Okay, I'm coming." I saw the imagery of her and her adolescent boy in three dimensions like a movie, but one projected holographically into my mind and my apartment in North Hollywood. She was literally swimming through the Zero Point Energy Field. What is this? Welcome to the Language of Miracles and the fulfillment of my promise to the great white shark queen.

COME SWIM IN THE ZERO POINT ENERGY FIELD

Picture a gargantuan spiderweb of silver light. Every living being is connected on this web. Now, let's expand on this idea. Instead of a two-dimensional web, let's picture this web in 3-D, as wide as it is deep and spreading out in every direction throughout the galaxy indefinitely. It's a sparkling ocean of electromagnetic energy that contains everything in our universe. It includes every living being and the history of every being. Not only is it made up of "matter," but this sea of electromagnetic energy occupies the space *between* the stars, and the empty space *between* your cells, and even the space between the nuclei and electrons in your atoms. Matter itself is almost completely insubstantial. It's made up of 99 percent empty space.

Now, instead of seeing the absence of matter as a vacuum, envision that this void, along with the rest of creation, is electric, vibrating, and alive. And not only that, but this ocean is *logging information* into a gigantic library of "records" (in microscopic interference patterns) as we move along through our history.

The Zero Point Energy Field theory facilitates the idea that all living beings are able to communicate naturally, through the laws of nature. Why? Because we are all parts of one big organism. If we are all simply puzzle pieces in one giant puzzle, doesn't it make sense that we should be able to connect silently with each other? Human beings are cells in the body of God, and so is every animal, every plant, and every star in the galaxy. When I say "God," I mean a loving and nonjudgmental infinite force. You could also call it Universal Intelligence, Divine Creativity, or Nature's Mind. I don't care what you call it; just call it. Your ability to communicate with animals will hinge on your ability to communicate with Universal Intelligence, because that relationship is your gauge for how well *you* communicate with *you*.

If we erased your body, and we erased the body of your cat, horse, or dog, all that would remain would be electrically charged energy fields — little clouds of spinning lights. You are made up of tiny packets of quantum energy that are always in communion with the world around them. Your dog is made up of these little packets of information, too. If we look at this with the new knowledge that we are all inside the Zero Point Energy Field, your animals are no longer separate from you. Take away the outer form and sharp edges, and there is no more division between what is you and what is not you. Your energy does not stop at your fleshy fingertips but can soar out into the world around you. Taken one step further, you and your dog or cat are not sequestered in containers or imprisoned in carbon bodies, isolated from each other by empty space. If we viewed space as an ocean of energy that is as tangible outside our bodies as it is inside our bodies, that would change everything, wouldn't it? You could wade out into that ocean and swim into your animal's energy field, where you would feel their physical and emotional aches and pains, and maybe even see the pictures in their minds.

This may sound outlandish, I know, but with our current understanding of science, there is no better way to explain it. I'm giving you *my* version of the Zero Point Energy Field, so let's talk for a moment about its scientific origins. Before the ZP field, the latest head-spinning theory was quantum physics.

Quantum physics is just the physics of the incredibly small. While Newtonian physics can suitably describe the orbits of the planets or the energy transformations during a game of pool, quantum physics describes how electrons surround the nucleus of the atom and other subatomic actions. At this point, you may be thinking that there's not that big of a difference between these two sciences. Hey, both explain how matter interacts with other matter, so what's the big deal? The difference is that the common laws of physics begin to deteriorate on small scales. For example, Nippondenso (Japan Electric) built a car that's only half a millimeter long. One could easily mistake it for a grain of sand if not for its gold color. At the scale of 1:1,000, physics is already changing. Oil would gum up the engine, and the tires wouldn't have enough traction to move the car.

Quantum physics tries to explain the behavior of even smaller particles. These particles are things like electrons, protons, and neutrons. Quantum physics even describes the particles that make these particles! That's right; the model of an atom that you were taught in high school is wrong. The electrons don't orbit like planets; they form blurred clouds of probabilities around the nucleus. Protons and neutrons? They're each made of three quarks, each with its own "flavor" and one of three "colors." Let's not forget the gluons, the even smaller particles that hold this mess together when they collect and form glueballs (not a very original name)....By learning how these particles act, scientists can better understand the matter that makes up the universe and the way it behaves (or misbehaves).

The discovery of quantum physics was a big "wow," but it left many questions unanswered. A small group of daring scientists all over the world continued to experiment, picking up where the pioneers of quantum physics had left off. These scientists revisited the mathematical black sheep, a few equations that had been booted out of the quantum physics family but not forgotten. These unwanted equations stood for the Zero Point Energy Field — the ocean of microscopic vibrations in the space between things. They realized that if the ZP field were factored into our natural perception of the material world, it would mean that our entire universe is one indivisible ocean of energy, one gargantuan quivering quantum field, and that each tiny piece is in concert with this glorious, divine symphony at all times. Here's the real kicker: These scientists discovered that we are not only connected but unknowingly exchanging information with the entire orchestra of life. We're already doing it. But most people aren't aware of it.

So, then, what exactly is a thought? It's an electrical charge. What is an emotion? It's an electrical charge. What is a sensation? That's right. It's an electrical charge. And I want to teach you how to recalibrate your energy so you may become so sensitive that you can sense the thoughts, feelings, and physical sensations of your world, especially of your animals. You'll become more aware of what you're already receiving. How do we fine-tune our intuition?

We must *will* our consciousness to be mobile and travel on waves, instead of viewing ourselves as isolated particles in a cold, disconnected universe. The fire that lights the fuse of intentionality is not in the head but in the heart. Intentionality is put in motion not by grasping these scientific concepts or by the need to comprehend and measure the world around us with our heads; the mysteries of interconnection are solved in the *heart*, and the only prerequisite for establishing intentionality and achieving communion with nonhuman animals is loving desire. We don't "cohere" with our thoughts, per se, but with our feelings. Your emotions establish who you will connect with and who you won't. The intentionality that comes into play is not a mere act of will but a commitment to be loving; and learning to love like that takes discipline.

Most of my students call it "building the bridge," but I call this tunnel of loving energy Lumensilta, a word I created from the Latin root *lumen* ("light") and the Finnish word *silta* ("bridge"). I call the act of "traveling" on this bridge Lumensonar. This enables my own brand of sonar, where I can connect with any animal, but the reference to sonar especially appropriate in honor of the oceanic animals.

You can train your mind to function in the wave aspect, not in the particle consciousness, where most of us spend our waking hours. Let's take a brief look at what the wave-particle duality is all about, because this is the simplest, most effective way to explain the different modes of operation where your consciousness can learn how to fly, or swim with sharks and actually hear them communicate. Let's join them in the waves.

THE PRINCIPLE OF WAVE-PARTICLE DUALITY

Albert Einstein proved that matter is composed of particles. A physicist named Thomas Young presaged Einstein's research in 1803, when he proposed the idea of the wave-particle duality after his discovery of a phenomenon called *interference*. Bestselling author Gary Zukav describes this beautifully in his book *The Dancing Wu Li Masters*:

> Young's double-slit experiment showed that light must be wave-like because only waves can create interference

patterns. The situation, then, was as follows: Einstein, using photoelectric effect, "proved" that light is particle-like and Young, using the phenomenon of interference, "proved" that light is wave-like. But a wave cannot be a particle and a particle cannot be a wave. The wave-particle duality was (is) one of the thorniest problems in quantum mechanics. Physicists like to have tidy theories which explain everything, and if they are not able to do that, they like to have tidy theories about why they can't. The wave-particle duality is not a tidy situation. In fact, its untidiness has forced physicists into radical new ways of perceiving physical reality. These new perceptual frames are considerably more compatible with the nature of personal experience than were the old. For most of us, life is seldom black and white. The wave-particle duality marked the end of the "Either-Or" way of looking at the world.

When we think of ourselves as waves — water, not ice — this big ocean of human and animal energy can join at any point and flow together in harmony. Our bodies and minds are separate from one another, and yet they are not. The nature of reality and the existence of matter therein is not dualistic. It is holographic, meaning that more than one definition of physical reality is correct at any one time.

Water makes a splendid analogy for consciousness. Water has three forms, but only one essence. The building block, H_2O, remains the same even if the water has taken the form of ice or steam. The same is true of your mind. I would equate resogenesis to the flowing-water aspect, where you're allowing your awareness to travel on a wave of energy in order to connect with an animal or another human being. The steam aspect of consciousness might be an even more refined wave, one that enables you to take flight in your own mind and "track" lost animals or "see" departed souls through the veils of heaven.

A skeptic has a mind like a chunk of ice. You don't have to. You can make choices. Your view of the universe has everything to do with your perspective, and your perspective is determined by how you choose to operate your own mind. Water responds to outer elements. Your consciousness also responds to outer stimuli, but you can train it to respond to inner stimuli as well, depending on the challenge. You can reconfigure your thinking processes so that your inner skills are multidimensional, adapting to solve the need at hand, just as a wave can be made up of particles and a particle can be part of a wave, depending on the circumstances.

What does this mean if all of life is interconnected and we humans are murdering the benevolent police force of the ocean that maintains the equilibrium of all the animals and even plants in the sea? Do we feel that by ingesting sharks' fins — like all the dissected parts and pieces of the mighty tiger — we are somehow empowering ourselves? The truth is, from the way humans treat their species, the sharks have the right to kill every one of us who comes into their ocean. But they don't. They are actually showing great compassion and qualities of forgiveness that we do not bestow on them. Take a breath while I tell you the truth about shark fin soup.

Satan's Soup

In "The Reality of Shark Finning," a campaign hosted by Shark Friends.com, we learn the truth about the "delicacy" called shark fin soup. Shark finning is killing sharks every year at an alarming rate. It is estimated that one hundred million to two hundred million sharks annually are killed for their fins alone. This practice is mainly for supplying shark fins for the so-called delicacy known as shark fin soup.

Sharks that have been caught and had their fins cut off are not always dead when their bodies are thrown back into the sea. Without its fins, the shark simply sinks to the bottom of the ocean, where it dies. Such a horrible death for such a magnificent creature! How awful it must be for these animals...to think that when their body hits the water again, they will be safe, only to realize that they can no longer swim and will end up dying in the ocean, which was just moments earlier their safe haven and is now their doom.

Shark fins, once they are harvested, are then dried and sold in markets to individuals and restaurants to be made into shark fin soup, which is sold to the public (especially tourists) for as much as $350 per bowl! All of this killing for a bowl of soup! Also, shark supplements are used in Asian countries to cure everything from intimacy dysfunctions to cancer.

Shark finning not only is a cruel and backward practice, but also is a waste and a travesty on nature and must stop before the great equalizer of the sea is lost forever. Shark finning should be made a practice of the past so that children will be able to see and admire sharks in the future, for it would be a sad and tragic day when the only sharks that people got to see were the ones in books.

But beyond this, humankind cannot continue to abuse nature, or nature will strike back...and with brutal fury! Humans will become extinct if sharks disappear. Without sharks, the oceans will teem with fish and other ocean animals that live off the plant life in the sea. When this plant matter disappears, so will the vital oxygen that the ocean produces...then what happens? Think about it. There are no international regulations to protect sharks.

SHARKS: THE FACTS

Some great conservationists are working to rescue sharks from the dastardly practice of shark finning. The Shark Trust gives us the facts:

Shark finning is the process of cutting off the fins of a shark and discarding the body, often still alive, at sea. This wasteful and often cruel practice is currently the greatest threat facing sharks, contradicting all principles of sustainable shark fisheries management and conservation. Tens of millions of sharks are caught each year for their fins — an upper estimate proposes that the fins of as many as 73 million sharks are traded annually.

Shark finning is illegal in many parts of the world including Europe but in most countries it is still legal to buy and sell shark fins. Furthermore, weak legislation and ineffective enforcement often undermines shark finning regulations. While fins are very valuable, shark meat has limited commercial value, which encourages the exploitation of regulatory loopholes. Shark finning is rife with three to four times more fins being traded than can be accounted for in global fisheries statistics. The major source of demand for shark fins is the market for shark fin soup.

Most sharks grow slowly, mature late and give birth to a few large pups after a long gestation period. Consequently, shark populations decline rapidly when targeted by fisheries and recover slowly, if at all. Shark populations may continue to decline and some species may become regionally extinct. There are now 135 species of chondrichthyan (shark, skate, ray and chimaera) fish listed in a threat category on the IUCN's Red List, with a further 106 species listed as Near Threatened.

Shark finning occurs worldwide and is most common in high seas fisheries, hundreds of miles out to sea. Oceanic fishing fleets target valuable fish such as tuna, using thousands of baited hooks on miles of long-line, and freezing their catch on-board. Unfortunately, long-liners often catch several times as many sharks than they do tuna. Until relatively recently, this shark "bycatch" was considered a nuisance, and sharks were cut loose and allowed to swim away. However, as shark fins have become increasingly valuable, fewer sharks are being released. Bycatch is often not officially landed at ports; therefore data on the extent of the trade are limited. Where figures exist, they suggest that Hong Kong is the world's shark fin trading centre, accounting for an estimated 50%–80% of all fins traded worldwide. The EU has supplied approximately one-third of all fins imported into Hong Kong.

The Shark Trust has successfully campaigned on shark finning issues for over a decade and was heavily involved in the adoption of the EU shark finning ban in 2003. We were responsible for the UK Government's enforcement of a ban on the removal of fins on all UK vessels in 2009, and, as a founder member of the Shark Alliance campaign, heavily involved in the review of the EU finning regulation that finally led to the adoption of a fins naturally attached policy on all EU vessels in 2013.

We continue to work with governments and industry to tighten shark finning regulations and ensure compliance, whilst promoting the unsustainable nature of the fin trade: tackling both supply and demand.

WHAT DO SHARKS REPRESENT?

Mobility and nobility. Moving forward in our lives. Navigation without fear. Moving toward your dream with power, grace, and passion. Sharks teach us how to navigate the rough waters of life no matter how choppy the seas may seem. What are we eating in our soup? The hope of feeling like nobility — the knights of the ocean, armed and more than competent when a challenge or conflict comes along. Is it perhaps the desire to escape from life's pains and problems, to "swim away," that makes humans want to eat sharks? Ironically enough, shark cartilage is promoted to literally create more mobility in our bodies. Could it be that we also crave mobility in our minds and emotional states? Even in their endangered state, sharks also represent grace in the face of tyranny.

5 | Black Mamba Snakes
Dancing with Death

Shall I compare thee to a summer's day?
Thou art more lovely and more temperate:
Rough winds do shake the darling buds of May,
And summer's lease hath all too short a date:
Sometime too hot the eye of heaven shines,
And often is his gold complexion dimm'd,
And every fair from fair sometime declines,
By chance, or nature's changing course, untrimm'd:
But thy eternal summer shall not fade,
Nor lose possession of that fair thou ow'st;
Nor shall Death brag thou wander'st in his shade,
When in eternal lines to time thou grow'st,
So long as men can breathe or eyes can see,
So long lives this, and this gives life to thee.
— William Shakespeare, "Sonnet 18"

"Amelia, dah-ling, there's a black mamba waiting for you in the ladies'." This deadly snake business was nothing new to me. Usually when I landed in this African lion camp, the owner, whom I'll call Cassandra, would just greet me with something like, "Do be careful on your way back to your hut, dah-ling, because if you meet a spitting cobra, if they spit in your eyes, dah-ling, you'll go blind. So do wear your sunglasses to bed. Have a good night!" This was, of course, delivered with a wicked grin. But this black mamba announcement was actually a first. Cassandra continued with glee, "She must be waiting for *you*, dah-ling, because she arrived in the camp just this morning, exactly when your plane landed, and we've not seen her for months, so she must have come just to meet *you*."

I asked, "Is there...um...by any chance, a bathroom that she's not in?"

"Of course not, dah-ling. She's the keeper of the sacred Nile meridian, and she can go anywhere she wants anytime she wants. You could wake up in the middle of the night with her in your own hut."

Silly me. For those of you who don't know, the Nile meridian is the longitude line that connects the home of the lions in the Kruger Park with the Sphinx in Cairo. In certain circles, the mamba is thought to be a dark aspect of the goddess who could be the counterpoint to the lions and their light. (Some people might think these "circles" are rings of Froot Loops, but I'd been wading out in this psychic cereal bowl for years and floating with the best of 'em. I find these fruit-flavored crunchy people far easier to swallow than the milquetoast majority, and usually not only more colorful but sweeter, too.)

Of course, I went into the bathroom looking for the snake. I'd heard about this mythical mamba for years. I'd been visiting the lions in the Kruger National Park yearly to pay homage every time I flew to nearby Johannesburg and Cape Town to teach. This trip was the first time the mamba had shown up when I was there. I was disappointed to find the public restroom empty and mamba-less. And she didn't appear again during the three days I was there that year. For some reason, she gave up on me before I could see her.

The black mamba has a reputation for being the deadliest snake in the world, and the fastest land snake on earth, traveling at speeds up to twenty kilometers per hour. We need some musical accompaniment here, so I'll hum my favorite old Blondie song, "One way or another, I'm gonna find ya! I'm gonna getcha, getcha, getcha, getcha!" I asked Cassandra over dinner, "If by some chance she were to bite me (ridiculous, I know), how long would I have to live?"

"Well, dah-ling, that depends on how long you can control your breathing. If you can't control your breathing, you'll live about twenty minutes, and if you can control your breathing, you may live for *hours*." Whew. What a relief. I jest here, but the fact is that when a black mamba bites a human, it strikes multiple times, up to twelve strikes, each carrying 100 to 120 milliliters of venom. Two drops can kill a human being, and the mortality rate is 100 percent. The final moments or hours for a human victim are ugly ones, where one goes blind and becomes paralyzed as the venom kicks in. An antivenom drug exists but isn't very effective, and most victims don't get to the hospital in time. Cassandra went on to comfort me by saying only one person had died that year from a black mamba attack, and the fool had poked the coiled snake with a stick to try to move her. I took mental notes: *It is best not to try to move them. It's even better to not poke them with a stick*. Then, with her own brand of certainty, Cassandra assured me that this particular mamba was the singular guardian of the Nile meridian and the lion camp and that she was indeed the queen of all black mambas everywhere. Such declarations are not uncommon in this mystical camp. So of course, this made my desire to see my first black mamba even stronger. Thus, in danger or not, I spent the next three days looking for the mamba. I was very disappointed when she didn't slither up.

Ah, but the next opportunity was only a year away. I had been staying in a hut with my then-boyfriend, Jeff, and we managed to get through the entire week mamba-less. On our final day we moved from an open-air hut, where anything and everything could and did crawl in from outside — primarily gargantuan insects but no snakes — to a proper house that had glass in the windows and doors that locked. As I was about to find out, being in a sturdy wooden house created a false sense of security. We unpacked bags of groceries in the kitchen, thankful to be in a house that had a kitchen. Eager to explore the house, we waltzed out of the kitchen and into the living room, which was separated from the kitchen by a glass door. Jeff disappeared into the bedroom with the luggage, and I turned around, ready to come back into the kitchen to get a pop out of one of the bags. Something had called me back into the kitchen. Maybe it was more than the desire for a grape soda. I looked down and noticed that one of the cabinet doors was opening...all by itself. This was a cupboard door right where I had been standing to unpack the groceries.

What came out of this cupboard put the fear of God even in me. First her big gray head poked out of the door, and then the door opened slowly, an inch at a time. Her body started rising out of the cupboard, dancing through the air, elevated weightless in space. She was a very big snake. And as you may know, the mamba has a "smile" painted on its face, like the Joker in *Batman*, and the inside of its mouth is black. So mambas are sinister-looking — and rightly so, because their bite is certain death — but they also seem to be mocking you with this laughing expression just before they kill you.

I was surprised at the level of panic I felt as the adrenaline started coursing through my veins and every hair on the back of my neck stood up. She continued to move up into the air, swaying and rising. And my panic continued to escalate. Now, of course, this uncontrollable fear is against everything I teach and know to be true about the attitude to take when greeting wild animals, no matter how deadly. But for the first time in my life, I truly couldn't control my fight-or-flight instinct. It seized me completely. Fortunately, I was also captivated by her beauty, and this feeling of awe and reverence for her allowed me to keep my wits about me enough to not do something really stupid…like scream. Or run. But I had some foolish moves yet to make.

I opened the door between the living room and the kitchen very carefully, and then I tiptoed across the kitchen floor only a few feet from her and opened the kitchen door to the outside — wide open so that she could see the open air in the front yard clearly. I crept back through the kitchen and manned my watch station behind the living-room door, where I hid shivering. I said to her, "There's the door. Now please leave."

I tried to remember my skills. I visualized her dropping to the floor and slithering out the door. Despite the fact that this was insanely rude of me, and the feeling behind it was the opposite of everything I teach, I was uncontrollably afraid, and I hoped she would make a quick exit. She obeyed me without question — she dropped to the floor and started sidewinding herself toward the open door. The length of her massive body was shocking, at least eight feet, and as the long, sinewy body slithered out of the cabinet, it just kept coming and coming and coming, making wide graceful S curves across the kitchen floor. She was simply massive, and in a moment of unthinkable stupidity, something in me snapped. I had a knee-jerk reaction where an old, silly damsel-in-distress program kicked in. In lost-little-girl mode, I did one of the most idiotic things I've ever done in my life. I screamed for my boyfriend to come "save me." He rushed into the room, saw the colossal snake, and picked up the doormat. Then he did the stupidest thing any human could ever do. He smacked the tip of her tail with the doormat. Now, at this point, she was almost out the door — all eight feet of her. But when she felt the attack on her tail, she flew — and I do mean *flew* — across the room in a full-scale aerial attack.

God knows where she got the torque to do a one-eighty on the floor and hurl herself six feet in the air across the kitchen like a bolt of black lightning, targeted directly at his face. The speed of the assault was horrifying, but more shocking still was how she stopped herself mid-air just inches from his nose. She hung suspended, right in front of his pale eyes. Her body filled the length of the kitchen, but somehow she had managed to contract her body, coil back, and cut off her momentum just before her fangs reached his face. She dropped at his feet with a soft smash of pure muscle gone limp on the tile. It was the most chilling sound I'd ever heard — like a dead body falling to the floor. But no one was dead. She spared his life. Without turning around, he backed away. And she let him. She didn't strike. She whirled her head around to the direction of her safe haven in the cabinet and, in a flash, opened the cupboard door with her chin. The entire length of her body followed like a whip of melted steel. Like quicksilver, her eight-foot-long body disappeared under the kitchen sink.

Somehow I came to my senses and said to my shell-shocked boyfriend, "Please leave me alone with her. Let me handle this."

And to his credit, he did exactly that. Whether it was faith in my ability or just the uncontrollable panic that this snake instills in any human being, I don't know, but he high-tailed it out of the kitchen and left me alone with her. He and I had retreated into the living room in horror, shut the door to the kitchen, and allowed her to go right back into her hiding place. Something in me shifted, and I remembered who I was. This time I vowed to do everything right.

I opened the glass door to the kitchen. I dropped to my knees a few feet in front of the cabinet where she hid. The kitchen cabinet door was shut and the stillness in the room was eerie, as if time had stopped and life beyond this moment ceased to exist, but I'd left the door to the outside world open. I remember hearing birds chirping through that open door and seeing particles of dust whirl in the atmosphere, still electrified by her flight. I remember that the sunlight in the room was too bright, whitewashed in the presence of death, as if the gates of heaven had already opened and I had been ushered into the blinding light. There was no going back.

In my mind, I "asked" her to come back out, while I visualized her opening the cabinet door. I knelt there for I don't know how long. I was in a slow-motion dream. Several minutes must have gone by before the door started to open again, ever so slowly. She peeked out tentatively, probably no less afraid than we were. We'd done a great job of scaring the hell out of her. Once again I saw her incredible face, and she began to lift her head right in front of my eyes, but this time I refused to see her as an evil menace. I saw her as the goddess that she was. Her graceful neck and regal head arced up until she was again showing herself, but this time meeting my gaze as I knelt in front of her. I apologized for my horrendous behavior. I told her she was indescribably beautiful, perfect in every way, and that I'd spent years wanting to meet her, but now that I was actually having that honor, I was grateful that she allowed me in her territory. I thanked her for wanting to see me, and I told her I was sorry that humans were afraid of her and failed to see her beauty.

You might not believe that black mambas can smile — what with the creepy grin already painted on their lips — but even snakes have facial expressions. I could see a change come over her face. Her eyes softened, and she danced before me, grateful for the wave of love and admiration I was emanating. You might also think I was a crazy fool to kneel four feet in front of Africa's most dangerous snake — courting death, tempting death. But if that's the case, you fail to see the point. I was already dead. I was looking death in the eye. If she had wanted to kill me, with one lightning strike I'd be dead. If I did not find a way to escort her out of the house, either my boyfriend or I, or even both of us, would most certainly be killed if one of us stumbled on her late at night.

But aside from that agenda, this meeting was important. I told her that I now knew without any question that she was indeed the queen of the black mambas and that I was sorry to have upset her, but now I was so grateful to be in her presence. I assured her that she was the most beautiful snake I'd ever seen. Then I thanked her for her benevolence and told her that I was proud of her for being so dangerous. At this, she smiled more and danced gracefully. I admired her for a moment, an hour, an eternity — I didn't know what was happening back on earth. We were somewhere else together, in a cosmic dream where no one could hurt us, another world where we would naturally never think of hurting each other.

Eventually I dropped my focus back down into normal reality for the sake of our safety. I realized that if someone came crashing in on this sacred moment and broke our spell, she could startle and become dangerous. I suggested that when she was ready, she could drop to the floor and exit out the open door. I told her that she must be very careful to keep on moving, because if any human tripped over her, especially on the porch late at night, they might try to kill her. I visualized her slithering out the door and all the way across the porch, disappearing into the bush. I explained to her that if a human found her, she would be in great danger. I knew that Cassandra would never harm her, but one of the workmen at the camp might not share Cassandra's sentiments about black mambas in his path, especially not if the men got spooked late at night in the dark. So I encouraged her to keep moving until she was safely out of sight from the humans.

She relished the moments of being in communion with me. We had a peaceful moment of prayer together, just admiring each other, just loving each other, being respectful of each other's ferocity — but also of each other's tenderness, joy, and hope, and the melancholy of being misunderstood. We had a moment of sharing some knowledge of injustice, of vulnerability, of being plagued by the fears, prejudices, and misperceptions of others. I told her that it was the greatest thrill of my life to get to meet her face-to-face after all these years. I knew she heard me. I could see it in her eyes. Then when she was ready, she dropped to the floor ever so softly and started crawling toward the sunlight through the open door. I didn't rush her this time. Nor did I call anyone to come rescue me. I just let her huge body slither and snake and make *S* curves for what seemed like forever until she found her way out of her dark hiding place and into the sunshine, safely away from the humans who could do her harm. Would that we all find our way into the sunshine.

The Death Walk

So what happened in that moment when I dove into such an uncontrollable trance, such a bottomless state of bliss, that I had no fear, no logical thoughts, no course of action other than to drop to my knees and simply love her? I might call this a shift operating from my higher self, a concept I teach. We all must locate this higher level of consciousness when we want to communicate psychically with animals or each other. Arnold Mindell, a Swiss psychologist and author of *The Shaman's Body* (HarperSanFrancisco, 1993), might say I was operating from my shamanic "dreambody," or what he calls "second attention," as opposed to first attention, where my only awareness would be of my own ego and its limitations. He calls this other self a "double," which I interpret to mean that we all have a spiritual doppelganger that is closer in essence to the Creator than our personalities, and this "double" can make choices with more focus and less fear, simply concentrating on the task at hand.

Although its presence is always available, because this double is superimposed on our normal waking selves, most people only experience it in crisis situations. Remember that Mindell renamed this double the "dreambody," a term I like even better, because it suggests that we can learn how to access another dimension of our identity that houses the powers of the subconscious, usually available only when we are asleep. I encourage my students to become aware of this spiritual aspect of themselves even in ordinary moments of day-to-day reality, so that its powers are readily available when we need them most, such as when we need to communicate with animals. But in every situation in life, recognizing this presence allows us to make better, less emotional, choices with the assistance of our newly found God-self. *The Shaman's Body* was a cult hit twenty years ago and caused quite a stir back then, but I only just discovered it while teaching in Portugal, and it's a big wow! Just listen to how perfectly this passage explains what I went through with my "demon" (the fear I felt when I met the snake), and shines light on my meeting with Ms. Mamba:

> If you wrestle your demon, you find moments of pleasure, freedom, and exceptional energy — whether you win or lose the battle with yourself. Perhaps best of all, you have moments of feeling real and congruent, free from the fears and symptoms of phantomhood. Now you know you have a double and sense your shaman's dreambody. But sometimes you forget these experiences and wonder just how much of the dreambody can be lived in this life. On the one hand, your love for the world tempts you back to pester and play with everyone else. But on the other hand, the ecstasy of experience may entice you to leave forever.

Carlos Castaneda's Don Juan saga scales more wild territory in each progressive book. In the last pages of *Tales of Power* (Simon & Schuster, 1974), Don Juan explains to his apprentice that the place in which they stand is their last crossroads together. Few warriors, he says, have ever survived the encounter with the unknown, which his apprentice is about to face. The *"nagual"* is so intense that those who go through the final encounter find it unappealing to return to the *"tonal,"* "the world of order and noise and pain."

Mindell offers the terms "warriors" and "apprentices" to describe those of us who are on a spiritual path, willing to fight for what we love and believe in while we seek lost pieces of our own souls. And for the other term, I had to do some sleuthing with the help of Merriam-Webster:

nagual
a. a personal guardian spirit or protective alter ego assumed by various Middle American Indians to reside in an animal or less frequently in some other embodiment.
b. the animal double or guardian itself.

Wikipedia takes the definition one crawling step further:

> In Mesoamerican folk religion, a *nagual* or *nahual* (both pronounced [na'wal]) is a human being who has the power to transform either spiritually or physically into an animal form: most commonly jaguar and puma but also other animals such as mules, birds, or dogs and coyotes.
>
> Such a nagual is believed to use their powers for good or evil according to their personality.... Nagualism is linked with pre-Columbian shamanistic practices...which are interpreted as human beings transforming themselves into animals.... Mesoamerican belief in tonalism, wherein every person has an animal counterpart to which his life force is linked, is also part of the definition of nagualism. In English the word is often translated as "transforming witch," but translations without the negative connotations of the word witch would be "transforming trickster" or "shape shifter."

We will explore the concept of this "witch," a source of power not just outside of us but within us, but what struck me about the dictionary definition was the word *guardian* after I'd been told that in some African mythology the black mamba is known as the sacred guardian of the Nile meridian. I admit that after this encounter with the nagual, I found it challenging and depressing to go back to a humdrum life in Los Angeles, a way of life that Mindell might call "phantomhood." I was surprised at the depth of my feelings of hopelessness and disappointment when I got back to America. I was feeling truly lost. Fortunately, Mindell, an insightful therapist, goes on to make rational sense of my seemingly irrational emotional reaction:

> Remember those feelings of wholeness that accompany the discovery of the dreambody? It is difficult to leave such an experience and go back to ordinary reality. Returning from a wonderful vacation, a meaningful relationship, or an intense inner experience is painful, because you fear losing the connection to your whole self. Thus you experience difficulties after your encounter with the nagual. Returning to the state of ordinary affairs — the world of the tonal, where dreams, body processes, and secondary processes are not valued — is not easy. Don Juan warns his apprentice that if he does not choose to return, he will disappear, as if swallowed by the earth. But if he does choose to return, he will have to wait and finish his particular task on earth. Once this is finished, the apprentice will have command over the totality of himself.
>
> All connected to the myth of consciousness have at least one task in common — to develop the second attention and revitalize the one-sidedness of our awareness, enabling ourselves and others to live more fully. Castenada's task, for example, was to bring the powers of the night into the day via the teachings of Don Juan.

THE POWERS OF THE NIGHT INTO THE DAY

When I discovered Mindell's mesmerizing book, I realized for the first time that there may have been other ways to react to the black mamba in the kitchen. A more "normal" person may have run out of the house screaming to find Cassandra and insist that we be moved to another camp because there was a snake in the house. Or perhaps a more normal reaction would have been to (again) run out of the house screaming and try to find someone more qualified to remove the black mamba from my house.

But in this moment of ecstatic crisis, neither of these thoughts occurred to me. In this dreamlike altered state, no other thought entered my mind but the task in front of me. My only option, as I saw it, was to get on my knees, just a few feet from her face, and tell her that I loved her. My job was to face death and not just accept it but worship it, because death, too, is God.

I now realize in retrospect that any other course of action may have gotten me killed. Had I run screaming, she could have chased me and in one lightning strike killed me. Or if I had had her forcibly removed by someone who "knew more" about snakes than I do, she could have killed them or returned that night to greet me on my way to the bathroom. This is not the bathroom attendant one hopes to find in a hotel loo, no matter how posh. No mints, no tissue, no squirt of cheap perfume. And the tip she might expect could be more than a few coins dropped resentfully in her tip jar. In what currency do we pay the demon? How do we pay off our inner demons when the scariest of all nightmares suddenly becomes real?

TIPTOE THROUGH THE TWILIGHT

Where do we go when we get "lost" from this world? Yes, it could be a world more beautiful, more scary, more magical, where the rules aren't the same as what we've been taught. Where did I go when faced with death? Mindell might say that after the first snafu with the boyfriend and the doormat, I found my way back to my "whole self." This is what I meant when I said, "I remembered who I was." That is an identity blended with the dreambody, the higher self. From this more sublime vantage point, I found it easy to fall into her beauty, devour her ferocity, worship every curve of her wicked smile, every sway of her cocky dance. I left myself behind and fell into her. I fell into loving her. I fell in love with her. Do you catch my meaning? Do you want to learn how to "talk" to your animals and actually perceive the messages they relay as they "talk back"?

Only if you fall in love with your cat or dog, your horse or your parrot, so that they become not some disdained object outside of you that stands to be judged or corrected, but someone you can fall into and love completely — someone you can love and identify with at all costs — will you hear them "speak." They must become someone you respect and take seriously, so much so that you're always willing to take their side. This is what I do with the cats and dogs I work with. *I take their side.* With the most glorious Olympic show horses on earth, *I take their side.* They win gold medals because *I take their side.* So if you have a four-legged loved one at home that you defend, protect, and adore — someone who requires more compassion than you are willing to give, but you give it anyway, honoring their feelings, their relationships, their trauma, even when they require that you search the depths of your soul to see their point of view — then you will know what it means to be on your knees in front of a black mamba. She saved me because I *took her side*, knowing that I was an inconvenience in *her* house, not the other way around. Honoring her point of view proved that I was willing to show the qualities worthy of being saved: compassion, respect, tenderness, humility — and these same qualities apply to the treatment of our domestic animals no matter how "tame" they may appear to be.

A lesson about being "tame." What does it mean to be tame? Did I turn my back on her and ask my knight in shining armor to come save me, or let my need for a man's love skew my intuitive wisdom the way I had done with the tigers? Did I defer my own stealth sense of inquiry and intelligence to a man or any other human being? With the tigers, I had. With this snake, I also had — but only for a moment. The old programming of "conform if you want to be accepted," "lie if you want to be loved," suddenly was replaced by a much larger sense of knowing. Then my true "common" sense kicked in: not the sixth sense but the first sense, when the God within me jumped out and became the primary operator of my reality, and He said, "Let me handle this." In that instant, I chose not to be tame.

Am I learning? Ever so slowly. Are you learning? Just watch. Remember my elephants: their noses. Something gooey and foreign, totally unknown, rough on the outside, the "finger" of a massive majestic giant comes searching toward your face. Do you flinch? Or do you trust that God is here too, perhaps bringing you something more beautiful on the other side of the fear than you ever could have calculated for yourself? Did I hope, "Please don't kill me"? Or did I hope, "Please step into my heart and touch me"? Both, maybe. But did I ever hope, "Please go away"? No. I only hoped, "God, come near." Because God created this animal, too; therefore, it was a divine creation. I only thought: "In all your forms — scary forms; terrifying forms; scaly, winged, aquatic, and slithering; terrifying, huge, mammoth, and ancient — come near and touch me. Whisper to me your secrets. Let me be the keeper of your secrets."

Are there words for this awe? For a reverence so great that I think my heart, body, and mind are going to explode into a trillion smithereens? If my only thought is "Come love me as I love you," and it always is, what happens then? What would happen if you could generate that reservoir of love and call on it in times when you were desperate, confused, or afraid?

What do you love?

Let's play a little game called:

I LOVE

I love really strong filtered coffee in big mugs. I love espresso. I love kettles that make hot water. I love electric adapters that make those kettles work. I love ceramic coffee cups. I love little silver spoons. I love local honey. I love honeybees. I love fresh sour lemons squeezed into my water every morning. I love the sound of birds singing: Hadedahs are my favorite, as they fly overhead in the middle of an African night, irritating everybody but me, waking me with a smile. I love to feed wild birds, to share my breakfast with pigeons and songbirds in the morning. I love to pray. I love churches. I love classical paintings of angels in medieval churches. I love to lie in bed before anyone else is awake and start my day with a blissful prayer of thanks. I love pine trees. I love tall sycamore trees and the way they smell. I love jacaranda trees in bloom and the carpet of violet blossoms they leave all over the Johannesburg streets. I love workout clothes. I love dance clothes of every sort. I love the soreness of my back when I stand up and stretch, moving my hips for the first time every day and beginning each day with my first morning dance. I love the rhythmic pounding of my feet on a treadmill. I love stationary bicycles in the gym. I love rock 'n' roll. I love pounding music, be it from hip-hop, funk, disco, hard rock, punk rock, oldies, or the latest hottest bands. I love to sweat. I love to dance. I love R & B first thing in the morning. I love rattles and drums around a big bonfire. I love Native American flutes. I love people who suddenly announce they are musicians and burst into song in public places. I love saxophones played in the depths of the London and Paris subways. I love jazz piano and jazz pianists. I love men who can sing and play the guitar. I love half-melted dark chocolate. I love people who can tell jokes around the dinner table. I love cats of every shape and size. I love lightweight laptop computers that remember my every thought. I love to cook. I love to eat. I love caramel apples. I love sharp kitchen knives. I love having scissors. I love hot showers. I love good soap. I love Mr. Bean movies. I love roses, the morning's first sunlight on roses, dewdrops on roses, and yes, raindrops on roses. I love whiskers on every creature that grows them. I love small rodents. I love animals with wings. I love finding feathers because it makes me think angels are watching. I love tiny prey animals. I love finding tree frogs in my luggage. I love gigantic whales and their mammoth smiles. I love sharks with big teeth. I love things that scare me and make me squeal with delight. I love things that go bump in the night. I love waking up with hippos in my front yard. I love finding elephant poop on my doorstep. I love finding notices taped to my bathroom mirror that say, "Please do not leave food stuff in the tents because elephants will damage the tents." I love signs that say, "Please be aware that the monkeys and baboons will remove all your belongings from this open-air bathroom." I love sleeping in a tent in Africa and smelling the night air. I love big fluffy white pillows. I love stars, especially the Southern Cross. I love candle flames. I love needing a flashlight. I love vervet monkeys who steal the toast off my plate at breakfast. I love airplanes. I love sparkling pools of water on the tarmac glistening and reflecting the sun just as my plane takes off. I love airports with their hustle and bustle. I love buying new lipstick at the airport. I love having accessibility to the whole world. I love real books and the smell of paper and ink, and the feel of real books in my hands. I love pen-and-ink drawings and watercolor paintings. I love to draw cartoons. I love writers who send my imagination reeling and remind me that there's magic but also order in this universe. I love Tom Robbins books. I love Middle Earth. I love words. I love to write them. I love to write them for you to read. I love a flickering candle in front of a picture of Jesus that I can gaze at every night as I fall off to sleep.

Okay, you get the idea…

Now it's your turn to list 133 "I loves."

THE MONSTER IN ME

Can I say, "I love horror movies. I love making them"? "I love the monster in me"? Well…it's taken me a while to admit to a string of scandalous horror movies I starred in in the 1980s. Scott, one of my most insightful fans, a drag queen in Atlanta, Georgia, creates a character that is very oh-so-seriously scary. He approached me at a Days of the Dead movie convention for an autograph, wearing the most outrageous costume I'd ever seen. His character is a possessed clown. His kind gay demeanor couldn't be any further from the villain he plays for fun. He once said to me, "You humanize monsters. That's your job. Sharks, tigers, snakes. Monsters. And you side with them and give them feelings."

He gave me a new perspective on my shameless acting career and also my unconscious drive to defend the underdogs, the other "scary" animals on this planet, because apparently as a child, I must have felt like one of them. The misfit, the outcast, the lonely misunderstood tiger or shark or, in this case, poisonous snake, represents the part of us that feels different from the other kids, yet it's where the love is, where the soul is, where the supernatural connection to God is, because it's outside the conscious reasoning mind, and yet it *is*, and there's nothing any of us can do to make it go away.

In my movies, I played the most terrifying female demon in movie history, and I can say that with no ego, but only in understanding that it must be true — that this thing that flew out of me one night was so universal and resonated with so many of my fans on an archetypal level that I now have an entire website devoted to nothing but their tattoos of me on their bodies. I am, of course, in full disgusting demon makeup in almost all of these tattoos, and when I ask the fans in person why this vicious unconquerable force of evil that I invented means so much to them that they'd have my pockmarked, fanged, demon face tattooed on their chests, arms, legs, or backs, be they male or female, they always have the same answer: "I don't know."

But one fan, Chris McGibbon, who's writing a book about the movies, did come up with a more conscious description: "You protected me as a child," he said. "Angela protected me." This explanation fascinated me, so I started accepting more invitations to these conventions, intrigued to talk to my fans about their feelings. Fans terrified to meet me, standing in front of me trembling with tears, said things like, "I drove three days to meet you and slept in my car" or "I had to have a shot (of whiskey) before I could even stand in your line, I was so afraid to meet you." I began to pry the truth out of these people, and they all seemed to have something in common — this need for a ferocious savior. One told me that she'd hide in her bedroom as a child watching *Night of the Demons* over and over to drown out the screaming of her parents in the next room, and that when her stepfather came into the room to rape her, she used thoughts of Angela to comfort herself. She was using my character as an emotional anchor to help her cling to fantasies of interference. She told me it was these fantasies of my helping her fight back that helped keep her sane. This same story came from a fan who was a gay man — now a dear friend of mine — who said that the characters in the movies were his "friends" as a child, the only friends he had, and once again there were these words: Angela defended him. The Kali-inspired destroyer goddess was the emblem of courage and justice for these abused kids, and that's why they wear tattoos of me on their bodies. Or maybe some fans just like it.

Why do I mention this in the snake chapter? In *Night of the Demons 2,* written for me by Joe Augustyn, I was the only character brought back from the first film. Steve Johnson, the most celebrated special-effects wizard in Hollywood, who had won an Oscar for *Ghostbusters*, turned me into a thirty-foot snake. I spent twenty-seven hours in special-effects makeup and broke a Hollywood record. I was transformed into a giant anaconda who could stand up and hover like a cobra. To this day, when I see the film, I don't recognize myself and can't believe that it was created before CGI. Steve Johnson tied the tip of my tail to a string of dental floss — which was invisible on the screen — and he stood off-camera whipping my tail around. The effect is utterly devastating, and I admit that when I try to watch the scene, I can't see through my fingers plastered over my eyes. I remember at the end of the twenty-seven-hour shoot, when I'd been strapped into a trench and glued to a teeter-totter, so that when the teeter-totter stood up, my unrecognizable reptile body would "fly" and "float" in midair, the director, Brian Trenchard-Smith, said to me, "And now, Amelia, you're going to throw a fireball."

"Are you going to set my hand on fire?" I asked, because Steve had indeed set my fingers on fire in the first film. (I'd had six seconds before the gel burned through to my skin, and I had to douse my burning fingers into an ice chest full of ice water.)

"No," my director said. "We're going to do it in post."

"Post? What's that?" I asked.

Nothing about my being a snake was faked — nothing on the outside or inside. You can see the outside when you rent the movie. But the inside is something different. It comes from such a deep place inside me. Those of you who are my movie demon fans know that the most famous dance scene in my movies was in part 1, where I choreographically shape-shifted into a black jaguar. Carlos Castaneda might have called that my big naughty feline nagual caught on camera. This connection to nature and magic was the source of my power, and why my likeness is tattooed on kids' chests all over America. Even if you can't grasp the shamanic qualities of my energetic transformation, you can see the feline qualities in my choreography as I crawl across the floor with slapping paws.

But the anaconda transformation is different. I'm not remotely human in this scene. The snake I portray is unapologetic. I'm an indomitable deadly force of nature, my life has been threatened, and I'm about to strike, ready to kill everybody in sight. In retrospect, I can see that I really might have been dancing with my scaly reptile nagual, the energy that voodoo high priestesses tap when they shape-shift into another form to create a portal of energy for the entire community. These shamanic shape-shifters and priestesses take on this possession as an extreme act of healing for their community, and some members of the congregation of my church do it every Sunday, possessed by the Holy Spirit. I did it on film, not knowing that it could touch the hearts of so many abused kids in this world.

A Safe Place

Why are movies made in Tinseltown such a safe place for so many people? Could it be that on the silver screen, actors can create an archetypical haven for all our viewers to find an outlet for their most ferocious wildness as well as shattered helplessness, where their only hope of survival is an allegiance with a raw Kali force? Angela gave my movie fans a safe place to put this passion and pain. Kali, for a definition, is the Hindu goddess of death and destruction, wife to Shiva. In her malevolent role as a goddess of death and destruction she's depicted as black, red-eyed, bloodstained, and wearing a necklace of skulls. She chops off people's heads (which is not very nice), but in her most dazzling depictions, she surveys the universe as she rides on the back of a tiger (which I think would be very nice).

I'm honored and flattered that so many movie watchers sense that I, the owner of all that primal force, am protective and good at heart. I would never decapitate someone, but I would very much like to ride around on a tiger. We all need a place for our fantasies. My movies gave me an avenue to express all my feral wildness and to honor the unnamable parts of my psyche that are connected with nature, no matter how "ugly" and "scary."

Could it be that if I didn't have it within me myself, I couldn't have gotten down on my knees four feet from a black mamba dancing in my face and say, "You're beautiful and I love you. And I'm sorry for what the humans have put you through"?

"I Don't Like Spiders and Snakes!"

I've found in my life that there seem to be two species that produce blind irrational fear in human beings: spiders and snakes. These are the most common prejudices I find on earth, and I believe that some of this terror may come from past-life experience where humans have some mystical memory of the deadliness of these beings. When defending them, which I do often, I will say that this spider or snake is just an innocent critter trying to make a living in the world. We make this very hard for them. Most spiders and snakes are not poisonous, but the fear of them seems to be hardwired into human DNA, and they invoke such terror that it's beyond rational control.

I experienced that for a minute with my mamba friend, so I had to remind myself that I'm not just a nincompoop Muggle bumbling around on a planet covered in poisonous snakes. I had to remember who I am — one of God's children — and let the spirit of God's grace shine through me even in the most terrifying of moments. I had to acknowledge that what James Joyce called "otherness" is an illusion, and if I honor the "otherness" in me, I can see that she also saw me as "the other" and melt the illusion of separateness into one flowing stream of energy. I danced with her soul. And when I did, she let me live, but the encounter also gave me new life. I can only hope that the encounter gave her some life force in return. I had to go into a "not all snakes are bad" state of mind in order for her to let me live, and I hope she slithered off with a new "not all humans are bad" opinion as well.

ANIMAL STEREOTYPES

One of the ways I can break through the blind panic my students have toward these animals is by joking that humans are afraid of animals that have "too many legs" and also afraid of animals that have "no legs." Why do we have such prejudices against animals who have more legs than we do or fewer legs than we do? The humor of it seems to challenge the fear for a moment and shine a bit of reason into the darkness like a shard of sunlight through a cracked window. The other way I challenge the fear is by countering the idea that "this being is a snake and I hate snakes." This being is an individual, who will react to a particular situation (an encounter with you!) in a fresh new moment that has never happened before.

There is no scientist who can tell me "Snakes act like this" or "Hippos act like that," because no scientist has ever been there with me in the moment I encounter a particular snake or a particular hippo for the first time — one who may not behave in a fashion that any snake or hippo has ever acted before, because it's never encountered me before, nor has it encountered you. I grew up in Texas, where rattlesnakes abound and were then, and still are, shot on sight. My own father shot one under our trailer when I was a kid. I grew up in the world of "Rattlesnakes act like this...," so the information I'm about to give you is *new*, not only to this world but even *to me*.

I had to acquire a sense of compassion for spiders and snakes, probably just like you will have to, because in truth, they have not always been my favorite animals. When I started my career as an animal communicator, I found quickly that I could have no prejudices about insects or snakes because people were emailing me asking me what to do about them, and I had to extend the same God consciousness in dealing with them as I do with anything else. I was soon to find that I would not only learn to tolerate snakes but also love them. And I mean truly love them.

So let's explore this integration. Before we talk about them as individuals, let's put a different lens on your point of view. Let's start by viewing them as male and female. Now that spider up in the corner of your bedroom is just a young mother trying to make a living in the world, and that sac of eggs is her most precious treasure, so if you wanted to have a heart and take care of that young unwed mom and her unborn kids, you might extend some compassion to her instead of just seeing her as a "spider." At least now she is a "she," and this gives her some more identity and a way to identify with her a tiny bit more so that you're creeping toward love and compassion.

I knew the mamba was a "she," and I knew that if I didn't love her, I'd be vanquishing the most important part of myself, not the angelic parts of myself that my ego has claimed — the aspects I don't acknowledge yet and struggle to excavate into the light. She represents the part of me that is in shadow, the dangerous part, and that's what brings me to this conversation about what she means to me. When people are afraid of snakes, they think of them as sexless terrifying beings who do not have feelings, do not fall in love, do not grieve, do not feel lonely, scared, or threatened. Nothing could be further from the truth.

This mamba was the closest thing to a real-life witch I have ever encountered, so I want to share with you some ideas from one of my favorite books, *The Witch and the Clown: Two Archetypes of Human Sexuality* (Chiron Publications, 1987), by the beyond-brilliant Ann and Barry Ulanov. I devoured this masterpiece in my late twenties, the same time I was playing a witch in the movies. I now realize it was this integration of my own dark side, my *shadow*, that makes it possible for me to work with some of the world's most "shadowy" creatures and meet them with great reverence and even love. Most humans view poisonous snakes as "not feminine" because they are deadly, and God knows, I was not acting very feminine by facing off with her, at least not in the traditional sense of how we categorize femininity. This passage gives us a way to not stay stuck in a perspective. Although the authors are talking about "the witch," I think there is no more perfect way to describe my mamba, as well as all the other snakes we fear.

WHICH WITCH IS WHICH?

Let's apply this passage from *The Witch and the Clown* to the witch inside the snake, and the witch inside you:

> The witch is an archetypal picture of the masculine element within feminine identity, of that opposite sexual dynamism that belongs to the feminine personality. She is an easy butt for grudges, a made-to-order container for blame, even in emancipated societies far removed from witch-diviners, witch-hunts, witch-trials, and executions. There she stands, always in an exaggerated pose, a caricature of what society and culture call masculine, of power, intellect, logic, and precision. Even more challenging, she embodies these elements in her own peculiar feminine way. Thus her logic is one of association, not of cause and effect; her precision, one of focused intensity, not conceptual clarity. Her power is that of nature's secret life, not society's; her intellect, that of the unconscious, not of reason. She personifies an issue faced by all women, one way or another: how to integrate this contrary sexual dynamism, with all its unmistakable masculine characteristics, within a feminine identity.

The black mamba ushered me into "nature's secret life, not society's," and brought me into an alignment with nature where my adversary's intellect helped me discover a new way of relating to animals, to the world around me, and even to myself: "that of the unconscious, not of reason." This was where true safety lived, you see. The following passage eloquently parallels my surprise encounter with my inner and outer witch:

> For women, the witch is a major missing piece of sexual identity, a culturally elaborated piece, even in its most exaggerated and caricatured forms. In her negative guise, the witch offers a picture of a woman possessed by the masculine elements in her. The witch is masculine in appearance, with whiskered chin and strident manner. She shuns the traditional female roles of helpmate and hearth, supporter of the dependent and needy. She goes after her own power and power over others. She wants secret knowledge and the craft to use it for her own ends. She wants weapons that will force others to do her will. She thrusts her ambitions at us. She must be acknowledged as a superior being, whose purposes others cross at their peril.

I propose that because humans haven't integrated their inner witch — and the authors go on to explain that men too have the archetype of the witch buried inside them — some people might project this exaggerated negative portrait onto wild animals like my snake. Some men project this caricature onto lions; perhaps that's why they must feel the need to murder this part of themselves, to conquer their own wildness and ferocity, or maybe they feel that they gain power by hurting innocent animals because they themselves have been abused in some way — by their fathers most likely — and rationalize that "hunting" a lion or elephant or shooting a "dangerous" snake somehow makes them more of a man.

I related to the snake as a person and ultimately decided to defend her instead of harm her because I identified with her feelings of being an outcast. The Ulanovs write:

> The environment ascribes to her powers that are altogether outside the conventional definition of female — a trafficking between the seen and the unseen, the determination and skill to color outside the lines drawn by social custom and constraint. That is her crime — not consorting with the devil, not embezzlement of the emotions, not rape, not cannibalism of children. She poses a danger because she enjoys contact with the hidden secrets of nature; she knows things, she goes after things. But her human environment is spell-fixated and blames its spell-binding power on the witch as if it were entirely her doing, whereas in fact her scapegoat role, designed by the community, is clasped in a secret handshake by the whole community.

Tell me this isn't true of my mamba friend; it seems our crime is that we enjoy "contact with the hidden secrets of nature." In my moment of euphoria, she and I shared our secret. For a few unforgettable moments, we were not alone. The "trafficking between the seen and the unseen" is my profession, and "the determination and skill to color outside the lines" is a perfect way to describe Animal Communication. My teacher was the mamba, and I was willing to let her take me as far outside the lines as she wanted me to go. My ability to completely disassociate from "social custom and constraint" let me go with her as I slithered right behind her into the secrets of nature's mind, not humans' rules — into the darkness, into the hidden secrets of nature. And in the same moment, I allowed *her* out of the box of fear, hatred, and prejudice. For the first time, she was praised for her beauty in the light — a light she deserved to bask in, where I could truly see her beautiful face, and love every crack and crevice, adoring and appreciating her closed-mouth smile. (If her mouth had been open...ouch! *Adios, amigos!*)

"Why do the witch and the clown remain so strongly alive for us?" the Ulanovs ask. "Because they are archetypes and as archetypes act as indomitable resources against a stereotyping that straps actual men and women into preformed sexual identities and will not let them loose." Most of us, especially women, are revolted by the sexual stereotypes. The most reductive ones define men as strong and tightlipped, never showing feeling, and women as soft, never going openly after power. Women lack intellectual power; men, feeling. These wooden simplifications should enrage us; many of us are committed to changing these demeaning, persistent typologies.

I'm addressing the idea of sexual stereotypes here because I want to ask you this question: Is it possible that we have somehow let our sexual stereotypes bleed into our perception of animals? Wouldn't it make sense to consider that perhaps our ideas of what a man is supposed to be — emotionless and stealthy — are the stereotypes we've put on our little leggy or legless animal villains?

We seem to think of certain animals as ferocious and emotionless, while we think of others as docile and angelic. I personally have known some bunnies that would kick your butt for fun, and I've even owned some hamsters that would gladly bite your thumb off. But we've been brought up with some stereotypes about animals that are simply unfair. What I'm challenging here is our tendency to think, "Here is an animal that can kill me, so it is bad," as opposed to, "Here is an animal that can kill me, but she is beautiful." In that moment where I got down on my knees in front of the mamba, I had to consecrate the differences between us and the emotions I felt around them, surrendering not to the idea, "This is what scares me about my world," but to the insight, "This is what scares me about myself." I had to honor the fact that she reflected the opposite side of my personality. In that way, I was not afraid of what could happen in the outer world. I had to acknowledge her presence in my inner world — and be able to say, "You are dangerous, but you are one of God's children, too."

This discussion of male and female sexuality could address the inner clockworks of Adam and Eve, but no chapter about snakes would be complete if we didn't talk about the mythical serpent, and what he represents, Satan. I'm going to once again refer to my beloved book *Edgar Cayce on Angels, Archangels, and the Unseen Forces* to give you some artillery in a battle with the devil. Of course, he exists, even as just a concept. All we have to do is look at the presence of laboratory experiments on animals, factory farming, global warming, the leveling of our rain forests, the pollution of our oceans, and the tragedy that the world is still at war to know that there is something terribly askew in the human psyche. Whether you believe there is a devil "out there" or you can acknowledge that there is a devil "in here," let's take a look at a very uplifting new way to view an age-old problem.

THE BATTLE OF GOOD AND EVIL

Christ incarnated so that there would manifest in our world a presence, a power, a love that would overcome any acts or manifestations of evil. Cayce's view of the destiny of Satan and his fallen angels was that, through light and understanding, all would eventually find their way back to their Creator. This concept differs vastly from the idea that evil is unchangeable and unredeemable.

There was a time, however, according to biblical lore, when Satan was not an evil adversary of God but an ally. In the book of Job, God is engaged in a dialogue with Satan, who came before Him with the "sons of God" (the first order of created souls who remained in harmony with God), and Satan reports that he has been treading "to and fro in the earth." In the biblical account, God attests to the purity of Job and wagers that he would never renounce Him. In a bizarre sort of chess game, God agrees that Satan can perform any test of faith he chooses, but he is not to hurt Job. It is interesting to note that when God and Satan reason out their game plan for Job, God says to Satan, "Behold, all that he hath is in thy power" (1:12). Satan then goes on a rampage, killing the servants, destroying Job's home, and stealing his cattle. But Job does not renounce God.

The book of Job indicates that the angels and archangels ("sons of God") spent time in creative activity and then returned to report their deeds to God. For example, after Job's first test by Satan, the Bible says, "Again here was a day when the sons of God came to present themselves before the Lord, and Satan came also among them to present himself before the Lord" (2:1). It is reasonable to deduce that Satan was still within God's grace during this period. "To present himself before the Lord" doesn't indicate that Satan was banished to utter darkness or that he hated God. Satan was acting as Job's adversary or coach under God's direction.

Satan announces that when a man's life is in danger, he will always renounce God under duress.

God ups the ante on the chess match: "And the Lord said to Satan, Behold, he is in thine hand; but save his life" (2:6). So Satan does what he does best: wreaks havoc in Job's life, makes him sick with boils, until Job curses the day he was born. He loses his family, his health, and all that is dear to him in life, but he does not speak ill of God, nor does he renounce Him. In the latter portion of the book of Job, God bestows upon him twice as much as he had ever lost.

The book *Edgar Cayce on Angels, Archangels, and Unseen Forces* states that the Cayce readings indicate that all souls will be tested so that they may be worthy to eventually be cocreators with God again: "Part of this testing is the choice of renouncing all that abhors love, peace, harmony. How can we choose love, peace, and harmony if we are not also faced with its exact opposite in our lives? Every day is an opportunity to choose what we will serve — the source of good or of evil."

When I brought up this controversial passage to my dear brilliant friend Dr. Bernie Siegel, he said, "In the beginning, God wasn't very nice." And from the sound of it, I'd have to agree.

If it's true that we're in God's boot camp on this earth, in training to resist evil in all its forms — including fear, jealousy, resentment, bitterness, cynicism, depression, regret, and guilt — and learn to be present in the moment with all our love, no one could be better teachers for us than the animals, especially if they have fangs and could kill us if we don't.

But I think it's the little niggly-piggly daily mental demons that harm us the most: the serpents of self-doubt, guilt, and helplessness that lead to jealousy or rage and, in turn, to a sense of self-entitlement seeking dominance or even revenge. These are the mental virus programs — the psychological worms — that weasel their way into the cracks and crevices in our minds.

The Forked Tongue

If there is a devil, he must use our own weaknesses to test us, and what may seem like self-inflicted harm is really just self-growth waiting to happen. From the looks of our world, it's been waiting for a long time. Whether this negativity is a "being" or a force of nature, it's one that must be resisted on a daily basis, because its counterproductive self-destructive power is profound. We must ignore those evil whispers. We must choose whom we serve. This wicked force, be it in a body or not, is *real*. It lies, it cheats, it steals, it manipulates, it deprives you of hope and happiness, and it empties your life of meaning.

We can be redeemed from these persistent mental and emotional evils, but this practice is just that: practice — a daily spiritual practice — and it takes discipline. We must choose light and love over darkness and despair, and we must choose it over and over in the course of a day, maybe even in the course of an hour.

Is it possible that our negative thoughts about ourselves and each other do more damage than we realize? Could it be that something so seemingly innocent as gossip could be tragically detrimental to our spiritual well-being? Of all the evils we endure on a day-to-day basis, engaging in hurtful gossip may be a pitfall more dangerous than we realize. *Angel* means "messenger." *Archangel* means "messenger of great importance." But the opposite of an angel is a devil who carries destructive lies and fears from place to place. That means if you have a forked tongue and love to gossip, you are acting out a shadow self that is the opposite of the angels. In the Night of the Demons series of films, I carried the possession like a herpes virus from kiss to kiss, from toxic lips that infected everyone else with it; then they did my killing for me, the bidding of the dark demon that had possessed me.

When we reach out to gossip with someone for reasons that fulfill unfulfilled desire — lust, but more often loneliness, a need to belong — the demon spreads itself from one lip to the next. And this is what we must look at now. From one word to the next ear, from that word to the next ear, the evil spreads like a virus, until it becomes known behavior built on common "truths" where the members of the group trust each other and trust the information carried for some inexplicable reason, no matter how contrary the information may be to the fundamental laws of life. We would not destroy our own environment, the very sources of nourishment we need for ourselves, our spouses, and our children. Yet we do. We would not destroy the very ground we walk on, the water we drink, and the air we breathe, but we do. We would not hoard animals or enslave them in ways that threaten our own survival, but we do.

So *evil* is in the word. It is in the spoken word. It is in the mouths of our politicians, news broadcasters, and writers for all newspapers, magazines, radio, and television. With the money from sponsors bringing dubious messages, relying on ratings became more important than the message itself, and the message in pure theater was lost; that message was one of hope, of community, of the virtues of goodness and service, of resolving conflict for the good of all, and of learning to master life's challenges to share that knowledge with future generations. That was the purpose of theater, film, and other forms of entertainment. It is now compromised. And for the record, in my films, before I got possessed, I was the only character in the movie encouraging the rest of the characters *not* to entertain any demons on Halloween night! The evil whispers of temptation won out over my moral message, and the evil spirits made my crimson lips their point of entry into this world. Oops. Gotta watch my mouth!

Carrying evil whispers is not a problem I would tag on poisonous snakes. They strike only when they feel their lives are threatened. They don't kill us to make purses, belts, or shoes out of *us*.

When I met my mamba, I had a split second to shift from terror to love, and I needed that love available. We must create a reservoir of this love so that it is there for us to drink, and to bathe in, splash in, and clean our energy when we become deprived of hope in a difficult world. God consciousness is the bank we must all invest in if we want some security in our lives. Staying stuck in fear is a choice. When we need major transformation in our lives, we must allow some old things to die in order for others to be born. To me, snakes are a symbol of change, and even the common depiction of the black mamba is an illustration of her with her own tail in her mouth, where something has gone "full circle."

BLACK MAMBAS: THE FACTS

I've summarized some sizzling facts for you from *The Encyclopedia of Life* and *National Geographic* sites so that you can get the straight scoop on my greased-lightning gal and understand how important it is that a lady like this never welcomes you with a kiss. The bite of the black mamba is known by South African locals as the kiss of death.

A single strike can deliver enough neurotoxic venom to kill fifteen grown men. Black mambas live in the savannas and rocky hills of southern and eastern Africa. They are Africa's longest venomous snake, reaching up to 14 feet (4.5 meters) in length. They are also among the fastest snakes in the world, slithering at speeds of up to 12.5 miles per hour (20 kilometers per hour). It takes its name not from the color of its scales but from the interior of its mouth, which is inky black and is displayed when it's threatened.

Black mambas are found in pairs or small groups. Several weeks after a pair of mambas mate, the female will find a good place to lay six to seventeen eggs. After she lays her eggs, the female leaves. The young snakes are about sixteen to twenty-four inches long when they hatch three months later. They reach maturity when they are three to four feet in length.

Black mambas are shy and will almost always seek to escape when confronted. They are fast, nervous, lethally venomous, and, when threatened, highly aggressive. They can strike from four to six feet away.

Before the advent of black mamba antivenin, a bite from this fearsome serpent was 100 percent fatal, usually within about twenty minutes. Unfortunately, antivenin is still not widely available in the rural parts of the mamba's range, and mamba-related deaths remain frequent.

What Do Snakes Represent?

Transformation. Sometimes we must "shed our skin" in order to move forward and embrace life's challenges with a newfound sense of courage. It's this connection to our own kundalini life force — the energy in our spinal column — that allows us to create new life for ourselves and, like a phoenix, rise from the ashes, no matter what we left behind.

6 | Bees

Children of the Sun

All things bright and beautiful,
All creatures great and small.
All things wild and wonderful,
the Lord God made them all.

Each little flower that opens,
Each little bird that sings,
He made their glowing colors,
He made their tiny wings.

— Cecil F. Alexander, from "All Things Bright and Beautiful"

Bees are a building block of creation. They are an extraordinarily important animal on this planet, without which major pollination, many flowering plants, and therefore many animals would cease to exist. Is it possible that the creativity and essence of God Himself are present in these tiny, seemingly impossibly crafted beings, and that's why their busy buzzing merits such authority?

Intimidating in every way, they also are masters of design, in their flight patterns, their crazy choreographed dances, and the building of their mathematically mind-blowing hives. And they make one of my favorite things on this earth: honey. So here we have a design that is the personification of comfort and life itself — something that looks hilarious, produces something delicious, and keeps every single being on the continents of this earth alive — and this being not only has intelligence beyond our wildest imaginings but a sense of humor evident in every aspect. I joke that God must have been drunk the night He designed the bee (maybe He had a beer and got buzzed), because if I were to tell you that I had come up with a cartoon character who has wings seemingly too small to support his bulbous body but — even on puny, disproportionate wings — can somehow fly, you'd say, "Earth to Amelia! Enough, already!"

But that's only the beginning. If I went on to tell you that my new cartoon character wears a ridiculous yellow-and-black-striped fuzzy jumpsuit and sports oversized boots, and that she flies into a flower and stuffs her boots with pollen, tracking it on petals as she flies from flower to flower until she flies home to unstuff her boots and create a nectar of the gods out of it — let alone that her home is a geometric masterpiece that she and her thousands of buddies created out of the goo oozing out of their bellies — you'd accuse me of getting a license for medicinal marijuana and tokin' on a fatty!

But even if you overlook the pollen-packed thigh-high go-go boots, there's still the issue of their cartoonish tongue. Honeybees slurp up nectar with their long, suction-cupped tongues. Their probing proboscis actually resembles a teeny-tiny elephant trunk. Of course. Coming or going, we're looking at a character that Walt Disney would have been ashamed to design. Go on to add that the majority of male bees answer to one queen, who incubates males at will only to have sex with her (let alone that the males lose their "fishin' tackle" and die immediately after sex), and you'd know that I might have indulged in this ridiculous character design just to invoke a few peals of late-night wicked laughter. (Oh, bee-have, Amelia!)

But any way you look at it, this being is too implausible to take seriously — and too important to our survival *not* to. Nothing like a honeybee could logically exist in our *normal* world! Thankfully, this fairy-tale creature not only exists but is the most essential building block in the food chain on this earth. Can they think and feel? Can they communicate with humans? Just wait!

Everything about bees is pure magic. Especially the fact that they come when I call them! But I only just found that out. For the last fifteen years, talk-show hosts and radio personalities have put me on the spot to ask me why the bees are dying. Many years ago, I was a guest on *Coast to Coast* — the most interesting late-night radio show in America, which was then hosted by the infamous and much-adored Art Bell. The show is now hosted by the wonderful George Noory, who not only has had me on the show twice but even flew me to Colorado to appear on camera in his new internet broadcast, *Beyond,* where I whispered with a wild mustang we brought right into the studio.

But this bee business began with Art Bell, when he caught me off guard and asked me why the bees are dying. Of course I said that bees are getting poisoned by the pesticides we humans put on their plants, but I also referred to the legend that back in the 1950s, Albert Einstein was said to have predicted that when the "bees are gone," the human race would have only four more years of existence on earth. In truth, Einstein did not write this. Although he could have quoted it. The prediction first appeared in the book *The Life of the Bee*, published in 1901 by Maurice Maeterlinck, who wrote: "If the bee disappeared off the face of the earth, man would only have four years left to live." Einstein probably referred to it in passing and made the terrifying prediction famous.

What an alarming thought, that someone could have predicted 116 years ago that bees might become endangered. Maeterlinck also wrote, "It is actually estimated that more than a hundred thousand varieties of plants would disappear if the bees did not visit them."

It has always been paramount to me to try to communicate with bees and find out how they can survive these dire straits and what my organic beekeeper students can do to help them. Please understand that I acknowledge their sacred place in our world, and I do not take this lightly, but I need to take you on a lighthearted journey now and explain my own personal miracle with them — not as an entomologist, because I am certainly not, but as a mystic and a curious writer. So flap your wings, rev your engines, and off we go!

My most astounding bee encounter took place three years ago in gorgeous Basel, Switzerland, where I teach every spring. I now have organic beekeepers who catch wind of my seminars all over the world and email me in advance to ask if I can speak to and help their bees, but this incident in Basel was one of my first experiences with an organic beekeeper who wanted her bees to be the focus of my seminar. I wasn't even sure it would work — that we could contact and "talk" to bees, being that they, like most insects, feel more like an alien nation to me than they do an animal kingdom. The woman turned out to be a "busy bee," emailing me obsessively and sending lists of questions that would make any psychic's head explode. Where other animal lovers might want to know what their animal needs in order to be healthy, this "bee" wanted to know what planet bees are from, how they came into existence on Earth, in what millennium they arrived on Earth and from what dimension, what is their ultimate purpose and long-term goal in the assistance of the human race, what is their future destiny once they've ascended this planet, and...and...and...you get the picture. Bzzz. Bzzz. Bzzz.

I say this with great fondness because I actually liked this woman very much and could relate to her cosmic consciousness and curiosity, but the length and nature of the questions were, I admit, worthy

of a chuckle as well as a serious lengthy investigation that would —
and will — take me the rest of my life.

When she arrived at the seminar in Basel, it all made sense. I
found myself looking down into the very round, unblinking eyes of
a short, round person who was gunning off questions at lightning
speed, questions that no one else would ever think of, after she had
made a beeline to the front of the room, dodging other students and
dive-bombing me to land on my platform as if everyone else were in
slow motion. I looked into her all-seeing eyes and realized then that
she wasn't a normal human — not a human spirit in a human body.
"Ah. A bee!" I thought.

I've met a number of people over the years who specialize in one
kind of animal rescue or study or another, and they often resemble
and even have the personality traits of the animals they work with.
I've known some horses-in-human-bodies, and I've seen quite a few
dolphins-in-human-bodies (you can tell by their wide smiles and
love for the ocean), and of course I've seen a multitude of cats- and
dogs-in-human-bodies, and even a few tigers (like me), but this was
the first human I'd ever met who was so obviously not human. She
was a *bee*! I suspect her spirit had taken the form of a human being
just so she could champion her nation.

I'm often accused of that myself — taking human form so I can
champion tigers — and I don't deny it, but this little bee cracked me
up. She was so incredibly excited that the following day — Sunday
— she was going to bring me a box of her bees. The entire group
was going to try to contact their collective consciousness and "talk"
to them. I admit I was excited, too. I've found a consistent phenomenon in teaching my annual seminars in Switzerland, and that's why I
fly across the globe to teach there every year: my Swiss students are
exceptionally switched on. For some reason, my seminars in Switzerland are usually filled with spiritually evolved people who want
to contemplate the nature of reality and the future of the galaxy with

the implications that once our endangered species ascends this planet and needs a new dimension to occupy within the Zero Point Energy Field, will we humans be worthy of populating such future worlds? While in many other countries, the students want to know, "Why does Fluffy pee on the rug?"

This was not a pee-on-the-rug kind of group, and we were all psyched to try to contact not only the bees in the box but also bee nations globally to ask how we could assist them so that they didn't go extinct...in which case, much mammal life on our planet would be threatened. Just to bee fair, I also have numerous bee-zarre traits myself, what with my passion for flowers and attraction to sweet-smelling candles, paled only by my rather obsessive adoration of honey, not to mention my flitting from country to country on a monthly if not weekly basis. I even went through a troubling phase as a toddler where I refused to eat anything that wasn't the color yellow, and I remember it like it was yesterday. God bless my baffled mother, who gave me a steady diet of bananas and scrambled eggs, but un-beeknownst to her, she may have had a child who was very bee-like. I also remember when I was two years old, learning how to read, and my mother held up a flashcard picture of a bee and asked, "What does a 'bee' say?" I said, "Bzzz. Bzzz." Then I danced around the living room to prove it. Thus I learned my A-Bee-Cs with the assistance of some bee-ings that I was very aware of, even as a toddler. How many of us humans did bees help teach to read and write? Lots, I'd wager. Who in the English-speaking world doesn't know that "A is for apple, and B is for bee"?

For many of us nature-loving humans, saving bees from swimming pools may have been our first association with saving a life. I don't think this can be downplayed. No matter how rough our situation was as children, or even is now, to be able to save a bee's life was (and is!) a way to feel utterly triumphant, blessed by God, and in the right place at the right time. It was for me as a child, as a little

Texan who saved countless bees from swimming pools, the most empowering experience of my life. I got to save one just the other day — a dramatic rescue where I had to leap into an unheated pool to rescue one who was almost a goner. And despite an avalanche of events happening in the world around me that were making me feel powerless, scooping that bee onto a big sycamore leaf and carrying her to safety made me feel like a million bucks! We don't have the opportunity to actively rescue a lot of other animals in our lives that we would like to save, but bees give us the opportunity to be heroes, and that's no small affair!

So I'm not criticizing this woman for her bee-havior but more likely praising her bee-attitudes because I have them, too. (If you think about it, bees and tigers look suspiciously similar in their stylish pumpkin-striped pantsuits, which are almost identically color-coordinated! Bumblebees and Siberian tigers match! Leave it to my totems to be slaves to fashion!)

I'd also like to hope that I'm pollinating this planet with some new ideas and that my buzzing around the globe for the last fifteen years has helped some real rare talents bloom. My most gifted and treasured students who now also practice as professional animal communicators are proof that mental pollination works, and these blossoming psychics are busy in their respective countries, pouring the sweet nectar of love for animals on anyone who comes close enough to be pollinated. And many of my readers will agree to being spiritually pollinated just through our sharing some life-sustaining ideas.

I had great hopes of cultivating the inner workings of this brilliant Basel-ian beekeeper and helping her stuff her mental pollen sacks with some new ideas. Over the six months leading up to this workshop, I'd received dozens and dozens of emails from this bee-woman (bees love the internet!), so no one in the room was more excited about this workshop than she, with the exception maybe of me.

She perched in a chair all day, engines idling, barely able to sit still, waiting for Sunday morning to come so that we could all behold her magnificent bees. I announced to the group that the following day was a very special day because I'd never had bees in my workshop before — at least not on purpose. I did have a few fly in the windows in my seminar in Hannover, Germany, many years ago, and I'd lured them out with coffee cups drizzled with a bit of sugar water. (Take note: If you ever have a bee in your abode that you'd like to expel, all you need do is put a teaspoonful of sugar and a little water in a glass, and the bee will go right into the glass, where you can rescue it and take it outside to safety. Bees shouldn't be exposed to foreign honey because it can carry viruses, so they should be lured out only with sugar water. It works like a charm.)

However, this weekend was going to be the first time I'd had bees at my seminar as our animal teachers, so the entire class was whirring with excitement. At the end of this day, the little bug-eyed lady gave me a precious offering from her own farm. I accepted her gift of delicious organic honey to take back to my hotel room and indulge in like a kid with her hand in a cookie jar. Honey. My passion. My obsession. I was in heaven. If there's one thing I simply can't live without, and must have every morning, it's organic honey. I even put it in my coffee every day. Divine. If I don't have it every morning, I go hungry, missing something, as if I don't have the right information to operate my body to get through the day.

You can imagine why I wanted to learn everything I could about bees and try to understand why I'm so attracted to them. So I was really looking forward to this meeting of minds and seeing what kind of new information we could all acquire from these mastermind engineers of life on earth. I suspected that they are mysteriously linked with the creators of three-dimensional reality on this planet, or at least far more in touch with the Divine Creator than we humans are, being that they help to sustain the entire system as we know it. That night, I was humming with excitement.

But the next morning, disaster struck. I arrived to find the little bee-woman fidgeting around at the podium, waiting for me, very distressed. With tears in her wide eyes, she told me she could not lure the bees into the box that morning to bring them to the workshop. They always returned to their box every day, but on this auspicious occasion — the one time we needed them — there were no bees to be found. She was devastated. The wind had gone out from under her wings, and she was even losing her ability to buzz. I wasn't feeling so buzz-worthy myself, worried that we as a species have so let them down, they wouldn't even lower themselves to come to my seminar and let us hold a meeting with them to hear their side of the story. Had we humans so failed them that they deliberately passed on the opportunity to talk to us and let us try to make things right?

I promised the bee-woman that we would use the photos she'd emailed the coordinator and we'd project them up on the wall so that we could still ask her little friends the (exhaustive) list of questions she'd proposed, and give her bees the hour delegated to their teachings as planned. The class and I spent the hour before lunch meditating on contacting the bees' collective unconscious (their "group mind" or the "soul of the species") to apologize for the toxins our people are dousing their flowers with, thank them for the invaluable work they do on our blue planet, and even experiment with getting counsel with their spirit queen. We told this divine golden queen in prayer that we love her and her people and want to make amends for how they are being treated and destroyed. We also took our best shot at the seemingly endless list of esoteric questions the beekeeper wanted answered, and even channeled messages of love and gratitude from the bees to their human keeper.

None of this helped the beekeeper. She had alighted in a chair and sat staring frozen all morning. Not one bzzz. Her batteries had gone dead. I was half expecting her to fall to the floor and roll over onto her back in her final death throes with legs quivering in the air.

I think the empty box had hurt her pride, and she felt abandoned by her own people when they didn't show up to keep their promise. She'd been emailing me for months, after all, so this was quite a blow.

But the bees had other ideas. We set about trying to talk to the photos on the projector, meditating on our wise little friends, but we were about to get a dose of bee wisdom that would make me want to soar on tiny wings.

I called the lunch break at one o'clock and was on my way out of the conference room when one of the students ran up to me shouting, "Ms. Kinkade! Come *quick*! There's someone here to see you! You've got to see this!"

I followed the student out the front door and into the street. This part of Basel is not countryside, mind you. I was teaching at the time in a very busy industrial part of Basel. The excited student shouted, "*Look!*" He pointed to my left, down the street, in the air.

A cloud of something was moving up the street toward me. A solid wall of something was making its way through traffic, above cars, and past very distraught pedestrians. I'd never seen such a big cloud of ... what the bzzz?

That's right. They came to my seminar, arriving right to our doorstep in a cloud of glory before our astonished eyes! One might assume that the beekeeper's bees did not want to go into the box and sit there stifled and inconvenienced all day to teach my workshop. So they sent *representatives*.

Apparently, our efforts had hit their mark. We had achieved contact. Now any of you naysayers can call it coincidence that the biggest swarm of bees any of us had ever seen just happened to fly straight to my door through the busy city streets in downtown Basel after we'd been praying for them and trying to commune with them for over an hour.

But I wouldn't say that out loud. Especially not outside in the springtime. And most certainly not if you're allergic. Those little gals can wield a mighty sting.

What did they say to me? Well, I didn't let them in, much to the relief of the owner of the seminar house, who had set up a café in the front of the building, but I did tune in to the swarm long enough to take in one mighty message before they roared off: "We can hear you, Amelia! You called us and we came!" And when the beekeeper came flying out the door behind me to witness the sight and stood next to me quivering with awe and pleasure, I heard them address her personally as they swarmed by, "We love you. We love you. We love you. Thank you for everything!"

Straight from the Bee's Proboscis

The world of bees is infinitely fascinating, and in researching it for you, I found that our scientists have — even in a treasure trove of information — barely scratched the surface of the knowledge hive. However, I am happy to report that despite our destructive behavior toward bees in the wild, many scientists who are conducting experiments on bees are doing so with the utmost care and respect. Of course we humans need to take more care to buy only organic honey and beeswax that is humanely sourced, to ensure that the honey the bees have stored to feed their young and feed their queen through the long winter is carefully rationed and not replaced with sugar water by callous beekeepers. Thankfully, there are many organic honey producers in this world who are meticulously caring for their bees with respect and even reverence, and the worst of the experiments that I read about involved simply placing a dot of paint on the backs of the bees to track their flight patterns, which the bees didn't seem to mind. Being that they were worker females, they might have only objected that their fluorescent painted jackets didn't match their corbiculae (the plural of *corbicula*, "pollen basket" in Latin or "go-go boots" in Amelia-speak).

But in all seriousness, a lot of scientists out there are doing great work and making huge strides to understand bee behavior, and every fact I discovered was more captivating than the last, so I want to take you on a journey down the rabbit hole — or, in this case, into the hive — as we explore the lives of honeybees.

Bee-witched, Bothered, and Bee-wildered!

Honeybees have one of the most seamless cooperative societies of any creature on this planet, a harmony achieved by the immaculate clarity of the roles and jobs of each member of the group. The experts at Arkive.org explain the three types of roles that honeybees play within the hive caste system on their "Honey bee" page, and my mother, Dr. Kinkade, who has doctorates in radiation biology and molecular chemistry, added a few corrections. (Yes, my mother is one very busy bee!):

> The honeybee (*Apis mellifera*) is probably one of the best known of all insects in the world, as it performs a vital role in the pollination of flowering plants, including our crop species. There are three "castes" within a bee hive: a "queen" (the reproductive female), the "drones" (reproductive males), and "workers" (non-reproductive females). All three castes are broadly similar in appearance; the body is covered in short hair, and is divided into a head, a thorax and an abdomen, the head features two large eyes, [three smaller ones,] and a pair of antennae. [It also has a long sticky tongue called a proboscis, and a pair of mandibles that act sort of like pliers.] The thorax bears two pairs of wings above and three pairs of legs below, and there is a slender

"waist" between the thorax and abdomen. The queen has a much longer and [slenderer] abdomen than the workers, and the drones can be identified by their broader abdomens and much larger eyes.

THE NURSERY IN NIRVANA

Brace yourself for this. Be prepared to bee humbled. I'm about to tell you something that is mind-blowing and, I'm sorry to say, proof that these little beings are in many ways more evolved than we are. Each honeycomb is made of small cells, called *brood cells*, which can hold honey or a single bee egg where the baby will pupate. That means the meticulously constructed hive functions as the bees' cupboard and also the bees' incubator.

The baby-having business of the bee is very different from the privileged life of a queen. While a female worker bee lays only a few eggs in her lifetime, a queen honeybee lays thousands. The queen places one egg into each brood cell in a special area of the hive used as a nursery. Okay, this is where you have to grab your feet because this piece of info will knock your socks off!

The queen bee has control over whether she lays male or female eggs! No, really! "Stop!" you shout. "It's too much! It's too crazy! It sounds like a fairy tale!" Yes, but it's true. If she uses her stored sperm to fertilize the egg, the larva that hatches is female (and will become a worker or, rarely, a new queen). If she leaves the egg unfertilized, the larva that hatches is male (and will become a drone). This means that female bees inherit genes from their mothers and their fathers while male bees inherit only genes from their mothers. Not what you're used to in the old run-of-the-mill mammal, huh?

The website How Stuff Works tells us:

The queen lays both male and female eggs, and after around three days, small white larvae emerge. Once the eggs hatch, the young "babysitter" workers take care of them for the first two days of their lives, feeding all the larvae a rich liquid known as "royal jelly." Workers are then fed on pollen and nectar, but only larvae that continue to be given royal jelly develop into queens. The baby queen feeds exclusively on royal jelly until she spins her cocoon. After six days the pupal stage will develop. Bee larvae molt several times before spinning cocoons, at which point the workers cap their cells with tiny plates of beeswax to protect them while they pupate.

You know what images these geometrical masterpieces of six-sided chambers evoke for me? Note the baby mummies in each golden honeycomb tomb, waiting to be reanimated once each larva "dies" by dissolving within cocoons filled with eternal manna from heaven (honey), left in each tomb by their ancestors to feed them in the "afterlife" when they are incarnated into their new (winged/upgraded) bodies. Building on this idea, the walls inside both types of burial chambers are painted bright gold — ours with gold gilt, theirs with wax — and our ancient version of the hexagram hotel is actually built in the form of a *platonic solid* (a pyramid), a mathematical component essential to the construction of the hexagram.

What song is running through my (little bit crazy) head?

Now, when I die,
Now don't think I'm a nut,
Don't want no fancy funeral,
Just one like ole King…

Tut, tut. Now, seriously, we're going to put on our thinking caps and pull out our time machines to explore some controversial new ideas at the end of this chapter involving the Flower of Life, and sacred geometry. I'll get back to the known bee-facts for a few more pages here, but I just invite you to gently observe that bees craft their wax condos — these architectural masterpieces — with no nails, plaster, or measuring devices, much less power tools. Each hexagram fits perfectly on top of, beside, and under the others. Remind you of something? "Now when I die, now don't think I'm a nut..." But it's true. The only structures we know of on this planet made of stones that fit together seamlessly in the historical time when we assume the (primitive?) humans didn't have power tools or forms of measurement for such large-scale objects, much less a means of lifting five million blocks of limestone for transport, housed the mummies of rulers like...

"King Tut, buried in his jammies." In truth, the Great Pyramid of Giza was built for Pharaoh Khufu in the fourth dynasty, or so we're told. Steve Martin's muse had his own golden bee chamber. (But what a lot of loot was left in this golden jewelry box in case the Little Boy King came back to life someday! There was enough beebread in there to keep Tut rich for eternity!)

And although I jest about the tomb analogy, let's not pooh-pooh the relevance of metamorphosis. It's another concept we humans tend to downplay or dismiss because we can't do it. I once saw my brilliant colleague Dr. Martha Beck speak in Los Angeles after I had the honor of helping with her dog, Cookie. Martha gave a lecture on imago cells that I will take to my grave (excuse the pun).

Listen carefully. This is life changing. In Martha's lecture, she used butterflies as an analogy for human spirituality, but the concepts lend themselves to bees, dragonflies, and all beings who work the magic of metamorphosis.

Dr. Beck tells us that after a butterfly larva spins a cocoon, the pupa disintegrates into a soup of cells — literally a half teaspoon full of liquid. She calls this goo "imago cells," after the Latin root of the word *magic* as well as *imagine* and *imagination*. And I will add *image*.

Now, if we apply the ideas of using your *imagination* to the act of being a *magus* or performing *magic*, magic would simply mean using the creative source or spark of God in the initiation of any creative act. A magus, like me, is simply one who can imagine and dream into reality an act or outcome that does not yet exist on earth. There's another name for this: *artist*.

Martha tells us that the butterfly pupa literally disappears in its totality and its body cells disassociate. But inside this fluid-filled cocoon, something more than a bit magical happens. Somehow at this stage, where there is literally no cellular organization left, cells turn from chaos back into order. The pupa's cells regroup, and something astonishing happens. A new body forms, unlike anything the little creature has seen before, but now it has wings. And all the rules have changed for this creature. It no longer creeps along, fighting for territory and food with other caterpillars on its leaf, indeed eating its environment out from under its own feet. (Now, you know where I'm going with this.) Once it emerges, winged, it sits on a leaf or flower in the sunshine, waiting for its wings to dry. It must orient itself because everything in its reality has been altered. It no longer eats leaves. Now it must fly into flowers and suck the nectar out with its new vacuum cleaner of a mouth. It no longer crawls along slowly — it can fly *really* fast. It no longer has to crawl in slow motion on plants looking for food to eat. Now its job is to find wind currents, updrafts that will help carry it to the next flower effortlessly. It no longer destroys the environment by eating the food out from under its own feet. Now it has a blessed constructive use in drinking nectar and pollinating plants. It is no longer a little chubby eyesore, the ugly duckling of insects, as it was as a caterpillar. Now it has rainbow wings like an angel, and it is one of the most exquisite insects on the planet.

Yes, I've arrived at the analogy. The human race needs to metamorphose. The bee larva, too, does nothing but eat and take from its environment, until it pupates and becomes a valuable, irreplaceable resource to plants and animals on earth. We need to metamorphose now, and gain some mobility, too. And although we don't sprout wings when we find our spiritual selves and our life's purpose, at least we can gain some mobility in our consciousness and become valuable shepherds of this earth and her animals. If we don't spiritually metamorphose soon, we're going to exhaust our natural resources, perish, and take all the animals with us.

Those ideas, of course, are just my opinion. Forgive me for being a buzzkill. I've written many meditations and lessons about human potential in my other books, so if you'd like to explore some of my spiritual teachings, run, don't walk, to the bookstore or order my books from Amazon. Start practicing your daily meditations, prayers, and affirmations so that you can transform your identity and start communicating with the animals around you. You'll be glad you did, and your animals will be grateful. But for now, let's put our striped fuzzy jumpsuits back on and return to the fun. Here are some delicious facts that we not only can all agree on but can *taste*. Welcome to the yummy world of honey manufacturing!

Don't Call Me "Sweetheart." Call Me "Honey!"

As I said before, honey is one of my favorite foods, and I think it is truly the nectar of the gods. Once I found out a bit more about its constitution and creation, I became even more certain that honey is the food of fairy-tale worlds. Most of us know that bees start making honey, which is their food, by visiting flowers. They collect a sugary juice called nectar from the blossom by sucking it out with their tongues. But here's where the fairy-tale character design begins: what most people don't know is that bees store this flower juice in what's called their *honey stomach*, which is different from their food stomach. No, really. I know it sounds nuts. Read on!

Honeybees live in hives. I admit that I, like some of my

generation, have been so divorced from the natural world, even where I grew up in rural Texas, that I've never even seen a beehive in the wild. Apparently that's where bees lived long before humans discovered honey and wax! Their biggest natural predator was, as all American cartoon watchers know, bears. So thanks to Yogi Bear and his sidekick, Boo Boo, even my generation knows that bees once lived in the wild, where bears would try to steal their honey. But it is no easy task, no matter how grizzly the bear! A typical beehive will house about sixty thousand bees, most of them workers, industriously making honey!

I'm ashamed to admit how easy it is for even me to forget where honey comes from and how painstaking it is to make, and just pretend that it comes ready-made in a jar on the grocery store shelves. And before this epiphany about how important bees are to our earth and our food supply, I was also prone to think of them as little pests to be avoided in the garden. I stepped on one once when I was a kid, wearing sandals on my way home from school, and boy did she let me know that she did *not* appreciate being between my toes. Ouch! I think we all have a story like that, so it's very easy to have an antagonistic attitude toward these little flying treasure hunters.

But I grew up in the South, moving from Texas to Louisiana at an early age, where honey is as imperative on your daily biscuits as the sugar in your "sweet tea" and the Tabasco in your gumbo. Lawdy, lawdy! Whar ah come from, honey is as indispensable on your dinner plate as...well, as grits! It was, and is, a staple food as far as I'm concerned. In recent years (I'm hiding my face in shame as I write this) I've also been prone to standing in a grocery store aisle and cursing the price of honey, saying things a minister simply shouldn't say. So why is honey so expensive?

- To produce a pound of honey, foraging bees have to fly a whopping fifty-five thousand miles!

- Foraging honeybees visit up to one hundred flowers per foraging trip in a single day!
- That's a lot of honeybees, working their little stingers off, because each honeybee will produce only around one-twelfth of a teaspoon of honey in its life!

Doesn't that make you appreciate those golden drops of liquid sunshine you might pour onto your pancakes? The bees literally spend every moment of their short lives making the honey we humans steal from them, and beekeepers go to great expense in setting up hives and keeping bees. In an era when supermarkets compete with each other on price, most of us consumers have forgotten the preciousness of miraculous honey.

I also have been guilty of buying the cheapest product on the grocery store shelf, but then I discovered, much to my dismay, that this cheap "honey" I brought home was not pure honey but diluted with corn syrup. This is becoming more and more common, especially in the third-world places I visit, like my beloved Africa.

Welcome to the Honey Hotel!

The next time you want to give a swat to a little "pest" threatening to restyle your hairdo, consider this: That little pollen smuggler is on her way back to the hive to feed all the infants in the hive when they hatch. The female worker bees collect the formula for a squillion little baby bottles. (Okay, there're really hundreds of incubator compartments in the hive, but this is the first food that will ever touch a baby bee's tongue and will give him the strength to empower his newly hatched body and venture out to pollinate our flowers.) Remember also that bees are responsible for one-third of the fruit and vegetables we humans eat. When the ladies return to the hive with their pollen baskets (go-go boots) full, they go about making honey to distribute to the hundreds of unborn bee babies, storing the rest to see the colony through the winter. What remains is a treasure-filled cupboard that humans will inevitably come rob. Now, do you still want to give that little buzz-kid a swat?

Honeybee workers born in the spring and summer will live only six or seven weeks, whereas those workers born in autumn may live four to six months. But their jobs are very important and we must never kill them, no matter how pesky they may be.

How do bees make honey? According to what I have learned, as spring and summer grace their territories, all-female worker bees venture out within a radius of four miles of their hive to collect nectar from the hundred closest flowers. Put that fly swatter down! She is very busy trying to save this world and its flowers, so we need to sponsor her foraging trips with all the encouragement we can muster! The male honeybees, the drones, do not forage, and neither does their queen. Which means that every single time you see a bee on a flower, she is a she. I hope that encourages you insect-challenged readers to have compassion for this working woman and not be afraid that she's going to sting you or get stuck in your hair!

But in "captivity," some beekeepers provide the bees with artificial, ready-made honeycomb frames to encourage the bees to focus their energies on making honey rather than making honeycomb. However, not all beekeepers support this practice. Some people are engaged in "natural beekeeping" which means allowing the bees to make their own honeycombs, as they would in the wild.

The nectar collected and stored in the cells still has a high water content, so the bees fan their wings to help the water evaporate until it reaches a water content of 17 percent. Once the nectar solution has become more concentrated, the bees cap the cells, building wax walls that insulate the honey. When beekeepers see these wax doors formed, they know the honey is ready to be harvested. Beekeepers then move in to rob the hives!

The honey that the bees have stored can keep in these capped cells indefinitely — without spoiling — for the honeybees to eat when they need it, and when they will not be able to forage. Of course bees can't forage in the winter when there are no flowers in bloom, so these capped containers of honey are the bees' coffers — the cupboard of "canned" goods to see the colony through the winter. During the winter, the colony will need to continue feeding around twenty thousand workers and their queen.

Does this help you understand the preciousness of honey? It is all the food that bees have to eat to see them through the winter and then feed all their babies when they hatch in the spring. Hopefully, a beekeeper will not remove all the honey from the hive and try replacing it with refined sugar. All the nutrients that bees need for survival are present in their honey, and not the sugar we humans can provide for them. Honey is ideal for bees — it is very high in energy, because it is full of nutrients as well as natural sugar. How can they exist on only one substance? And why is it so high in natural sugar? Well, they need a lot of energy. A honeybee's wings beat about 11,400 times per minute. What a workout! They also flap their wings to regulate the temperature in the hive, so they need to perpetually restore their energy to keep their wings flapping. Does this mean that they can tell the temperature, too, and even use their bodies as little thermometers as well as fans? Apparently so.

Let's sprinkle even more fairy dust onto this magical scenario. Bacteria and fungi cannot multiply in high concentrations of sugar, and this is why it keeps indefinitely. There is no expiration date on honey. It has a very long shelf life: like almost forever! Cra-zee, I know! It may crystallize and dry out, but it won't spoil. Convinced yet that bees are magical? I am.

Unfortunately, we humans have contaminated their perfect pristine food supply. Due to poor agricultural practices, bees nowadays are usually forced to forage on fields drenched in pesticides. In a perfect world, we would all not only buy nothing but organic honey but also even try to purchase from local beekeepers, which would ensure a healthier environment for honeybees and other pollinators.

This brings the biggest ethical bee question to light: Do we have the right to steal their honey at all? If the weather is warm enough for them to go out to forage and food is plentiful in the form of flower blossoms, it seems to me that humans can take honey in modest amounts without harm. In the wild, predation is natural. Other insects, mammals, and even birds (often with the help of another predator) will nip into the honey jar. I think the key words here are *moderation* and *consideration*. It takes great skill and consideration for a beekeeper to understand how much or how little honey can be taken to still ensure the colony's survival, as the bees must live off nothing but their store of honey throughout the winter.

How Do Bees Make Wax?

For this research, I looked for an organic beeswax-candle manufacturer, and the information I found was astonishing. I'm a great lover of scented candles, so once again a product that bees produce is one of my favorite things on earth. What I did not know, though, was that they secrete the wax out of their own tummy region and then have to chew it to create the wax they use to build the walls of their hives. Just listen to this, from BeeswaxCo.com:

> Worker bees, which live only around 35 days in the summer, develop special wax-producing glands on their abdomens....Bees consume honey (6–8 pounds of honey are consumed to produce a pound of wax) causing the special wax-producing glands to convert the sugar into wax, which is extruded through small pores. The wax appears as small flakes on the bees' abdomen. At this point the flakes are essentially transparent and only become white after being

chewed. It is in the mastication process that salivary secretions are added to the wax to help soften it. This also accounts for its change in color....

A honeycomb constructed from beeswax is a triumph of engineering. It consists of hexagon shaped cylinders (six-sided) that fit naturally side-by-side. It has been proven that making the cells into hexagons is the most efficient shape for using the smallest possible amount of wax to contain the highest volume of honey. It has also been shown to be one of the strongest possible shapes while using the least amount of material.

A Day in the Life of a Bee

Are you impressed yet? When do these brilliant beauties manage to accomplish so many head-spinning tasks? Let's put on our compound-eyeglasses and take a closer look at a day in the life of a female worker bee. This timetable comes to us from Howland Blackiston in his book *Beekeeping for Dummies*, 2nd edition, and you will see how much of a "dummy" Mr. Blackiston is not! I was gob-smacked by this schedule, and I think you will be, too. Here he shows us the calendar of the role of a worker bee, from the day she hatches out of her cell and turns around to clean the delivery room for the next baby hatched in her own infirmary!

House bee housekeeping (days 1 to 3)

Once a worker bee metamorphoses into an adult, she stays in the hive for about three weeks as a "house bee." One of her first tasks is cleaning out the cell from which she just emerged. This and other empty cells are cleaned and polished and left immaculate to receive new eggs and to store nectar and pollen.

Performing undertaker duties (days 3 to 16)

During the first couple weeks of her life, the house bee removes any bees that have died and disposes of the corpses as far from the hive as possible. Similarly, diseased or dead brood are quickly removed before becoming a health threat to the colony.

Nursing young worker bees (days 4 to 12)

The young house bees tend to their "babysitting" by feeding and caring for the developing larvae. On average, nurse bees check a single larva 1,300 times a day.

Attending to the queen bee (days 7 to 12)

Because her royal highness is unable to tend to her most basic needs by herself, some of the house bees do these tasks for her.

Collecting nectar for the hive (days 12 to 18)

House bees also take nectar from foraging field bees that are returning to the hive. The house bees deposit this nectar into cells earmarked for this purpose. The house bees similarly take pollen from returning field bees and pack the pollen into cells. Both the ripened honey and the pollen are food for the colony.

Fanning the beehive (days 12 to 18)

House bees also take a turn at controlling the temperature and humidity of the hive by fanning their wings. They're sort of like animated fuzzy ceiling fans.

BUILDING THE BEE HIVE (DAYS 12 TO 35)

House bees that are about 12 days old are mature enough to begin producing beeswax. The wax flakes they produce help with the building of new wax comb and in the capping of ripened honey and cells containing developing pupae.

GUARDING THE HIVE (DAYS 18 TO 21)

The last task of a house bee before she ventures out is that of guarding the hive. They are poised and alert, checking each bee that returns to the hive for a familiar scent. Only family members are allowed to pass. Bees from other hives are occasionally allowed in when they bribe the guards with nectar. These bees simply steal a little honey or pollen and leave.

BECOMING FIELD BEES (DAYS 22 TO 42)

With her life half over, the house bee now ventures outside of the hive and joins the ranks of field bees. You'll see them taking their first orientation flights. The bees face the hive and dart up, down, and all around the entrance. They're imprinting the look and location of their home before beginning to circle the hive and progressively widening those circles, learning landmarks that ultimately will guide them back home.

Sheesh! If you think you're busy working a nine-to-five job while raising kids, how about working 24/7?! No ice cream and reality TV for these gals! They never get to prop their six feet up on the couch and read a good crime novel. (I suggest my own, *Aurora's Secret*, by the way, if I can be so self-serving, because naughty as it is, it does involve talking to animals and understanding their points of view.) But if you ever wanted to pull out a can of Raid, I think this picture of the working girl's career will encourage you to spare her life, won't it? Now let's look at a day in the life and love life of a male drone bee, just for a giggle.

DATING, MATING... OH, BEE-HAVE!

The sole purpose of the drone's existence is the act of mating with the queen. Each colony produces several hundred drones so that the queen has a few hundred potential mates to choose from "on a Saturday night." The drones congregate around "hot spots" waiting for the appearance of new queens like a bunch of eligible bachelors in a nightclub. If they only knew what would happen to them if they scored, maybe they wouldn't be so eager to get lucky.

Bee experts say that the queen will usually make three nuptial flights, where she may mate with around twenty drones. (Va-va-voom! She's got her groove on. Talk about needing a sugar boost to keep your energy up.) Most of the drones will get overlooked and not have a hot date with the queen, which is a very good thing if you're a drone. If you are a drone who just had sex with the queen, you will not need a cigarette. You will need a "bee priest"! Immediately after consummation, the drone's reproductive organs are torn off his body and he dies on the spot. The queen flies off, wearing his genitalia still attached to her. (Ouch! That smarts!) You've got to hope these drones die happy with smiles on their little round faces.

If drones escape without being chosen for a date with their queen, they may live up to four months. At the end of summer, the male bees leave the nest and do not return. They spend the rest of their lives feeding on nectar from flowers, trying to mate, and occasionally competing with other males for territory, where they get into tiny fistfights. Oh, I've seen this behavior in the parking lots of some Texas country and western taverns where I go to line-dance. In the human version of this scenario, the nectar is Jack Daniel's, and the old cowboy's boots feature horse poop, not pollen, but the aftermath of the aging lovelorn is the same.

Truth be told, drones are totally harmless. If you've ever been stung by a bee, it was a little girl with a nasty temper or a working woman who felt threatened or harassed. The queen, too, can sting, but the drones are born without stingers, so ready-made are they to be the boy-toys of their "cougar" queen. Some scientists believe that drones help to incubate the brood of unborn bee babies, which would make them babysitters as well as sperm banks, so their presence is extremely important for the hive. I've never spoken to a drone personally, so I can't confirm that they babysit the unborn children. The most memorable conversation I've ever had with an insect was not with a honeybee. It was with his cuter, more cuddly cousin, the bumblebee, who is famous not for making honey but for his wonderfully scary buzz. Why do bees buzz, you ask? Two reasons: first, their rapid wing beats create wind vibrations that produce a buzzing sound. The larger the bee, the slower the wing beat. The lower pitch makes it sound louder, so hefty bees seem to buzz louder than smaller bees. I'd like to share a story about a very big-boned gentleman I encountered quite by accident who had a very big baritone buzz.

"I'M THE C-A-S-A, THE N-O-V-A, AND THE REST IS F-L-Y"

Even though the focus of this chapter is the honeybee and I'm not including the other hundreds of kinds of bees, we can't talk about the bee buzz without mentioning the most buzzworthy musicians, the genus *Bombus*.

According to a July 4, 2005, article by bee expert Gard Otis in *Scientific American*, "Why Do Bees Buzz,"

> Some bees, most commonly bumblebees (genus *Bombus*), are capable of vibrating their wing muscles and thorax (the middle segment of their body) while visiting flowers. These

vibrations shake the pollen off the flower's anthers and onto the bee's body. Some of that pollen then gets deposited on the next flower the bee visits, resulting in pollination. The bee grooms the remainder of the pollen onto special pollen-carrying structures (on the hind legs of most bees) and takes it back to the nest to feed to the larvae.

Isn't this scientist telling us that the bumblebee actually sings? Of course he does. But do scientists know what's he's singing about? Even those entomologists who are funk-challenged have observed that the DJ Bombus sings a low R & B song to the flower he wants to pollinate, vibrating his chest against her swooning stem until he literally knocks the pollen out of her. Now remember, the DJ Bombus wears roomy knee-high go-go boots, not unlike a P. Funk previously mentioned in this book, who doesn't fly like a bee but landed in a spaceship shaped like one, only to sing and wow the ladies with his low, rumbling voice.

When bumblebees vibrate flowers to release pollen, the vocal buzz they produce is surprisingly loud. Honeybees (genus *Apis*) are incapable of buzz-pollination and are usually quiet when foraging on flowers. However, some flowers are not easy to penetrate and have adapted to pollination only by pollinators capable of buzz-pollination. Tomatoes, green peppers, and blueberries all have tubular anthers with the pollen inside the tube. When the bumblebee vibrates the flower, the pollen falls out of the tubular anther onto the bee's fuzzy back. Consequently, bumblebees pollinate these crops much more efficiently than honeybees.

I had a bumblebee try to put the moves on me even this morning. Just as I was spooning honey into my first cup of joe, a jumbo-sized Bombus flew in through my bedroom window to make sure I was awake. Either he'd heard I was writing about him, or he had mistaken my pink pajamas and rose-scented night cream for something pollenilicious, because he got all up close and personal with me. First he peeked down the top of my Victoria's Secret satin PJ top to check the size of my morning glories. I shooed him out of my shirt, but by doing so, I only initiated a dogfight. He shot skyward. Charlie at two o'clock! He did a barrel roll and dove down to my muffin tops to see if my chrysanthemums were in bloom. When I swatted him with some vigor, he flew off for a moment, porpoising all over the room, and then he banked around my lower back and zoomed in on my sidesaddles to see if my pumpkin patch was in flower. When I whirled around, flailing and screaming, he dive-bombed my head and caressed my hair, mistaking my blonde morning Afro for a hibiscus bush, only to get sent sailing toward the ceiling with one mighty swat. He hovered up there disillusioned. Had he been hit? Was that smoke coming from the cockpit? He called a Mayday and dove in a hammerhead, zzzzzzzing louder and louder at my counterattacks, all pistons firing. Time to buzz the tower! He circled around my head to show me how handsome he was before he came in for a landing. Here it was. The full-court press. I felt his little ailerons tickling my ear, and then he nuzzled my neck and pressed his fat furry fuselage against me. He was convinced that I was air-traffic control! Once again I dodged his advance, and he outsmarted me, shooting just out of reach over my head.

"Listen, top gun! You omnipresent pest!" I screamed, squirming and flailing my arms like I was shooing off a flock of geese, "I'm writing a book about you guys! And I've never tried to talk to one of your people! Why won't you *talk* to me?!" Suddenly, he cut his engines, dropped down to my eye level, and hovered in my face. We stood locked for quite a while, staring eye to eye — my two eyes gazing into his five eyes (two compound eyes with a hundred bazillion components, and three extra "normal" eyes just for good measure).

"This is serious, Romeo! Do you and your nation have a message for the human race?" The little master blaster turned up the volume on his internal boom box, and I was a bit worried that he was getting annoyed with me and would just settle on my nose to give it a mighty sting. God knows I'd have deserved it because I'd been really rude, treating him like I was practicing badminton. Fortunately I wasn't very good at it, so he wasn't harmed. But he was buzzing really furiously now, and I tried with every ounce of my strength to quiet my flustered emotions, quiet my mind, and open my heart so that I could tune in to his song. But I just couldn't hear anything. There were no transmissions from this little flyboy. No contact with the tower. The airwaves were dead.

I finally managed to tune my radar into his mind-set, and then I heard it: "I said a hip hop, the hippie the hippie, to the hip, hip hop, and you don't stop the rock it to the bang bang boogie, say, up jump the boogie, to the rhythm of the boogie, the beat. And me, the groove, and my friends are gonna try to move your feet."

Ah. Just as I suspected. Straight from the yellow-striped mother ship! The Bombus is the flying funkasaurus of insects. I moved my feet all right, and managed to get the Bee Funk out into the garden to rap "Bumble's Delight" (his version of "Rapper's Delight") to the hot-pink bougainvillea blossoms, who would really appreciate his advances. Can we even fathom an alternative reality where color and scent and loveliness prevail? Am I crazy? Do I really think that bumblebees are so in awe of the beauty of the flowers they seduce that they snuggle up to them and sing them love songs? Indeed, I do. And if we humans are nothing but dark shades moving around these beautiful, agile creatures in a dimension so murky that they don't even perceive us, I pray that we never fail them so completely that we break through the sanctity of this innocence. Even I can't rise to the level where I can eavesdrop on the inner sanctum and hear the thoughts of DJ Hip Hop Bang Bang Boogie. Or vice versa. Maybe he thought I was the meanest cherry tree he'd ever seen.

So perhaps at the end of the day, the Bombus doesn't think much about communicating with humans. Furthermore, he may not make as much honey as his little workaholic cousin the honeybee; but with his sweet-talking rap (although he didn't get any action out of me and my fragrant pink striped pajamas), the DJ Bombus succeeds in pollinating some of the shyer fruits and vegetables. Bumblebees don't live as long as honeybees, and the bumble does not waggle, but the Bombus seems to have more fun.

SONGS IN THE KEY OF BEE

I might have mentioned that I started my career in Hollywood as a dancer in the movies, on television, and as a rock video queen. Remember that when I was a backup dancer for stars like Donna Summer, she once flew me in a helicopter from gig to gig like a bee. Dropping me off directly on the Greek Theatre stage in Los Angeles caused quite a buzz. As I mentioned earlier, I made cult history starring in B movies with my "demon dances," and the glory of my dance career was choreographing those cheeky dances myself. I spent many years thereafter training dancers and teaching ballet, jazz, tap, and even gymnastics to children. I still salsa dance and cha-cha-cha in salsa congresses all over the world, so naturally for me the most fascinating aspect of bee life is their dance ability. The very idea that they communicate through dance — as I once did — only makes me more fascinated with these little beings; and the notion that their little ballets convey important information — and that they can obviously "talk" to each other — is a fact that bugs some very important scientists.

The latest debate is yet another issue that I can relate to after my brief career in Hollywood as a classically trained ballerina and jazz dancer who did *not* sing. I once sat on Ray Charles's piano bench when I was working as one of his backup dancers and sang into his ear. I suspect it may have been the only time he wished he were deaf instead of blind. I do *not* sing. But the latest findings might indicate that the buzz of a bee as it dances changes notes and also relays important information. Apparently, the bees sing *and* dance. But there's a big difference between who can sing and dance in the bee world: unlike many of our male Broadway performers, the only member of the troupe that does not sing and dance is actually the only queen.

Ah, if only I were much smaller, perhaps my dancing would still be considered an honorable profession no matter what my age, and my terrible singing would fit right in with the crooning of my fuzzy pals.

Waggle All Summer Long!

In an article titled "How Honeybees Communicate with the Waggle Dance Talk," on HiveandHoneyApiary.com, bee experts tell us:

> Honey bees perform a group of movements, called the "waggle dance talk." They do this to inform other worker bees of the exact location of the food source. When they are successful in locating good food supplies, they then return to their hive and perform a dance on the honeycomb.

The NC State University report titled "The Honey Bee Dance Language" provides more detail:

> When an experienced forager returns to the colony with a load of nectar or pollen that is sufficiently nutritious to warrant a return to the source, she performs a dance on the surface of the honeycomb to tell other foragers where the food is. The dancer "spells out" two items of information — distance and direction — to the target food patch. Recruits then leave the hive to find the nectar or pollen.

Distance and direction are presented in separate components of the dance.

When a food source is very close to the hive (less than 50 meters), a forager performs a round dance. She does so by running around in narrow circles, suddenly reversing direction to her original course. She may repeat the dance several times at the same location on the comb or move to another location on the comb to repeat it. After the round dance has ended, she often distributes food to the bees following her. A round dance, therefore, communicates distance ("close to the hive," in this example), but not direction.

There aren't a lot of human dances to compare this to. Square dancing and the Texas two-step go round and round in circles, but those dances are never performed solo. Being that I am a dancer of Native American Cherokee and Choctaw descent, this "round" bee dance evokes visions of my ancestors dancing to drums, going round and round a fire. Think of it this way: if the food is close to the hive, the little bee will dance like a Native American at a pow-wow, circling a campfire, stomping in rhythm to the drums, while the drummers sing trance-inducing chants. "Hay-yah-yah-yah, hay-yah-yah-yah." Put a few feathers on this bee's head and a pair of moccasins on her feet, and you have my great-great-grandmother conveying a story to her tribe through circular dances. Okay, it's a stretch, but you must admit, it evokes a certain mood. The very idea of Native Americans dancing around a fire at night with shadows chasing them soothes my soul and makes me wistful for a time I'd love to remember. Imagine housewives telling stories to their children about nature and life, praying to the spirits of Father Wolf and Mother Bear, honoring the sun, the moon, the rain, and the stars — instead of watching reality TV, eating ice cream, obsessing on cell phones, and taking antidepressants. These bees and their ringlike dances and the thunder-drumming of their tiny wings make me long for a simpler world I wish I had known.

But the circular dance is reserved only for indicating good eating near the hive. Say the bee wants to convey more complicated directions for great pollen farther from the hive. There are two more complicated dances for particular distances. Does this mean that bees can measure, log distances, and count meters as they fly back from flowers? Well, let's go back to the experts at NC State:

> Food sources that are at intermediate distances, between 50 and 150 meters from the hive, are described by the sickle dance. This dance is crescent-shaped and represents a transitional dance between the round dance and a waggle dance.
>
> The waggle dance, or wag-tail dance, is performed by bees foraging at food sources that are more than 150 meters from the hive. This dance, unlike the round dance, communicates both distance and direction. A bee that performs a waggle dance runs straight ahead for a short distance, returns in a semicircle to the starting point, runs again through the straight course, then makes a semicircle in the opposite direction to complete a full figure-eight circuit. While running the straight-line course of the dance, the bee's body, especially the abdomen, wags vigorously from side to side....
>
> While several variables of the waggle dance relate to distance (such as dance "tempo" or the duration of buzzing sounds), the duration of the straight-run portion of the dance, measured in seconds, is the simplest and most reliable indicator of distance. As the distance to the food source increases, the duration of the waggling portion of the dance (the "waggle run") also increases.... For example, a forager

that performs a waggle run that lasts 2.5 seconds is recruiting for a food source located about 2,625 meters away.

As far as the choreography is concerned, I've seen something similar to this on catwalks at Paris Fashion Week. Fashion models are forbidden to waggle for fear that they will fall from their mile-high stilettos and break their necks on the catwalk, yet a bit of waggling occurs nonetheless, depending on the height of the heels. Now, take that figure-eight configuration as if we were looking down on ice skaters cutting that perfect figure eight into the ice as they practiced. This is the pattern that each bee makes as she gives direction not to Vivienne Westwood's new fall collection but to the new batch of pollen she happens to be wearing in her stylish overstuffed go-go boots. Add what appears to be a sense of overwhelming joy and crazy shameless booty shaking, and then get this — the duration of the booty shaking seems to be in direct proportion to the distance that the new pollen is from the hive. As our scientists estimate, two seconds of waggling is almost identical to two thousand meters from the hive. Three seconds would be three thousand meters, and so on. That's the duration aspect of the dance. Now let's talk about the angle of the catwalk. Put on your thinking cap. This is going to hurt. The NC State report tells us:

> Although the representation of distance in the waggle dance is relatively straightforward, the method of communicating direction is more complicated. The orientation of the dancing bee during the straight portion of her waggle dance indicates the location of the food source relative to the sun. The angle that the bee adopts, relative to vertical, represents the angle to the flowers relative to the direction of the sun outside the hive. In other words, the dancing bee transposes the solar angle into the gravitational angle.... A

forager recruiting to a food source in the same direction as the sun will perform a dance with the waggle-run portion traveling directly upward on the honeycomb. Conversely, if the food source is located directly away from the sun, the straight run will be performed vertically downward. If the food source is 60 degrees to the left of the sun, the waggle run will be 60 degrees to the left of vertical.

Because directional information is given relative to the sun's position and not to a compass direction, a forager's dance for a particular resource will change during a day. This is because the sun's position moves during the day. For example, a food source located due east will cause foragers to dance approximately straight up in the morning (because the sun rises in the east), but in the late afternoon, the foragers will dance approximately straight down (because the sun sets in the west). Thus, the location of the sun is a key variable in interpreting the directional information in the dance.

Got all that? Ready to jump up and do it? Altogether now... five, six, seven, eight! Let's see if I can find an analogy to make it simpler. Envision this: The returning bee sets up her catwalk facing away from her newly found drive-through Jamba Juice shop. But the dancer choreographs her straight line not from where the Jamba Juice shop actually is but from the angle of the sun in relationship with the audience in the hive. What this means is that the returning worker bees set up their model on a catwalk dance, aligning the catwalk stage with the angles of the sun. That's right. These surfer bees are even good at *math*! She conveys trigonometric information with her dance. In choreographing her dance, the bee is in fact using her own body as a stopwatch, a compass, a protractor, a triangle ruler, and a sundial...all at the same time. Feel stupid yet? I do.

"These Boots Were Made for Walkin'!"

Now, take into consideration that these blonde bombshells are living the good life in their thirty-one days of summer. When they're not collecting pollen in their go-go boots, they're dancing to explain where the good eatin' is, and when they're not dancing, they're building their dream home out of the wax oozing out of their bellies. That's right. Wax spews out of their skin so that they can surf on their own architecture.

Jump back, Bombus! I spoke to one of these blonde California girls who was busy chowing down on an orange grove in Malibu last summer, and I asked her how she and her beach blanket buddies were making out with the grub these days. I asked her if she had a message to convey to the human race. A few of her golden peeps joined in with a few lines from the Beach Boys' "Surfin' Safari":

Early in the morning we'll be starting out,
some honeys will be coming along.
We're loading up our woody with our boards inside
and headin' out singing our song....

Ah, punked again. These little surfer girls are too far advanced to talk to meat-headed giants, even animal psychic meat-headed giants. They're busy being Godalicious gorgeous top models and having fun. What use do they have for a boring troll like me? I explained that I also am a bit of a dancer and choreographer, and I'd be really honored if she'd waggle a few steps for me. I waggled around the tree to try to encourage her to join me. But her boots were full and she had better things to do. Time to hurry home and shake her groove-thing! I'm sure she added a few extra dance moves when she got back to the hive to indicate to her girlfriends, "Dude! I just found the most totally rad orange grove! Sick! I was totally in the pocket when I, like, look up and there's this, like, paddlepuss raking over me, totally washing-machining my zonal path. I was like, 'Dude! Excuse you!' But she made me rail-bang the petals and break a nail on the way out of the riptide. You Wahines have to, like, so totally turtle roll around this stupid human who'll be spazzing out in your way. Like *she* can dance! *As if!*"

And we humans are inconvenienced by sharks in our neighborhood when we go surfing. Imagine how these little bee surfers feel about us. Most humans smack them with fly swatters or squirt them with Raid.

After honeybees have performed the waggle dance talk, they may also share part of the food that they found with other bees in the colony. Rad! Looks like it's time for a barbecue on the beach in their yellow-striped bikinis after a long day of dancing in flower dust and surfin' on belly wax.

Seriously now, I'll stop waxing poetic. But I can't help it. There's nothing on earth I love more than a beautiful dancer. We're going to get back to the facts about bees according to human history, not just according to Amelia's wildlife.

Scientists tell us that because honeybees are social insects that live in a colony, they have to communicate with each other. Note the words "have to." Not "want to" or "get to" or perhaps "could have private conversations about sacred geometry because no group of humans on the planet could build a massive structure composed of perfect hexagrams with no training whatsoever." The begrudging words are "have to." But even so, what this means is unprecedented. First of all, entomologists are admitting that honeybees communicate with each other. This alone is landmark. These bees are obviously giving each other directions like little tour guides. But where scientists disagree is if honeybees give these directions exclusively through their groovy dance moves or if they also use odor cues, being that their go-go boots are full of pollen from the best new flower-garden restaurants in the area. Most scientists agree that the mapping out of flight paths is conveyed by both bee ballet and alluring aromas.

However, some killjoy scientists argue that the dance is meaningless and that these bees are actually only communicating by the smell of the take-out doggie bags they've packed in their thigh boots. Pshaw. I hate to be judgmental, but do you know how stupid that sounds to me? That's like going up to Baryshnikov after he danced the starring role in *Don Quixote* to tell him you could only follow the story line because you could smell the tapas on his breath. I'd like to see one of these scientists aim his tuchas at his favorite restaurant in relationship to the angles of the sun as it journeys across the sky, set up a catwalk for himself, and pantomime for me exactly where the restaurant is while hip-hopping like a rock star.

A Blow to the Human Ego?

Aristotle first noted the waggle dance talk around 330 BCE. But another great mind who noticed the dances and studied them rigorously for years came to believe that bees could communicate through their choreography. His waggle-wondrous discoveries captured the hearts and imaginations of the world, and even some scientists waggled right along with him. In 1967, Karl von Frisch, a German zoology professor, published the book *The Dance Language and Orientation of Bees* (Belknap Press/Harvard University Press), providing five decades of research studies on how honeybees communicate. His landmark research and years of commitment paid off. The research in decoding the waggle dance language won him the Nobel Prize in 1973. In an article in the February 2010 issue of *Max Planck Research*, Tina Heidborn cites the observations of Tania Munz, from the Max Planck Institute for the History of Science, who is currently writing a book about von Frisch:

"The discovery that animals could communicate in such detail and, moreover, symbolically caused a sensation," says Munz. "However, von Frisch's discovery also brought up some serious questions about the self-image of humans. If even such lowly animals as insects can communicate so brilliantly, what were the implications for the perceived difference between animals and humans? For centuries, language had been the sole preserve of humans (at least as far as humans were concerned). It was seen as the boundary that divided *Homo sapiens* from the other living organisms on earth. Von Frisch's findings eroded this self-image."

To this I say, "Good. It's about time!" If we don't allow our overinflated sense of superiority to start to fade away, how will we ever be receptive to the lessons that nature and all her creatures have to teach us?

BEES: THE FACTS

The U.S. Department of Agriculture estimates that the total number of managed honeybee colonies has decreased from 6 million in the 1940s to only 2.5 million in 2015 due to colony collapse disorder and other environmental factors. Honeybees are vital parts of our ecosystem, acting as highly efficient pollinators of our food crops and of wild flora. We need them to keep our crops healthy, so they are vital to our existence on earth. But in recent years their numbers have been decreasing by the billions. Not only do they act as a keystone species in our environment, but beekeeping, honey production, and honeybee pollination is worth about $14 billion annually in the United States.

Pay attention, folks. This is important!

And an August 19, 2013, article in *Time* magazine titled "Mass Deaths in Bee Colonies May Mean Disaster for Farmers — and Your Favorite Foods" begins,

You can thank the *Apis mellifera*, better known as the Western honeybee, for one in every three mouthfuls of food you'll eat today. From the almond orchards of central California — where each spring billions of honeybees from across the U.S. arrive to pollinate a multibillion-dollar crop — to the blueberry bogs of Maine, the bees are the unsung, unpaid laborers of the American agricultural system, adding more than $15 billion in value to farming each year. In June, a Whole Foods store in Rhode Island, as part of a campaign to highlight the importance of honeybees, temporarily removed from its produce section all the food that depended on pollinators. Of 453 items, 237 vanished, including apples, lemons, and zucchini and other squashes. Honeybees "are the glue that holds our agricultural system together," wrote journalist Hannah Nordhaus in her 2011 book, *The Beekeeper's Lament*.

INSIDE THE GOLDEN STARGATE

Scientists have provided us with some amazing concepts about the workings of nature's world, and I'm not going to discount any of the amazing research I've found about bees. (Except the idea that their dance is meaningless.) But what I am going to do is suggest that you may have some tools for exploring the natural world around you, and even the spiritual realms within you, that do not rely on the findings of our predecessors. Many scientists have provided a color-by-numbers model for explaining the world around us, one that does not factor in human and energetic interchanges between humans and animals (the observer and the observed) but relies on conclusions made by the observer as if the animal under study were not being observed. I appreciate the merits in this and I understand the endeavor — to describe the animals and insects as if there were no observer interfering — and I believe it's a noble cause. However, this coloring-book model of how to explore the world around us and fill in piece by piece each question that arises scientifically does not cater to the inner workings of the human psyche. There's no place in this coloring book for your soul to interact with the information you're taking in.

Some of the puzzle pieces that scientists have identified and put together are absolutely brilliant — like the study of the bees' dances and how they measure distances to the food source through their choreography. The work defining how the queen bee has control over the DNA of her young is equally stunning. Scientists like Dr. Karl von Frisch have already pushed the envelope and threatened the collective ego of the human species by suggesting that bees are far more advanced than humans in many aspects, including how they communicate with each other. But even at that, there are unconscious preapproved ways of approaching science, and I feel that there are forbidden subjects, spiritual connections that we have never explored before. In fact, there seems to be an invisible knowledge barrier around these ideas that has entrained us to look the other way when we come too close to finding something new.

I have never been one to color inside the lines, and I'm not about to start now. I can tell you that on a personal level, every time I think about infant bees, left to pupate in perfect hexagrams within Metatron's Cube, with six golden walls surrounding them and an indestructible "nectar of the gods" that is seemingly eternal (honey), my mind goes to the Great Pyramid of Giza. When I was thirteen years old, I weaseled my way into the king's chamber, squirming on my belly through passages with ceilings too low to stand in. This alone made me feel a bit like a bee larva. I inched along until I found myself in the bowels of the Great Pyramid of Giza and entered the king's chamber. I have personal experience of the pyramids as well as the temples of Sekhmet in Luxor.

I can tell you only that the feeling I get — one so mystical and intuitive that I cannot express it in words easily — is that the connections between the sacred geometry of the pyramids, tombs where the kings left their bodies to be embalmed as mummies in order to reanimate later (this was the popular belief at the time), and these golden incubators that store hundreds of bee eggs and incubate the little masters of sacred geometry are unexplored territory.

What I know for certain is that some big, beautiful consciousness created the universe, and He is so big and beautiful, this Divine Designer is beyond our egoist comprehension. And His glorious consciousness is present in every creature everywhere, no matter how great or small. Aliens or no aliens, the Lord God created them all. But He's left us in charge of taking care of them all. Each little flower that opens, each little bird that sings. He made their glowing colors. He made their tiny wings. Can we save them before it's too late?

What Can We Do to Save the Children of the Sun?

Fortunately, of all the animals I've written about in this book, the future of bees could be the most uplifting. The endangered status of the bees can be reversed. The solution is really easy. And it's really fun!

One of the most detrimental things we can do at home is to plant lawns of grass, and worse yet, to spray pesticides on our lawns. Green manicured lawns ensure that bees will have nothing to eat. Occasionally a dandelion or two pops up in your lawn, and humans are very likely to go out and "weed up" the wildflowers, or worse yet, dump weed killer on the odd flowering weed that appears unwanted. We humans are very likely to ignore the bee climbing into that dandelion or buzzing around that accidental weed. We've put a lot of value on something that has no value. And we spend a lot of time and money nurturing and watering (and mowing!) utterly useless lawns of green grass that are actually detrimental to the bees we depend on for our survival.

So here's a solution that is beautiful, fragrant, and good for the environment: Rather than planting grass lawns in front of our houses, if we humans planted meadows of wildflowers, we could give our sacred friends some clean food. They need clean nectar and clean pollen from uncontaminated wildflowers. Even if you're not willing to sacrifice your manicured green lawn, you could plant a small wildflower garden in your side or back yard, or even plant a bee-attracting wildflower patch in a big clay pot.

If everyone everywhere planted nothing but a bushy pot of beautiful wildflowers outside their homes, which would tempt our precious bees to transport the nutritious clean pollen, we could re-store their population and be very proud of ourselves. Wildflower seeds are practically free. If you include a few packets of wildflower seeds in every Christmas and birthday card you send, tape them to packages on every gift you give in the holiday season, and even have wildflower-planting parties in the springtime, in a year or two we may really have something to buzz about.

In *The Sacred Cookbook: Forgotten Healing Recipes of the Ancients* (Three Seed Productions, 2013), Nick Polizzi writes:

> In the Old Testament of the Bible, Israel was referred to as "a land flowing with milk and honey." The sacred writings of India and Egypt mention it. The Pharaohs were buried with it. John the Baptist ate it along with his locusts, and in ancient Rome it was used to heal wounds from battle....
>
> Reverence for this sticky gold turns up in the written and painted history of almost every human tribe and civili-zation in human history. According to Cheyenne myth, the first men lived on honey and wild fruits and were never hun-gry. In Hebrew, the word for bee is *dbure*, stemming from *dbr*, which means "word." The ancient Hebrew texts refer to honey as "the truth," because it is perfect in its original

form, needing no refinement whatsoever. The collection of honey by bees is considered a divine miracle.

In the Vedas, honey is considered an actual god.

The temple of the Egyptian god Osiris was also known as "the mansion of the bee," and apiculture originated in ancient Egypt.

According to this new definition of *word*, is it possible that the famous reference in Genesis, "In the beginning was the word and the word was God," could also be interpreted as "In the beginning was the word and the word was "bee"? The DJ Bombus would certainly like to think so. Let's do everything in our power to get him and his buddies off the endangered species list.

WHAT DO BEES REPRESENT?

Creativity through endless energy. They teach us that it is through our sacred connection to nature and our own souls that we find endless reservoirs of energy. They show us how to embrace roles, love our jobs, take pride in craftsmanship, never be lazy, and do beautiful work for the greater good. Bees are the weavers of physical reality, and they never shirk their responsibilities or question their place in the universe. They work joyfully and show us that we can all find valuable work and productive roles in society. Bees mirror our abilities to build and to invent new structures in our lives while working in tandem with others. Through lives of cooperation and service to the greater good of the species, we find infinite amounts of energy.

Bees show us that spring will always come, no matter how long the winter, and spring will come again to our hearts if we work hard, stay healthy, and honor the cyclical nature of the seasons in our lives. When we stay in harmony with our own internal rhythms and work joyfully, no job is a burden. Bees show us how to keep busy doing God's work and assisting the planet. But most of all, bees teach us how to create sweetness in our lives, and to appreciate the earth's endless bounty of beauty. And they remind us to jump up and dance no matter how silly we may look! *Sweet!*

7 | Whales
The Council of Elders

MY FIRST MAGICAL ENCOUNTER with whales happened many years
ago just north of Cape Town. I had been teaching a weekend workshop there and having some health problems — tummy trouble, as
one is prone to suffer when one travels to third-world countries.
One of my students, Wynter, offered to take me to Michael, her
sangoma, a doctor trained in the traditional ways — all herbs and
energy work (no Western drugs). This man was also a very famous
medicine man. He has since retired to start a family, but his influence
on my life was significant, because he could not only body-scan me

using the methods I teach for animals, tell me about my past and future in depth, channel angelic energies, and shape-shift into animals, but also manipulate the weather.

I admit that I've had a lot of success in contacting weather spirits over the years, and I'm perpetually amazed at how beautifully they cooperate with me. Michael made me feel a little bit more normal, and this alone may have been the best medicine for me, just to feel a little bit less like a petunia in an onion patch. A lot of the supernatural faculties I employ are old hat for him, so he was at the time the perfect doctor for not only my body but my soul.

But on this occasion, the magic didn't come through this man. It came through the whales themselves. Here's the story: I was juggling to get an appointment with Michael, which was near-impossible, because he had not only a fully booked appointment calendar but also sick people without appointments congregating in his waiting room for hours for an opportunity to see him. At the same time, during these last few days of my trip to Africa, I was trying to coordinate my schedule with a whale-watching tour off the coast of Hermanus. The boat trip was equally precarious because the trips were completely subject to the weather. I really wanted to do both — to see Michael and also see the whales, but I wanted to do it in that order.

Unfortunately, I couldn't get an appointment with the doctor, so I scheduled a whale-watching trip. An unexpected storm appeared out of nowhere. The wind kicked up, a magical event I now associate with witch doctors because over the years I myself have learned how to generate storms on occasion when the weather spirits choose to cooperate with me. But back then, my hopes of a sunny day were being overridden by a medicine man who made the wind go wild! The phone rang. It was the boat company calling to say they'd have to cancel the whale-watching trip that day. The phone rang again. It was Michael calling to say he had an opening. I went to see the marvelous doctor that day instead of the whales. He told me he wanted to see me again before I left, but I protested, saying I wanted to go out on the boat on my last day in Cape Town to meet the whales for the first time before I had to fly back to America. I saw the expression on his face. He didn't like this idea. He wanted me to be treated one more time in person before I left.

I scheduled my seat on the boat for the next day anyway. The next day, oops. The wind again. Crazy gale-force winds came roaring across the sky out of nowhere. Argh! Time to go back to the doctor. Very disappointed, I called his office to make another appointment right after the whale-watching company called to say the boat trip was canceled again — two days in a row because of mysterious crazy wind. Begrudgingly, I went to see the doctor again and take another load of foul-smelling herbs for my very busy tummy.

After my appointment with the witch doc, I was pouting and lamenting that I didn't get to see the whales. "But I really wanted to see the whaaales! You mean I have to drink all this icky stuff and I still didn't get to see the whales? When am I ever going to get to see the whaaales?"

Then the miracle happened. Wynter and I were en route from the doctor's office to the Cape Town airport, where I'd have to fly back to London whale-less and wailing, when a surprise traffic jam brought all the cars driving along the coast to a standstill. As you can imagine, this isn't what one hopes to find on the highway on one's way to the airport when one has an international flight to catch. But I didn't curse very long.

People were parking their cars in the middle of the road to jump out and look over the railing on the highway. We pulled over and hopped out, excited to see what all the hubbub was about. I followed the gaze and pointing fingers of the excited people to the beach, where two gigantic whales were playing in the waves. I'd never seen whales so close to the shore in my life, and never dreamed they would come this close to land. The two huge adult whales were in a frenzied game of cat and mouse, chasing each other around and around in the waves, making massive yin-yang patterns with their bodies. They were in so close that I thought they'd just stand upright on their tail fins and waddle right up the beach.

"They came to see you off!" Wynter said. "You couldn't go to them, so they came to *you!*" I tried to dismiss it because it was too good to be true, but when I tuned in to them, I could actually hear them calling to me, and everyone watching saw them wave their fins in the air and slap their tails, insistent on getting my attention.

I knew nothing about whales at the time, and thought they might be the popular southern right whales, the very ones who bless the coasts of Hermanus every year to thrill tourists who fly from all over the world to see them. But on closer investigation, I saw that they were treasured humpback whales, those magical lords of the ocean so famous for their songs. I would have been lucky to see humpbacks if I had been able to go out on the boat. And here they were, thrilling me.

We didn't have a profound conversation, but their happy dance with fin-slaps and tail-lobs said it all. In this first encounter, if we could have put their signals into English words, their message would have been nothing more than, "Hey, Amelia! Howzit going, Amelia? Look at us! Watch us dance! Woo-hoo! Woo-hoo! Don't be a stranger! Come back soon!"

When I boarded the plane, I was still buzzing with adrenaline, and nothing or no one could have wiped the smile off my face. But I didn't make much of the encounter. Any skeptic could have dismissed this first sighting as coincidence.

The second encounter was not dismissible, nor was it a happy one. Many years later, I was living in Seattle, and my then-boyfriend and I planned a whale-watching trip in the Puget Sound between Seattle and Vancouver. Note that I was going out on the boat only as a tourist, and I foolishly thought this would be fun, an excursion we were going to use just as a holiday.

The day before the boat was scheduled to leave, I tuned in to the ocean, searching for the animals I was about to meet. I zeroed in on a pod of five orcas. Yes! Just what I wanted to see! I'd never, and to this day have never, seen an orca in the wild, and I was tickled to pieces that they appeared to me and might take a meeting with me the next day. Then I picked up something on my radar that was far more mysterious. Again, I'm no whale expert. I don't know a whale from a sardine, so what appeared to me really threw me for a loop. He was huge. I don't mean a little bit huge. I mean huge beyond the boundaries of hugeness.

He was separate from the pod of orcas, still far off the coast, and he was making his way to Puget Sound. To see me? I couldn't say. But he had an agenda and he was on a mission. I can say he was a he, because he identified himself as a teenage male, or maybe what we would think of in human terms as a guy in his early twenties just old enough to go to college or join the army.

I asked him what he was doing off the coast of Seattle, and the nearest word I can use to describe his answer is "Reconnaissance." I asked him if he was alone, and he said "Yes." I tuned in to his personality to see whom I was dealing with here, because this was my first conversation with a whale. I got the distinct feeling that he was the equivalent of a young human Marine, a warrior trained in special forces, some sort of ninja so highly skilled with senses so keen that he could travel great distances alone to scout out new territory for his community.

But the way he looked! Sheesh! All I can say is that his body resembled a huge floating oyster shell, the size of a battleship.

"Good night! What *are* you? And are you really *alone*?"

He didn't have a name in English for his species, and I'm thankful for that, because what humans have named these majestic beings is so disgusting and condescending, I think it was best that he didn't know what humans call them. He assured me that he was truly alone; as I scanned the waters, I didn't find another like him for miles, and I mean many, many miles. He also showed me his map and trajectory, and I saw that he had crossed the ocean alone, swimming alone for weeks, and was targeted to hit Puget Sound the next day — the day my boat was going out! I apparently was going to get to meet the Rambo of the whales, so I was over the moon.

"Where are your people stationed?" I asked.

"Hawaii," he answered.

"You swam all the way from *Hawaii*? All by yourself?" I was incredulous.

"Yes," he answered.

"What are you looking for?"

"Food. Fresh food."

The feeling I got was very different from the vibe of the five orcas. He was shaped very differently, and he was a totally autonomous person, supremely peaceful and confident in his abilities, as if he were the top commando working for the CIA. Most if not all of the magic I felt with him can't be conveyed in words, but when I tuned in to what he was doing, I felt like I was in the computer room in a futuristic *Star Wars* movie where the computer panels of a spaceship are running scans on twenty different screens and the computer programmer is able to fire all screens simultaneously while he effortlessly navigates the starship.

I also got another spine-tingling feeling — and this is totally beyond our human capacities for reasoning — that as he was taking in the information about the new territory around him, he was sending the program back home, so that his pod back in Hawaii could watch his tour through his eyes. He was functioning as a camera that could log information and relay the data back to his people, who could watch his discoveries in real time simultaneously, as if they were watching a news broadcaster live on location on television.

I asked him about this. "So whatever you see, you can broadcast it back home?"

"Yes."

"And what will you do if you find food?"

"We will relocate the pod from Hawaii back to Puget Sound."

Okay, hold on to your hat. Because the wild ride has just begun, and as I said, this is not a happy story.

That night, as I innocently — or stupidly — anticipated my meeting with these whales, something terrible started to happen to me. I kept trying to mentally track the five orcas in an attempt to contact their leader to ask them to meet with me the next day. I succeeded in identifying the boss of the pod, and it was a female matriarch, but something horrible happened inside my head. I felt like I was in the kind of war movie where we relive what happened to the soldiers on the battleground in Vietnam. I tried to sleep, but every time I dozed off, I'd hear thunderous crashes that made my ears want to explode. By midnight, my nervous system was so shot, I felt like jets were dropping exploding bombs all around me. The pressure in my ears was excruciating, and I started to cry. Everywhere around me there were bombs, bombs, bombs, and as I tried to escape them and keep my family safe, there was nowhere for us to go. Terrorized in a churning sea of violent crashes and explosions, I kept feeling more frantic and upset.

All night this went on. Every time I tried to fall asleep, the thunder of bombs and horror would begin again, making me feel like my eardrums were going to start bleeding from all the explosions.

My poor boyfriend tried to tell me it was just my imagination, but by two AM, I was still in tears and too agitated to sleep. Living with a psychic isn't easy. This wasn't the first time he'd endured watching me up all night reacting to invisible demons he couldn't see, and I'm sure that having the whale trip spoiled by my freaking out about underwater experiments was not his idea of a good time. Early the next morning, exhausted, with raw nerves and bloodshot eyes, I set off to catch the whale boat that was going into the Puget Sound.

I tried to keep it together. When I'm in public, I never tell strangers who I am or what I do. I don't have an ax to grind, and I'm a very private person when I'm not working, but something came over me this day. A young woman introduced herself as our tour guide, and she explained her wealth of credentials as a student studying to be a marine biologist. I'm not one to pull an unsuspecting person aside and say, "Look, I'm a psychic, and blah, blah, blah." But maybe I was just too exhausted and out of my mind from the hellish night I'd endured, so once the boat took off and I had a moment alone with this lovely girl, I seized the opportunity. I pulled her aside and said, "Look, I'm a psychic. You may not believe in any of this, but there are five orcas out there and one teenage male who is another species. I don't know what he is, but he looks like a giant oyster. He's still out of range, but he's on his way over here."

As God would have it, the girl didn't even flinch, and she was actually excited to talk to me about my impressions.

"Where is the teenage male from?" she asked.

As I said, I didn't know bupkis about whales or their territories. So this seemed so outlandish that there was simply no way I could be right. I took a deep breath and closed my eyes. I was about to say something so ridiculous that I couldn't even bear to look.

"Hawaii. He says he's swum all the way from Hawaii all by himself."

Her eyes widened and brightened, as a smile shimmered across her face.

"*Really!?* They're coming *back*?"

She confirmed that a pod of five orcas had been seen in the exact area only days before. I told her the head of the group was a female matriarch, and this lovely girl confirmed that her crew had seen the matriarch in recent weeks when they had precious sightings of this group.

However, she did not know what the young male was, and she said that no other species of whales had been spotted in the Sound recently — but she seemed to have high hopes...and a secret. She was obviously going to hold her tongue until he showed up.

I sat huddled in the back of the boat and let the wind blow through my hair, wishing it would blow the congested feeling in my brain out of my head and take with it the waves of panic, frustration, and fury, but I still couldn't shake the feelings of being terrorized by explosions.

When I felt the boat drift very near the pod of five orcas, I took the guide by the arm and said, "We're almost right over them now. They're beneath the boat." She confirmed that this was near the spot where they had been sighted the day before. I asked her if the military had been conducting underwater experiments that could be causing explosions to upset these whales and their sonar. She said, "There are three military bases here, all around us, and yes, they're doing underwater experiments."

I asked the matriarch of the orca pod to bring her people up so that we could see them, but for the hour we were out there, we never saw one orca. Of course, I was dying to see them, as all the tourists were.

"Won't you please surface?" I begged.

"Can you help us?" I heard the transmission from the strong matriarch.

"No," I sent the message with a wave of great sorrow.

"If you can *hear us*, then why can't you *help us*?" she demanded.

"I think the human military must be conducting the experiments.

And whatever they're doing must sound like explosions to your sonar. I can't stop them. No one will listen to me. I'm so sorry."

"To hell with you then! Why should we surface to meet *you*?!" she said. And I felt the pod swim away in a burst of fury, away from me and my boat. She was utterly furious with me, and rightly so, because for the first time in her life, she found a human being on the land who could pick up her sonar, and I was utterly worthless to her and her people.

My heart sank. I felt like I wanted to throw up. Her response was completely appropriate. I wasn't worthy of being entertained by this goddess of the sea and her family just so that the tourists could snap pictures. There was no point in allowing me to ego-trip that I'd contacted her. She didn't owe me a circus act. I didn't deserve it. And after the way we're treating these animals, no humans deserve that reward.

I was totally miserable and sat back down, feeling like I'd had a sucker punch to the stomach. But I didn't pout long, because everyone on the boat started shouting with glee and pointing fingers in the opposite direction. An unexpected visitor had arrived, and boy did he arrive. Splashing and spurting water out of his blowhole, a colossal whale was spotted on the horizon, swimming toward our boat.

My leviathan surfaced to make sure that I saw him and to thrill the pants off of everyone on the boat. I was still clutching the guide's arm when we spun around to get a glimpse of him.

"I know this sounds crazy that he says he's from Hawaii. But he's here on a reconnaissance mission to see if he can move his pod up from Hawaii. He wants to see if the food is good up here now."

The guide confirmed excitedly, "It's a sperm whale! They haven't been spotted in this area in over three years! Their food supply diminished three years ago, and they all disappeared for Hawaii!"

"They want to come back!" A lump formed in my throat. Tears came to our eyes as she grabbed me and hugged me. If the food supply had replenished itself enough to lure them back, that was a very good sign for the ecosystem in the Puget Sound.

My Rambo wasn't terribly close, but I could see even in the distance that he was a handsome chap with a winning smile, and it was the pattern of barnacles on his back that reminded me of an oyster shell. He and I only had a few moments together before he dove out of sight, but before he left, he swam along in tandem with my boat, joining up so that my boat seemed to be swimming right along beside him.

I've used a lot of adjectives in this book. I can say words like *thrilling, awe-inspiring, phenomenal, most magical moment of my life,* and so on. But the truth is, there are no words for this. This Jedi Knight of the whale world contacted me so that I could hear him; and he swam quite a distance — timed everything perfectly — to surface within the limited range of my sight so that he could meet my boat. For this honor, I have no words. Unfortunately, I also have no words for the American military who may be inadvertently torturing our sea life. I could use a few, but they are not appropriate to come from the mouth of a minister.

Many people have emailed me over the years asking about whales and how humans are interfering with their sonar; how many whales are beaching around the world, dying mysteriously; and how, tragically, we can see pictures all over the web of dolphins bleeding to death with blood pouring out of their ears.

What can we do? I don't have the answers yet. So my plea to all of you readers is not a lecture from an expert, but a global plea to insist that our military and corporations stop performing underwater experiments and mapping that kill our whales and dolphins or leave them alive with sonar patterns so disoriented that they cannot function.

My students and readers have sent emails asking if there is a safe place on this planet for us to "send" the whales, to transmit the information that there is a safe piece of ocean far away, out of the range of our military and their ongoing crimes against nature.

I've heard that a sanctuary exists off the coast of the Canary Islands, a military-free zone, where our sonar-driven sea life can get some peace. Since my heartbreaking encounter with the orcas, I've been trying to transmit this message, and I've been asking them to explore new territories in search of pristine, safe territory as far away from the human race as possible.

Fortunately, I've had one more enthralling meeting with these glorious beings since that heartbreaking trip in the Puget Sound, and my last encounter with whales to date is thankfully a joyous story with a happy ending. A year or so after my harrowing message from the orcas in Seattle, I was living once again in Los Angeles. A reader of my books reached out to me over the web, a German veterinarian named Gaby, who was very excited that I was moving back "home" to Southern California. Having retired from her veterinary practice, she now does holistic work with horses. We met and became fast friends, and I even drove down to stay with her a couple of nights at her home in charming San Juan Capistrano, where we talked about how much I wanted to go out on a whale-watching expedition off the coast of Dana Point, where all the tourist boats go out to see the migrating whales.

She told me that she happened to be friends with a man who captained one of these boats, Captain Larry, who worked for Captain Dave's Dolphin and Whale Watching Safaris. (Larry, sadly, has retired from the company he was working for at the time.) Captain Larry even met us for a drink so that Gaby could introduce us and try to explain what I do. I downplayed my reputation because I can never predict when or how my appointments get made with sharks or whales. With this man who made his living taking tourists to see whales, I didn't want to make outlandish claims if there was a chance I could disappoint.

Larry rather laughingly blew off "what I do," as most men do who make their living spotting wild animals, but he assured me that he'd take me out on the boat, and no matter what, we'd have a wonderful time. The company offered a 100 percent money-back guarantee on their excursions, so that if you as a tourist saw no whales that day, you'd be given a free ticket to go out on the boat and try again another day.

We set the date for a couple of weeks in the future. The date was very near Gaby's birthday, so she decided to invite ten women and make a party out of our whale-watching adventure. She set the party date on the boat for a Sunday. I was planning to drive down on the Saturday before the party, go out on the boat, and pray that we saw whales on Sunday afternoon.

Having been shunned by the alpha female of the orcas, that femme fatale of the ocean who refused to even give me a glimpse of her glamorous black-and-white tuxedo, I wasn't expecting much. I know for a fact that the American military are also doing experiments off the coast of Southern California, so I certainly never dreamed that a pod of whales would greet me with big smiles and open fins. But then God swam in and gave me a big tail-lob on the head! Splish, splash!

On the Friday morning before the party, I was sitting quietly working at the computer when five colossal whales "swam" into my office. I was busy minding my own business when they blasted into my airspace. A quantum email from five noisy leviathans is kinda hard to ignore.

"Oh boy, here we go again," I thought. "Phantom fishy business!"

"What can I do for you?" I asked. "And are you all coming to meet us on Sunday?"

"No. You've got to come on *Saturday*! We'll be gone by Sunday!" one of them insisted, speaking for the whole group.

"But the party is on Sunday! Can't you wait until Sunday when we all go out on the boat?" I asked.

"No!" the spokes-whale insisted. "We're in a hurry! You've got to come *tomorrow* if you want to see us!"

Now, these whales were big. I don't mean a little bit big. I mean big. The size of small sailboats. They were a different type of whale from anything I'd ever seen before — not as big as the sperm whale or as chunky, but these whales were long, dark, and sleek. Once again, it was a pod of five, and I asked about their numbers again just to make sure.

"How many of you are there?"

"Five! We're in a hurry. You've got to change your plans!"

They swam off and out of my mind. I know what you're thinking — it sounds like I was already out of my mind, but after the encounter with the whales in Seattle, I knew better than to challenge this vision. I called Gaby.

"Gaby, you've got to change the date of the party! The whales were just here! There are five gi-normous whales coming to meet us! But they said they're coming *tomorrow*, not Sunday! They're just passing by and they're in a hurry. They say they can't wait until Sunday."

Gaby not only trusted me and my crazy prediction, but she spent the next hour calling the other nine women to cancel her birthday party, but not before she called Captain Larry and told him the news. She booked us two spots on his boat on Saturday instead of Sunday. I threw a few things in an overnight bag and high-tailed it into traffic to try to get down to San Juan Capistrano that night so that I could be fresh and ready to go out on the boat the next day. Thankfully, I didn't spend another agonizing night tortured by underwater explosions.

The next day, I was a bit dismayed to see the crowd of at least fifty people waiting in line to board my boat, but Captain Larry appeared and sneaked Gaby and me past the long line and up into the captain's deck, where we had a private tour. Talk about VIP treatment!

I confess, though, I felt a bit tested by this salty old seaman, and I knew I'd be the brunt of many jokes if my five phantom whales didn't show up. It had been a slow few days for whale sightings, and even sightings of one or two whales in the distance were scarce. This was a whopper of a tale that five giants would appear out of the sea in totally calm waters. I also admit that even after all these years, there are still a few butterflies that make their way into my belly when I'm waiting for a wild animal to keep an appointment with me. The sea was calm and there was not a whale in sight for the first forty-five minutes or so, but I just kept reminding myself of the incident in South Africa when the queen of the great white sharks finally showed up an hour after the captain wanted to turn back. Once again, I sat looking like a lunatic, meditating and praying in Dr. Spock-like mode, with fingers to the temples, sending my puny human sonar as best as I could.

They heard it! Suddenly, I saw the crowd on the deck beneath me going crazy. A very large whale had surfaced and was now mugging and posing for pictures. But then the other side of the boat got some action. Another whale popped up on the other side, capturing the attention of the crowd. And then right in front of my eyes, another surfaced! And then another!

As the fifth whale surfaced behind the boat, there was an eerie feeling in my stomach I'd never experienced before. The whales were under the boat, diving and playing all around it, and they were so almighty colossal that with a head-butt or flip of the tail, they could easily capsize the boat. But of course, they didn't. Larry cut the engine, and we floated in the center of five mammoth whales surrounding the boat. He informed me that they were fin whales and that a pod this big was not an ordinary occurrence.

Again, words fail me as I try to describe the sensation I

experienced in their presence. I felt as if I were surrounded by a council of gods. It was as if Apollo, Zeus, Mercury, Hermes, and Athena had suddenly landed their fiery chariots from heaven and became real on earth. And then these five gods and goddesses joined hands around me. The five whales seemed to all "cut their engines," too. They floated in perfect stillness in a circle all around my boat. The peace they instilled in my heart and the benevolence they emitted made me feel as if the archangels had suddenly manifested and blasted every molecule of water in my body with serenity, strength, and hope. Perhaps "hope" is not the right word, because whales feel like they already have it all. There's a sense of grace and gratitude in this *allness* that humans don't emulate. So it's not hope, but a sense of faith in their capacities and place in this world, a confidence that they're so powerful that everything's going to be all right, an electric ability to communicate instantaneously, effortlessly, and a feeling of oneness with other beings of their own tribe.

These are feelings I don't have when I'm trying to communicate with humans. There's something unique about the all-knowingness of whales, and when I tune in to it, I feel more safe and secure than I've ever felt in my life. This council of elders hovered around the boat for some time before one finally dove and the others followed. They didn't speak to me in words the way my clairaudience usually interprets information. What they did to me was a mystical form of fine-tuning, as if they struck all the fluids in my body with a tuning fork, bringing everything I thought and felt — indeed, everything I was — into one unified field of coherent joy.

That day, I felt like I'd been a disconnected plug my entire life, dangling on a dead wire, and suddenly five fin whales appeared out of nowhere and without even needing to think about it reached over and plugged me back into an electrical socket. The currents of energy flowing through my body felt better than anything I'd ever felt in my life. I was at the center of a five-pointed star, as five bolts of lightning entered me from every direction. They got inside of me, beamed their sonar into me from all five directions, *did something to the water inside my body*, and upgraded my energy field. Everything in me that had felt insecure, sad, fearful, and inconsistent just magically dissolved. Instantly, every atom in my body was singing, floating effortlessly in an ocean of happiness.

Of course, Gaby was thrilled and Captain Larry was blown away, but I couldn't explain "what they said" or why they took the meeting. Maybe they just showed up to give me a gift: this "zap." And because the communication was a two-way street, I could body-scan them, align myself to resonate on their frequency, and have the opportunity — even just for a few moments — to know how good it feels to be a fin whale.

So far, these are the four encounters I've had with whales, and to date, they only include humpback whales, the orcas who never revealed themselves, the sperm whale, and the five fin whales. I hope to encounter many more whales in my lifetime, and I might even be able to take you out on some whale-watching trips in Cape Town in conjunction with some shark diving with gorgeous and fearless Lesley Rochat.

I'm going to share some research about the kinds of whales I've met, but more fascinating still, I'll share some ideas about sonar, not just the kind of sonar that whales use with each other, but the kind of sonar I use in communicating with all animals everywhere. In this chapter, we're finally going to explore some concepts about intuitive communication, and I'll share techniques so that you can start practicing "talking" to animals at home, too. Your four-legged family members will appreciate your efforts, and no one deserves to be heard more than the animals who love you.

I'll explain in laymen's terms the Zero Point Energy Field, and being that it is also an ocean, this chapter about the ocean is the right time to introduce it. There is no better analogy than a whale's sonar to explain how we all can learn to use extrasensory perception associated with "supernatural" abilities, because the concept lends itself so beautifully to humans' latent ability to pick up frequencies in communicating with all animals everywhere, not only sending information out but learning how to listen and receive information as it comes in.

And of course, we'll take a look at whale songs and what I think they're actually saying to each other. But first let me just outline for you some fun facts about the kinds of whales I've met and spoken to so far.

HUMPBACKS

The humpback whale gets its name from the humongous arch in its back when it surfaces. These winsome whales are black and gray in color, 14.6 to 15 meters in length, and easily recognized by their long, tapered winglike flippers. When they fling themselves into the air in their famous acrobatic maneuvers, they can make a mighty splash because they weigh in at thirty thousand to forty thousand kilos. With one little cannonball, even a baby humpback could splash all the water out of your swimming pool! These lovable leviathans are called "songsters of the sea" because of their musical talent in composing, singing, and sharing intricate melodies. We'll explore more about the composition of humpback rhythm and blues later in this chapter.

According to my favorite charity for the rescue and preservation of whales, Sea Shepherd Conservation Society, humpbacks are found in all of the world's oceans. Most populations of humpback whales follow a regular migration route, summering in temperate and even polar waters for feeding, but wintering in tropical waters for mating and calving. (This clever arrangement makes me smile and reminds me of many of the smart retired human "snowbirds" I know who spend their winters in Palm Springs and take off for colder climates in their campers in the hot summer months.)

Humpback whales migrate northward from the Antarctic through South African waters on their way to the tropical waters off Mozambique, southern Madagascar, and Angola every year in April and May. This is why I saw the two frolicking on the beach off the coast of Cape Town when they came to see me off on my way to the airport. These awesome animals have incredible powers of endurance, traveling over 3,100 miles (5,000 kilometers) during each seasonal migration with almost no rest along the way. During migrations, they cover over 1,000 miles per month.

I wonder if this is why they sing and improvise new tunes along the way, to entertain themselves the way my brothers and sisters and I did on long road trips across West Texas when I was a child. One time my family drove for three straight days, and I remember we kids and our mother sang a lot in the car, rewriting lyrics and making up silly rhymes to pass the time. Maybe the ocean's big baritones are just singing together on their "road trips," to pass the time and entertain the girls. Their cruising speed is only 3 to 9 miles per hour but can go up to 16.5 in bursts when they feel they are in danger. Fortunately, they can also dive deep — they've been known to dive to depths of seven hundred feet and hold their breath for up to thirty minutes!

But generally, they stay close to shore because their feeding, mating, and calving grounds are close to shore. Tragically, the fact that they are very slow swimmers made these gentle giants easy targets for early whalers. The International Whaling Commission gave them worldwide protection status in 1966, but large illegal kills were made by the Soviets until the 1970s, and it's heartbreaking to know that Japan, Norway, and Iceland are killing whales to this day. Marine scientists believe the humpback population is now about thirty thousand to forty thousand, which is less than 35 percent of the original population. What a travesty that human whalers could annihilate so many of these mighty musicians.

These astronomic beings have gastronomic tastes, because they feed on some of the minutest creatures in the ocean, so small that they wouldn't fit on a cocktail fork. Humpbacks feed on krill, small shrimplike crustaceans, and various kinds of small fish. Each whale eats up to 1.5 tons (1,361 kilograms) of food a day. Could you imagine swimming around in an ocean of seafood jambalaya and feeling like God put everything you could ever need in the gumbo pot? What a different paradigm to live in a world where we all felt that we were well provided for in an abundant universe! No wonder they sing happy songs all day!

And what a whale of a good time they can have when not being chased by whalers, because these jolly Goliaths can *dance,* too! Humpback whales are acrobatic and even aerobatic whales. They can rocket completely out of the water (breaching) and swim on their backs with both flippers in the air. The hip-hopping humpbacks also engage in dance moves called tail lobbing (where they raise their huge flukes out of the water and then slap them on the surface) and flipper slapping (using their flippers to slap the waves like they're beating a bass drum — *boom!*). But the true photo-op-of-the-century for any whale-watching photographer would be to catch a humpback spy hopping, which means the whale pokes its head out of the water for up to thirty seconds to take a look around like a periscope. Of course, these behaviors must have secret meaning for humpbacks, but the flipper slapping is an obvious sign of joy, sort of like a high five is to happy humans.

Humpback breeding occurs mostly in the winter to early spring near the surface and in warm, tropical waters. This romantic vision makes my mind float off in a sea. The choice of romantic vacation spots for these colossal charmers is not that different from ours. The tropics are the singles-resort-of-the-sea for the jumbo-sized legless set. Maybe their finned fantasies don't include luxuriating in hammocks under the stars, tied to Tahitian palm trees, but the seductive males serenade the females with enticing love songs.

What humpback bachelorette could resist? Whatever the boy humpbacks are singing, it certainly does the trick. Each female typically bears a calf every two to three years, and the gestation period is twelve months.

As I researched humpback babies, I discovered that the newborn humppies consume about one hundred pounds of their mother's milk each day for a period of five to seven months until they are weaned to solid food. (There's a fact that could make Elsie the Cow hide her udder in shame! Could you imagine how much *cheese*... Okay, we don't really need to go there.) What we can assume with some certainty is that humpback mamas are wonderful mothers, and because of this long nursing period, the bonds between mother and child must be very strong.

Of course, the most fascinating aspect of their lives for me is their composing, but we will explore that further in a passage I have very scientifically named "Deep Blue Doo-Be-Doo-Be-Doo." For now, let's get a glimpse of a whale of a different color — my little James Bond whale, the spy who loved me, the battleship-sized Marine who met me in the Puget Sound.

SPERM WHALES

Sperm whales are the largest whales with teeth, and they have the largest head of any animal in the world, measuring an epic twenty feet long, ten feet high, and seven feet across. This tremendous head is about one-third of the whale's body length and is often covered with circular scars that were made not just by barnacles but by the suckers of the giant squid that they hunt and eat. (Thus the resemblance to the giant "oyster shell" I saw when I tuned in to my brainy Barnacle Bill!)

These stately whales have the largest brain of any creature known to have lived on earth. (No wonder my James Bond could send his psychic sonar so strong as to signal me even in my little blonde ape brain!) Unfortunately, though, their heads also hold large quantities of a substance called spermaceti (suspicious, Italian…and funky!), which may be essential for their well-being. It is this very mystery goo that attracted the attention of whale killers. Whalers once believed that the oily fluid was sperm (Oops, not a rocket scientist in the bunch, I'm afraid! And it makes me wonder how much trouble these anatomy-challenged men had on their wedding nights…), but scientists *still* do not understand the function of spermaceti. One common theory is that the fluid — which hardens to wax when cold — helps the whale alter its buoyancy so that it can dive deep and rise again. These stupendous whales can dive like submarines! Sperm whales are known to dive as deep as 3,280 feet in search of tasty squid. But remember, they are mammals and must breathe air. These stellar swimmers can hold their breath underwater for up to ninety minutes!

When it comes to their kitchen table, their fare is very different from that of their humpback cousins, who dine only on hordes of krill hors d'oeuvres. A sperm whale's lunch can put up quite a fight and pop the whale in the eye with one of its many arms. These big-toothed whales feast on thousands of pounds of squid (and fish) a day — about one ton (907 kilograms). Now that's an octopi pie! Once again, my mind wanders back to human food and my favorite Cajun restaurants in New Orleans. Could you imagine how much coleslaw, hushpuppies, and tarter sauce we would need to dress a ton of fish?

But these appetites belong to athletes of epic proportions. These big eaters need this energy to swim fast — unfortunately to escape human hunters. So while a sperm whale's cruising speed is about 3 to 9 miles per hour, it can swim up to 27 miles per hour when fleeing whaling boats. If only they could escape faster!

Adult males grow to be about fifty to sixty feet long, weighing about forty to fifty tons. That would mean my James Bond Marine could have been fifty tons of fun! Females are smaller, about thirty-three to forty feet long, weighing a svelte fourteen to eighteen tons.

And if you thought the size of their brain was impressive, wait until you hear this! The four-chambered heart of the average sperm whale weighs almost three hundred pounds, about as much as two grown human men! No wonder Mr. Bond and I had a love-at-first-sight experience. Let alone the size of his immense brain, just think of the size of his heart! I could have fit inside that heart and still had room to go-go dance as he serenaded me an original love song. (That's the only kind of Bond girl I would ever want to be — one who had captured the heart of a sperm whale.)

But the real Bond girls stick together and travel in packs. Female sperm whales and their young appear to travel in pods of up to twenty while the macho males may roam solo or move from group to group. Sperm whale reproduction does not vary, dependent on the seasons, and they breed all year round. (That means they don't need piña coladas and tropical vacations. They stay sexy in every season.) The gestation period of a sperm whale calf is longer than that of a humpback. A sperm whale mama stays pregnant for a whopping sixteen months, and the baby is born tail-first near the surface of the water. The newborn instinctively swims to the surface within ten seconds for its first breath with the help of its mother. This makes me wonder if these mammals aren't far more equipped for life in the sea than we humans are for life on the land. While it takes us two-leggeds months to learn how to walk, or even to crawl, these illustrious whales adapt to their environment in a splash. Within thirty minutes of its birth, the baby whale can swim. The newborn calf is about thirteen feet long and weighs about one ton. (Try to find a baby bonnet to fit on *that*!) A female sperm whale will give birth to about seven to ten calves, and often with the help of midwives. Frequently, other whales assist in the birth. While nursing, the baby calves drink forty-five pounds of milk each day and aren't weaned until the age of two years. Undisturbed in the wild, these whales can live to be forty years old.

Humpbacks aren't the only songsters in the sea, but if the humpbacks are the jazz aficionados, sperm whales remind me of a Latin band with a hot percussion section in a salsa dancing club. They produce a series of clangs or clicking noises that scientists believe they use for communication or echolocation. Tragically, humans found other uses for these miraculous beings rather than studying their vocal patterns and trying to learn about their communication techniques. Sperm whales were the prize trophies and mainstay of whalers in whaling's eighteenth- and nineteenth-century heyday. A sperm whale was immortalized in Herman Melville's *Moby Dick,* in which sperm whales were cursed with the reputation for being violent man-eating sea monsters. These docile giants were targeted for oil and ambergris, a substance that forms around squid beaks in a whale's stomach. Ambergris was — and remains — a very valuable substance used in perfumes. (Trust me when I tell you, I never knew what ambergris was made of, and when I found out, I read the ingredients on every bottle of my favorite perfumes. The bottles containing ambergris are now at the bottom of the trash barrel, where they belong. I love perfume, but I never dreamed that it hurt my precious P Funky whales, and perfumes containing ambergris will never grace my neck again.) Thanks to horror stories like *Moby Dick,* many people dismiss the slow, cruel murdering of these majestic animals to extract the "sperm" inside their beautiful heads. (With the way humans treat these magnificent animals, one must question who here really is the "dick-head.")

ORCAS

Orcas are known for their smart black-and-white coloring and long dorsal fin (the fin on their back). Their glamorous tuxedos make them popular with humans, and they are immortalized as stuffed animals and cartoons, but they are also unfortunately the stars of some shows where humans keep them captive in small, cruel tanks. Often referred to as "killer whales," orcas are not whales at all but are in fact considered the largest species of the dolphin family. They weigh up to six tons (5,443 kilograms) and grow to twenty-three to thirty-two feet (7 to 9.8 meters). That is almost as long as a school bus. The largest orca ever recorded was thirty-two feet long. The orca's large size and strength make it an absolute powerhouse and one of the fastest marine mammals, able to reach speeds in excess of thirty knots (about 34 miles per hour). Shazam! That's one well-dressed torpedo!

According to the International Union for Conservation of Nature's (IUCN) Red List, orcas, or "killer whales," don't ever attack human beings. The legacy of their ferocity is fueled by their astonishing ability to hunt large marine animals, such as sea lions and whales. With their stunning black and white coats and round, cheerful faces, they remind me of giant floating panda bears, but the diet of a killer whale couldn't be any further from that of tranquil vegetarian pandas. Killer whales have winning smiles with massive teeth, which can grow up to four inches (ten centimeters) long. Orcas will prey on almost any animal they find in the sea and even off the coastline! If you've ever seen video of these whales cornering sea lions on ice floes in order to tumble the ice floes and eat the sea lions, you will see that once that imposing grin appears next to a sleeping seal, that seal is a goner. Orcas can fly into the air and snatch their prey off of land! Orcas are apex predators, at the top of the food chain, which means that no other animals (except for humans) hunt orcas. Killer whales feed on sea birds, squid, octopuses, sea turtles, sharks, and rays, and they work together as a team to catch larger prey or groups of prey such as schools of fish.

These cunning carnivores can live in any climate and adapt to temperatures from the warm waters around the equator to the icy waters of the North and South Pole regions. They can also travel incredibly long distances and have been tracked from the waters off

Alaska to those near central California (a distance of more than two thousand kilometers or twelve hundred miles).

My research from the *National Geographic* "Killer Whale (Orca)" page tells us that orcas are very social and live in pods, which usually have up to forty members. Orcas also work together to care for the young in a pod; young females help the mothers care for their young. (So despite their ferocity when hunting, a loving social behavior is displayed here that is actually more sensible and caring than that of many human females, who leave most other young, struggling mothers to fend for themselves.)

A female orca will give birth every three to ten years, to one offspring at a time, with a gestation period that lasts about seventeen months. According to the IUCN, the orca's population is unknown, and therefore the organization cannot label the animal's conservation status, though some populations are protected.

I believe that the orcas, like the whales, are the elders of this planet and deserve to be protected so that we can learn from them, but many humans do not share this belief. Civilizations around the world kill orcas for various reasons. Some people kill them for food, while fishermen see the animals as competition that must be killed to protect the fish population. Contaminants in the ocean and seas, such as chemicals and oil, also pose a great threat to orcas.

But it's not too late for us humans to learn about their mysterious methods of communication. Scientists have discovered that orcas use echolocation to talk to each other and hunt. This means they make a sound that travels through the water until the sound waves hit an object. Then, the sound waves bounce back to the orca, echoing back the size and even the shape of the object. This ability enables them to detect where objects and other orcas are in the area. Although I did pick up on their sonar telepathically and was able to count the five orcas in the pod underwater, orcas are the only type of whale (or giant dolphin) I encountered who did not come to see me after we made psychic contact. Now let's take a look at the pod of five who did.

FIN WHALES

The fin whale has a brownish-gray color with a V-shaped head and can weigh as much as 130 tons. Could my five new friends have toppled my boat when they played ring-around-the-rosie, singing "Happy Birthday" to my friend? Indeed, each whale was the size of a sailboat! Measuring in at up to ninety feet long, fin whales are considered one of the biggest whales in existence, second only to blue whales and sperm whales. According to Whale Facts (Whale Facts.org), an online resource for information about whales, a single large adult fin whale (at seventy-five tons) can weigh as much as ten large elephants (at fifteen thousand pounds each). Despite the fin's massive girth, this whale is slender and streamlined, allowing it to reach speeds of over twenty-five miles per hour. And these graceful giants live very long lives.

It is estimated that a healthy adult fin whale can live up to one hundred years when undisturbed by human hunters. The only known natural predator of the fin whale is a pack of hungry killer whales, but even that fearsome threat pales in comparison with the damage done to them by humans. Extensive hunting during the whaling era threatened their entire existence, so much so that they are currently listed as a protected species by the International Whaling Commission. What a crime against nature that we humans are the biggest threat to these elders of the ocean, who at the astonishing age of one hundred years may have gathered great knowledge, but they die holding the secrets of the sea. How blessed was I to take council with five of these rare, breathtaking beings?

Fin whales are adventurers and can be found traveling throughout the earth's oceans all over the world. Their diet consists of fish, squid, krill, and crustaceans (so with this varied diet, they too seem to be swimming around in one huge global restaurant). Although little is known about their migratory patterns, scientists believe that fin whales frequent cooler waters during feeding season and then migrate to warmer seas during the mating season. They also sing, or at least speak out loud, communicating to find each other through loud low-pitched sounds.

Fin whales die from collisions with ships, water pollution, global warming, and overfishing, as these massive mammals struggle to maintain their food supply. Fin whales also can get caught in fishing nets, where they drown because they are unable to return to the surface for oxygen. Noise and chemical pollution may threaten the existence of fin whale populations. And despite the end of the commercial whaling industry and bans put on hunting marine mammals, some countries and companies still participate in hunting fin whales as a source of food. Yikes! We have some work to do to restore the valuable elders of our oceans in time for them to teach us how they communicate. Let's tune in to our oceans' most treasured teachers and see what we can learn now.

PSYCHIC SONAR: LISTENING WITH LOVE

I could spend a lifetime trying to explain what ESP is so that I can share my bizarre gifts with others, and I've made that my quest — I'm now on my sixteenth consecutive year of touring the world teaching Animal Communication, to try to awaken this brain chemistry in animal lovers around the globe. And this is the sixth book I've written on the subject. I was mentored by the astronaut Dr. Edgar Mitchell, founder of the Institute of Noetic Sciences, on his ideas about the recent discovery in quantum physics, the quantum hologram, which adheres to the mathematics discovered in the Zero Point Energy Field theory. I've spent years studying the quantum energetic connections between humans and the world around us to try to make sense of something quite unusual that's going on in my brain. But the truth is, there is only one answer to the question, Why do I have "extrasensory sonar"? I don't know. I have some theories, though, and I can tell you this: surfing the waves is a lot more fun.

So let's investigate this mysterious thing called sonar. If we can begin to understand how it works for whales, we may be able to rekindle some ancient part of our brain that lies dormant, waiting for this emergent faculty to spark back to life in us landlubbers. Let's do a little psychic spy hopping, stick our heads out of our usual mundane Muggle world, and have a look around!

What Is Sonar?

When an animal or machine makes a noise, it sends sound waves into the environment around it. Those waves bounce off nearby objects, and some of them reflect back to the sender. It's those reflected sound waves that you hear when your voice echoes back to you in a canyon. So, in short, sonar is a process through which we listen and obtain information from the echo. Whales and specialized machines can use reflected waves to locate distant objects and sense their shape and movement.

The range of low-frequency sonar is remarkable. Studies reveal that dolphins and whales can tell the difference between objects as small as a BB pellet from fifty feet (fifteen meters) away, and they use sonar much more than sight to find their food, families, and direction. Sonar is how whales "see," because they don't rely on their eyes or ears alone to navigate through their underwater worlds. They rely almost exclusively on their sonar. Human scientists have yet to decipher the songs of whales to discover their meaning, but I personally know that whales use sonar to communicate with each other (and with me). The ability to send and receive sonar is the most indispensable faculty that whales use in order to function in their lives.

I suspect that sea creatures who rely on their sonar can also use it to body-scan each other and even us. That's why a dolphin can determine if a woman is pregnant or a man has metal inside his body — because it uses sonar like an x-ray machine to run scans. A dolphin can see not only the outer shape of an object, its location, and its trajectory, but even the contents and inner workings of the object investigated. More evidence surfaces every day to suggest that animals who employ sonar, like dolphins and whales, can also use this faculty to determine our emotional conditions; thus more people are swimming with dolphins in order to achieve greater health benefits. I believe from my experiences with whales that they use their sonar to telepath with each other and that they also have a number of mysterious attributes that we humans have yet to discover, such as the miraculous healing abilities they demonstrated when the five fin whales zapped me with their lightning love frequencies.

ACTIVE SONAR

According to the National Ocean Service of the National Oceanic and Atmospheric Administration (NOAA), "Active sonar transducers emit an acoustic signal or pulse of sound into the water. If an object is in the path of the sound pulse, the sound bounces off the object and returns an 'echo' to the sonar transducer." In this way, the wave of sonar hits its mark, bounces off, and returns to the sender in a feedback loop, which the sender (now receiver) translates into information about the location, size, and contents of the object, as well as its rate of speed. "If the transducer is equipped with the ability to receive signals, it measures the strength of the signal. By determining the time lapsed between the emission of the sound pulse and its reception, the transducer can determine the range and orientation of the object."

PASSIVE SONAR

The National Ocean Service continues:

> Passive sonar systems are used primarily to detect noise from marine objects (such as submarines or ships) and marine animals like whales. Unlike active sonar, passive sonar does not emit its own signal, which is an advantage for military vessels that do not want to be found or for scientific missions that concentrate on quietly "listening" to the ocean. Rather, it only detects sound waves coming towards it. Passive sonar cannot measure the range of an object unless it is used in conjunction with other passive listening devices.

"IF I ONLY HAD A BRAIN"

I could never have predicted, hoped, or dreamed that I would be able to pick up on the sonar of whales. It's not like I could have written in my calendar: "Next Tuesday: intercept sonar from sperm whale on his way across the Pacific." But the fact that I could listen isn't all that impressive. What's impressive is that the whales can signal *me* even on the land. All credit must be given to them, because unlike humans, they may have bodies, minds, hearts, souls, and psyches that cannot be shattered into tiny pieces. Their mental puzzles must be immense! And so are their senses of humor. Maybe before they got through to me, they all met one weekend in their underwater Treasure Island casino, played Go Fish long into the night, and bet a month's worth of krill that one of them could contact a dense, blonde animal communicator on the land. In three different parts of the world, four types of whales succeeded, and I think they slapped fins later and spurted fountains out their blowholes while they had a long frothy laugh. I hope I'm a legend in late-night pod-lore. For all I know, there may be some comedic songs written about me by now. I sure hope so.

But seriously, if they can communicate this well with *me*, imagine how well they can communicate with *each other*! There are some new ideas hatching out there about intelligence and brain chemistry not just in humans but in all living creatures. How can the human race evolve if we don't reconsider one of our most timeworn, outdated concepts about human hierarchy? What is hierarchy in nature, anyway?

Everywhere I go, people ask me about the sizes of brains. A hive of bees would have brains like angels on the head of a pin, where whales have brains fifteen times the size of human brains. My smart spy friend, the sperm whale, has a huge brain that weighs about twenty pounds (nine kilos!).

One concept brighter than considering the size of the brain on its own might be to consider brain size in comparison with the rest of the body and how much of the brain is operative. This would make little house cats my first choice for the wisest souls on this planet, or at least the cleverest, because I suspect that their little plum-sized brains are firing on all pistons.

Let's take a look at some alternative ways to define intelligence and the myth of brain size ruling our levels of cognitive awareness. Come surfing with me now in new waters, with a different kind of surfer — one who believes the holonomic brain theory may be a better way to comprehend how our brains function.

I'm going to revisit some of the basic precepts I spoke about in *The Language of Miracles*, where I cited the discoveries of Dr. Karl H. Pribram, author of *Brain and Perception: Holonomy and Structure in Figural Processing* (Lawrence Erlbaum Associates, 1991), whose revolutionary research indicates that the brain may not be exclusively compartmentalized at all, but *holographic*. Unfortunately,

Dr. Pribram has not been an animal champion, but his discoveries may help build a case for nonhuman cognitive thought.

In an interview with Dr. Jeffrey Mishlove for the PBS series *Thinking Allowed,* Dr. Pribram expounds upon his claim to fame. In psychology and neuropsychology, he is known as the originator of the holographic, or holonomic, model of the brain:

> The holonomic brain theory is based on some insights that Dennis Gabor had. He was the inventor of the hologram, and he obtained the Nobel Prize for his many contributions. He was a mathematician, and what he was trying to do was develop a better way of making electron micrographs, improve the resolution of the micrographs.... Essentially, with electron microscopes we make photographs using electrons instead of photons. He thought maybe instead of main ordinary photographs, that what he would do is get the interference patterns. Now what is an interference pattern? When light strikes, or when electrons strike any object, they scatter. But the scatter is a funny kind of scatter. It's a *very well regulated scatter.* For instance, if you defocus the lens on a camera so that you don't get the image falling on the image plane and you have a blur, that blur essentially is a hologram, because all you have to do is refocus it.
>
> So one of the main principles of holonomic brain theory, which gets us into quantum mechanics also, is that there is a relationship here between what we ordinarily experience and some other process or some other order, which David Bohm calls the *implicate* or enfolded order, in which things are all distributed or spread — in fact, the mathematical

formulations are often called *spread functions* — that they spread out....

These quantum-like phenomena, or the rules of quantum mechanics, apply all the way through to our psychological processes, to what's going on in the nervous system — then we have an explanation perhaps, certainly we have a parallel, to the kind of experiences that people have called *spiritual experiences. Because the descriptions you get with spiritual experiences seem to parallel the descriptions of quantum physics.*

At this point in the conversation, Mishlove pulls out his verbal water wings and goes wading through the interference patterns of Pribram's genius:

But what you're saying, if I can try and simplify it, is that there's a level of reality at which things are what they appear to be. I look at you and I see a body and a face. That would be the *explicate* level, where things are what they *appear* to be. Then there's an *implicate* level, which is *just as real*, but if you were to look at it, it doesn't look at all like the other.

Pribram agrees: "We experience it entirely differently — *as a spiritual aspect of our being.*"

Later in the interview, Mishlove, now far out to sea, observes:

Many neuroscientists today — it's almost axiomatic, when they talk about the mind, which they sometimes do — they say the mind is sort of located in the brain. I gather that that way of putting it is totally discordant with your own view of things.

To which Pribram replies:

Yes. There are lots of different ways of phrasing this. One is that mental phenomena are emergent properties of how the brain works, and so it's almost like the brain is secreting vision and mind and all that. But maybe a better way of talking about it would be to say that mental phenomena arise through *the interaction* between brain and body and environment. That whole interactive thing produces an *emergent,* which we call *mind and spirit.*

Shazam! The word "spirit" flutters out of the mouth of a very traditional scientist! Apparently even Dr. Pribram and I agree on some of the most basic components of how we all perceive physical reality. In order to communicate psychically, you must disengage yourself from your *explicate order*, let your consciousness *scatter* into the larger paradigm of *implicate order* (where you perceive yourself not as a static being but an action in motion), then let your focus spread out to include other sentient beings within that motion. Honing your intuitive abilities means that the camera of your consciousness can learn how to view what's beyond the blur of ordinary perception.

Is it possible that whales might perceive reality within an implicate order where they literally operate on a more evolved wavelength than human beings? Could the concept of implicate order explain why the sperm whale told me he was on his way to meet me and the five fin whales insisted that we cancel the party because they were swimming past on Saturday, not Sunday? They found a way to contact me that did not involve Muggle technology, and I found a way to tune in and listen. So I think we humans have some catching up to do. For our purposes, in learning telepathic communication, we will move our conscious headquarters into the *spiritual aspects of our being.* Let's leave our frontal lobes behind for a while. From the looks of our planet, they haven't done us much good anyway.

Subconscious, Meet Superconscious!

There's a new way of looking at ourselves and our mental abilities, while factoring in the intelligence of the other animals on this planet and giving them credit for more intelligence than we have ever recognized before. The ocean may be the ultimate temple for meditation, because in its watery depths there are miles of silence reaching out not only around these ancient beings, the whales, but also below them. By submerging themselves, these submarine-like beings would and should enter a world of total silence. Were it not for human intervention, they would be living in an underwater paradise of timeless virtual domain. The fluctuations in frequencies in this realm of undisturbed silence would be easier to read than on land because water is a great conductor of energy.

I'd like you to entertain a new possibility where our magical abilities to communicate nonverbally with other beings don't reside in our subconscious, available only through hypnosis, deep meditation, trance states, and altered states that are available only when drug induced. I'd like to present the idea of *superconsciousness*, where we can integrate our normal rational thinking processes with the intuitive powers housed in the creative hemisphere of our brains. I suspect that whales succeeded in this integration millennia ago, or this higher state of awareness is the scope in which they've operated all along.

If whales are superconscious, I wonder if each faculty lends itself in the integration of operating the whole mind, whole body, whole soul, and whole heart together, effortlessly and simultaneously. We have much to learn from our elders, the whales. They taught me how to be a little more sensitive, to trust myself a little bit more, and to listen to nature's heart and Nature's Mind, not my own, limited as it is with thoughts and fears. I can't say that I'm superconscious just yet, but the whales helped me drift closer to a more peaceful integration of connecting with nature while remaining separate enough to analyze and make sense of the incoming impulses.

SUPERCONSCIOUS-FRAGILISTICEXPIALIDOCIOUS

The presence of "supernatural" powers, including what I teach — Animal Communication, mediumship, remote viewing, the ability to body-scan other beings both physically and emotionally (medical Gestalt and sonar), the ability to read records and patterns from the animal's or person's past, clairvoyance, clairaudience, clairsentience, uncanny healing abilities, helping animals or humans to manifest new situations and attitudes in their lives, and even the ability to help animals or people cross over to heaven — may simply be attributes lying dormant in all of our brains. Dr. Edgar Mitchell called psychic ability "an emergent faculty in the evolution of the human race," so, in other words, he believes that this sixth sense is part of our learning curve as we humans evolve into something more mature and attuned with Nature's Mind. (Or not.) In short, meditation and superconsciousness allow us to turn off the "computer programs" we're mentally running and listen to the minds of others. I believe that whales mastered this attunement long ago and may simply use a greater amount of their brainpower.

American inspirational author Orison Swett Marden said: "Deep within man dwell those slumbering powers; powers that would astonish him, that he never dreamed of possessing; forces that would revolutionize his life if aroused and put into action."

We all get glimpses of superconsciousness in our daily life, but deep perceptions of it can really only come to us in the stillness of meditation. Meditation is a state of intense inward awareness in which we learn how to still our thoughts and emotions so completely that we are no longer concerned with or even aware of the stresses and obligations of our day-to-day lives. It's a bit of a holiday in the midst of your busy day, a holiday for your mind and nervous system that I highly recommend. Only through meditation can we retrain our awareness to operate not from the conscious level, where we are aware only of our own thoughts and emotions, or even the subconscious level, where we can only access patterns from the past, but from the superconscious, where we can listen to information *coming in from the outside.* Superconsciousness is the direct experience of who we actually are when we are tuned in to our *higher self* (our God-self or our *spirit*).

In the silence of the superconscious level, we become aware of new subtle energies both inside us and around us. A whole new world of possibilities can open up to us. Entering this new realm of bliss, which the Eastern yogis call a *samadhi* state, a transcendent state of feeling connected with All That Is, can with proper training allow us to sense the emotions and thoughts of other beings, such as the animals we love. Our mind becomes more acute so that we can grasp bits and pieces of frequencies and thought patterns sent from other beings. And there is a new sensation that comes only from incoming information: Delight! Sheer delight! New horizons of talent, ability, and perception open before us.

We live in an ocean of energy, and as we open ourselves to these waves and dare to swim in this new connected sea, we grasp more of the subtle side of life. As our "inner eyes" flutter open, we begin to stop seeing only the outer edges of things and start to see the content and meaning, the soul-consciousness at the heart of everything. Only from this vantage point can we establish resonance with an animal and see its point of view. But you must find your way into your own spirit, not your personality, your opinions, your prejudices or preconceived notions, but your actual eternal shining spirit, which will enable you to find mobility of consciousness and build bridges to the hearts and souls of other animals.

Sustaining a state of superconsciousness is the ultimate goal of our spiritual evolution as humans, but even a rare glimpse of a super-conscious state can be the summit of an entire lifetime of searching for self-knowledge and inner peace. But what about animals? Undis-turbed by humans, do animals already feel these rich states of grati-tude and bliss simply by being alive on earth? Do sheep grazing on the green fields in the English countryside and lions sleeping on their backs, sunbathing in the African sun, experience states of connection to the earth, to each other, and even to God? If you have a house cat, you know this is true. Cats' capacity for tranquillity far exceeds ours. Or if you have a new puppy and get to witness the exuberance of play-ing chase in the grass, swimming in a pond to fetch sticks, or even eating — eating anything and everything — you know that he seems to have integrated a superconscious state of joy into his normal life.

Superconsciousness can lead you to the center of your intuitive heart, teach you how to listen to the silent voice of your true soul… and help you to achieve the highest, purest form of love as you meet — and embrace — your higher self.

But about now, you may have a few questions swimming around in your brain. If you're interested in learning more about Animal Communication for yourself so that you can learn how to commu-nicate better with your animals at home, please read (or reread) my other books published by New World Library, where I explore these ideas in depth. I know through personal experience that all animals communicate within the Zero Point Energy Field by means of quan-tum processes, allowing information like thoughts, emotions, and even physical symptoms and history to be transferred, traveling on the wave function, from one living creature to another.

We also vocalize words to convey ideas even when our words are not congruent with our emotions. In other words, humans can lie or withhold information, whereas animals are a lot more likely to tell me the truth, not hiding behind smokescreens of illusion. Animals vocalize, too, as well as telepath. Dogs bark, cats meow, pigs oink, horses neigh, and all of those vocalizations mean more to them than those sounds mean to us. But of all the spoken animal languages we hear, one stands out as the most magical mystery, the most haunting form of communication that still remains secret to our scientists. Why do whales sing? And what are they saying when they sing?

Deep Blue Doo-Be-Doo-Be-Doo

Would that we had a Dr. Karl von Frisch studying whales' songs the way he did with the dances of bees. What a wealth of information remains hidden deep within the ocean's depths. The most interesting and thorough studies I've found on whale songs have been conducted by a musician named Katy Payne. In an August 6, 2015, article for NPR titled "It Took a Musician's Ear to Decode the Complex Song in Whale Calls," Bill McQuay and Christopher Joyce open a window into the interpretation of whales' music in this underwater world.

The first time Katy heard whale calls, she wanted to *see* the sounds, to see if there was a discernible pattern, so she got spectrograms of the visual representations showing peaks and valleys. She discovered in the patterns what looked like melodies and rhythms. Katy had majored in music, and she was quick to discover that the pattern wasn't random. She noticed that the humpbacks' long, intricate songs could also change and evolve over time.

Katy and her husband, Roger, discovered that for the most part all the males in a local group sing the song in a similar way. But over time, some sections of a group's song gradually change — in rhythm, pitch, and duration — as the whales listen to each other and collectively take up variations. This evokes for me memories of the dueling scat battles of Louis Armstrong and Ella Fitzgerald. If you are new to these epic collaborations, these two masterful musicians used their own voices like horn instruments and went wild improvising jazz riffs: "Bomp-bomp-diddley a whee-bop-skip-a-doo-whop-a-bop-be-dah-shing-a-doo-wop." No words necessary when you can really swing.

Apparently these swingin' humpbacks have their own version of scat singing. The Paynes recorded this same humpback group's song two years later and found that it had evolved from six elements to fourteen. All the added sounds came at the end, like a musical coda. Why do these male humpbacks gradually modify their songs?

So many people over the years have asked me about the meaning of whale songs. Some stunning evidence surfaced in the last few years to indicate that a new whale song could originate in the Southern Hemisphere, and within six months this very song would be heard sung by the whales in the Northern Hemisphere. I've joked that these songs could be just like what we play on our radios. The whales could be singing their version of Madonna's latest hit.

Do our songs have words as well as melodies that convey experience and emotion? Of course our songs tell stories. So why would theirs be any different? Whales may simply be artists. Being that they were here long before humans were, how dare we insist that we are the only species that makes art? Wouldn't it be logical to entertain the thought that we humans were not the first artists on this planet? Couldn't an ancient species older than humans have been the first musicians? I've heard some mockingbirds do solos for hours that would put any human jazz artist to shame. So maybe they sing because they like to invent melodies.

Another theory I present is that their songs may be news broadcasts where they alert each other to important issues like nuclear spills in Japan; underwater earthquakes; threats to their species imposed by human military experiments; and the locations of ships, nets, pollution, and, on a happier note, good places to eat. Unfortunately, if this were true, I wish the whales could relay these warnings to each other more effectively to avoid whaling boats.

The next story gives us evidence that through vocalizations and even sonar, whales don't seem to be able to detect the presence of fishing nets, or perhaps whales are so focused on more beautiful things that fishing nets take them by surprise. But I promise there is no sad ending to this story. This victory reigns supreme, and it's an example of how all of us can assist animals in need if we have the courage, empathy, and patience to put our fears aside and dive into their struggle.

VALENTINA, THE HUMPBACK BALLERINA

In a waterfall of miracles pouring down on me in the last forty-eight hours, I found a video online last night while researching humpback whales called "Saving Valentina." I can tell you it is one of the most spine-tingling and triumphant victories I've ever seen caught on film. Michael Fishbach and his family and crew were out whale watching when they spotted what they thought was a dead whale floating in the water. As they approached her in their little boat, they found that she was alive — just barely. She was so entangled in a fishing net that both of her dorsal fins were pinned to her body and the net weighed down her tail so that it dragged fifteen feet below the water. In one of the most riveting candid videos I've ever seen, Michael and his crew spent over an hour feverishly cutting the net with the only knife they had available — a knife the size of a butter knife.

It was slow going. In the beginning, he dove into the ocean, swam to her, and struggled bravely to free the net that was suffocating her. With one slap of the tail, she could have killed him. But she didn't. Did she know he had come to save her life? Scared, desperate, exhilarated, he shouted back to his family on the boat that he needed some help. He swam back to the boat, radioed for help, and was told that help couldn't reach them for over an hour. This whale didn't have an hour. She was exhausted and almost dead. It's a wonder she hadn't drowned in the nylon fishing net that had her completely sewn up in a deadly cocoon. She floated like a mummy right next to their boat until Michael and his crew finally succeeded in freeing one of her pectoral fins. Suddenly electrified and humming back to life, she led them on a wild goose chase. She could move one of her fins! Someone had come to save her!

The crew followed her until she became tired out and willingly drifted back to the boat to allow the men to finish the job. After an exhaustive hour of laboriously hacking at the fishing net and loading it on deck to free the young whale, they finally cut the last bit of the hellish maze off of her tremendous tail. In the video, you can see her swim away only for a moment to check if she is truly free before she returns to give the men the floor show of their lives. In more than forty breathtaking breeches, she performs a euphoric dance in the water and the air, shooting up like a rocket launched out of the sea, twirling and spinning, laughing and slapping the waves with her fins and tail — it is the closest I've ever seen a whale come to giving a roaring round of applause. There's no denying what she felt: ecstasy. And there's no doubt in my mind what she was saying to the boatload of heroes who saved her: "Thank you!"

I can only imagine what this must have felt like to the saviors who watched her water ballet, cheering her on. Imagine the satisfaction these men must have felt — the thrill of seeing that she had come back from the dead unharmed and could now dance with wild abandon in a fountain of unbridled joy. Eventually, she swam away in freedom. In these short moments while I held my breath, praying for these men, I had already fallen in love with Valentina. To watch her swim off both warmed and hurt my heart. God only knows the emotions that must have been coursing through the men who rescued her. I have never seen anything like this, and I'd never dreamed that rescues like this were even possible. With eyes still flooded with tears, I Googled the organization that Michael Fishbach had founded, the Great Whale Conservancy, and sent him an email (gushing) to ask what my readers and I could do to support his work.

This morning I received an email from this valiant man, granting an exclusive interview for this book. I asked him if he felt that Valentina *knew* on some level that he and his crew could help her, and if he felt she was communicating with them as she waited patiently through the agonizing hour of slicing net from her body.

His response can help us all understand the importance of whales, not only to the ocean but to our world, too — the world on land:

> Let me begin by saying that I do not mince words and am very passionate about the whales and the oceans. The Great Whale Conservancy fights very hard for the protection of these remarkable and intelligent beings whom we never have really yet come to comprehend. I'd put nothing past them. They live in the oceans, which are the undisputed lungs of this planet.
>
> And we are now coming to understand that the great photosynthesis mechanism that the oceans' phytoplankton is becomes greatly enriched by the immense iron-rich feces deposits that these whales release in the surface waters. They literally are a conveyor belt of richness that allows the planet and all of its inhabitants to "breathe" sufficient oxygen. And this system does play a role in minimizing the horrific effects of our fossil fuel use, as the oceans dissolve and sequester more carbon that any other system on earth. We at the GWC are working as closely as possible with a

few "conservation biologists" to uncover more of how this system works and the level of difference it makes. We have a short paper in the works that will be released on this topic soon. We made a very big mistake when we killed all those whales during the awful era of whaling, that I can tell you for certain.

"Do you think Valentina knew you and your crew were trying to save her life? Do you feel she deliberately sought out your help?" I asked.

I try to be as honest as possible in answering these types of questions. First of all, she was immobilized by the net, so she did not initially swim to us, we motored very slowly to her, and then I swam the last short distance to meet her. For sure she could communicate with us. She was in my opinion a broken animal when we found her. Her spirit and life force were mostly gone. In the beginning, I think I "woke her up." That spirit and life force began to return, and initially she was frightened, but of what I can't say. Whales are not meant to stop or be immobile, and this was a very young whale who had not been on her own for very long. What I can tell you for certain is that she cooperated with us completely. We had physical contact with her (that is, the boat and her body) on at least five different occasions. Never once did she so much as flinch. She did try to swim away as she became a bit more free, but that was in an effort to return to her world, the mysterious world of a humpback whale, and never did she try to do more than swim away as body parts became usable again. Eventually she was free, and she certainly expressed the joy of being alive, whale alive. Was she thanking us? I can't say for certain. It's tempting to say she was, and we felt like she was, but really none of us can be certain. We can be certain she was thrilled to be free and expressed that in a very humpback way.

All of this brings into focus another horrific problem on the high seas and the coastal ones: ghost nets drifting here and there and killing marine life. Whale entanglement is a nasty business and a big problem. Whale disentanglement is not the way to solve this problem; getting humans to be more responsible with their nets is. In the United States, it is actually illegal to attempt to disentangle an entangled whale. It is considered harassment and in violation of the Marine Mammal Protection Act. In other countries laws are different, but disentangling a whale is potentially a risky business. People have lost their lives attempting this.

Then I asked, "Do you offer whale excursions, so that my readers and I can come with you to meet and learn about whales?"

Yes, I bring people to see whales, and in fact our research boat in Baja California is full of such people every year. The public is invited to spend a week at a time with us in Baja, where we house and feed them and take them to share in our work and experiences with the whales. This we may also begin to do in Brazil and possibly Northern California soon, but in Baja this upcoming season will be our 20th of doing this.

I plan to join the great captain one day soon, and I hope you do, too. What I learned from this interview was that by their very existence, whales keep the oceans of this world nourished, alive, and flourishing, even with the nutrient-rich waste they excrete. Unlike humans, whales give back to this earth more than they take. Their bodies themselves are transformers of energy, taking only what they need and excreting something so valuable that it sustains the life of phytoplankton to feed future generations of sea life. There is beauty coming out of both ends of the whales, songs from their lips and the essential food for others from under their tail fins!

And if that weren't enough, their ability to create photosynthesis in the oceans, which Michael calls "the lungs of the planet," helps neutralize the damage we humans are doing to the atmosphere by helping to manufacture oxygen. Even with the horrors we inflict on them, the elders of the planet are trying to ensure the future of life on Earth, not just for them but for all species everywhere. As hard as we try to destroy them and their world, they are busy trying to save us and our world. You see, no matter how badly we humans behave, we cannot taint their intrinsic grooviness. Nature's crooners will continue to sing love songs to creation as long as they live. Rather than forcing all the whales to take their last breaths, wouldn't it be lovely if humans learned to sing along?

WHALES: THE FACTS

According to a September 29, 2013, article by Megan Gannon for *Live Science*, "Sonar Blamed for Mass Stranding of Melon-Headed Whales,"

> Four years ago, about 100 melon-headed whales mysteriously entered a shallow lagoon system in northwest Madagascar and became stranded. Now scientists say the creatures' demise was likely brought on by sonar used to map the ocean floor for ExxonMobil.
>
> Previous research has suggested that sonar can be harmful to marine mammals. The underwater noise can mask the

calls of dolphins and whales and scare them away from their feeding grounds. Naval exercises using sonar have been linked to a 2008 stranding of at least 60 dolphins along the coast of Cornwall, England.

But researchers say the new findings from Madagascar mark the first time a marine mammal mass stranding has been closely tied to high-frequency sonar mapping.

From May to June 2008, about 100 melon-headed whales (*Peponocephala electra*) swam into Madagascar's shallow, tidal Loza Lagoon system, a highly unusual environment for the toothed whales, which usually stick to the open ocean.

An independent review panel made up of five scientists considered a wide range of possible explanations for the mass stranding, including disease, toxins, vessel strikes, storm conditions and unusual acoustic events.

The panel wrote in their newly published report that on May 29, 2008, a day before the first stranding occurred, a survey vessel contracted by ExxonMobil Exploration and Production (Northern Madagascar) had been using a high-power 12 kHz multi-beam echosounder system to map the ocean floor about 40 miles (65 kilometers) offshore....

The 12 kHz sonar emitted by the survey vessel is within the frequency of best hearing sensitivity for melon-headed whales, the panel wrote. But these sounds at the 120-decibel level would be well above the hearing threshold of the whales....

"Implications go well beyond the hydrocarbon industry, as these sonar systems are widely used aboard military and research vessels for generating more precise bathymetry (underwater mapping)," Howard Rosenbaum, director of the Ocean Giants program for the Wildlife Conservation Society, said in a statement.

"We now hope that these results will be used by industry, regulatory authorities, and others to minimize risks and to better protect marine life, especially marine mammal species that are particularly sensitive to increasing ocean noise from human activities," Rosenbaum said.

ExxonMobil, meanwhile, disputed the findings.

Allow me to explain why man-made sonar hurts whales: The frequency that both whales and the military use falls between 100 and 500 Hz. Whales send out signals between 160 and 190 Db; the navy has tested its sonar signals at levels up to 235 Db. This hertz frequency is too loud for whales and dolphins, and hurts their ears and brains.

Not only are the frequencies too loud for whales; they are very difficult to escape. Instead of sending out one focused beam of sound straight down, the devices send out many beams of sound in all directions and are able to determine the direction of each packet of sound. The LFA (low-frequency active) sonar being tested by the military can travel thousands of miles and could cover 80 percent of the earth's oceans by broadcasting from only four points.

Using multibeam sonar, oceanographers can "illuminate" a swath of the seafloor many miles wide, and thousands of measurements of the water depth are collected every few seconds.

But what scientists have discovered and agree upon is that sonar is how whales "see" and also "hear." They cannot function without their sonar. This is why human military experiments are so detrimental at best, deadly at worst, to our sea life. The United States Navy is also transmitting underwater sonar that scrambles the messages and the minds of our whales and dolphins, and can even kill them. This is the answer to why so many whales have beached themselves in recent years or wash ashore dead. They beach themselves to escape the deafening noise that humans are creating underwater. Some sea life who rely on their sonar would rather commit suicide than be subject to it. Dead dolphins who still have blood flowing from their ears have washed ashore.

The Ocean's Heroes

There are some organizations doing spectacular work to protect whales, and at the very beginning of my journey, I had the honor of speaking alongside one of the ocean's greatest champions, the founder of Sea Shepherd Conservation Society, Captain Paul Watson. We lectured together at an animal rights conference in Chicago in 2001 just after my first book was published. I was still very green and a little bit shaky back then, but this man showed me how to capture an audience and unleash the wrath of God in front of a huge crowd of people in defense of the animals who can't stand at that podium and speak for themselves. When this mighty captain recapped stories about protecting whales from illegal Japanese whaling boats, his bravery in the face of unspeakable cruelty had every audience member — big, burly men included — heaving with tears. I learned as much as I possibly could, as quickly as I could, as I watched this superhero speak. Like Poseidon himself roaring to life from the pages of a mythology book, Paul is unshakable in the face of corruption. With waves of righteous indignation pouring out of him to wash over the audience, he made a point that I will never forget: There is right and there is wrong. And nothing will ever change that. He will stand in defense of beauty, of innocence, of the dignity of noble ancient creatures until he takes his final breath, and he is willing to die for what he believes in. And so am I.

Fearless and uncompromising, Paul Watson set a standard that we all should follow — even if we can only contribute in small ways.

His years of struggle and persistence have paid off, and no one has accomplished more to rescue and raise awareness about the plight of whales and other tortured beings in the sea, who have been harmed and disrespected by humans. Sea Shepherd is leading the effort to defend and protect humpback whales from the harpoons of the illegal Japanese whalers in the Antarctic.

I look forward to the day when the matriarch orca will surface for me, not to entertain me or make despairing pleas for humans to stop torturing her family and her people, but to take a meeting with our people because we *deserve* it. We may still have a long way to go to be worthy to take council with these magnificent animals so that we can be apprentices of their masterful knowledge. But like Michael Fishbach, Paul Watson, and many other ocean warriors, I'll die trying.

I have a vision of the distant future where we humans have not just evolved enough to be devoted apostles of the ocean's council of elders but actually outgrown our violent nature and matured enough to be their *friends*.

WHAT DO WHALES REPRESENT?

Superconsciousness. They represent our capacity for spiritual growth. But they also represent intellectual growth, new mental capacities that make advanced communications possible without the crutches of technology. They teach us about communication and the vast possibilities of the human brain. In their ability to signal and communicate with others of their species (and even ours) across the ocean by utilizing a component active in their own brains, they show us that we may have potential to activate more of our brain chemistry and view "supernatural" talents as innate parts of our physiology, built into our human bodies, waiting to grow. They demonstrate that sonar may be an emergent faculty in the evolution of the human race. But most of all, their superconsciousness gives us a new goal — a way to live lives filled with clear communication, self-confidence, humor, and grace, all the while sending nothing but good vibes and beautiful love songs through our airspace. They show us the potential to be helpful stewards of the earth and give back more than we take. Whales teach us to live with abandon, sing loudly, smile widely — and, above all, not to be afraid to make a big splash.

BEAUTY IN ALL BEINGS

In Plato's *Symposium*, the great philosopher focuses his brilliant mind on the virtues of beauty:

> What if man had eyes to see the true beauty — the divine beauty, pure and clear and unalloyed, not clogged with the pollutions of mortality or all the colours and vanities of human life — thither looking and holding converse with the true beauty simple and divine? Remember how in that communion only, beholding beauty with the eye of the mind, he will be able to bring forth not images of beauty, but realities.... And bringing forth and nourishing true virtue to become the friend of God.

If Plato has set our goal to know the Divine by seeing the divine beauty in all things, would he not have agreed that there is wondrous beauty in each of God's creatures? Would he have seen animals with my eyes and agreed that there is as much beauty in my tiger, elephant, lion, shark, snake, bee, and whale friends as there is in any other form on earth? Would Plato also have championed my discovery that there is as much God consciousness in your dog, cat, horse, or parrot as there is in any church or any angel in this universe? Would our greatest Greek philosopher have agreed that we will find joy, peace, and spiritual evolution not by ascending beyond this earthly plane but by sinking deeper into it to glorify its beauty and unravel its endless wealth of secrets? I think he might have. Nature and her animals whisper only with those who see her beauty. Will the human race ever be worthy of being a true friend of Mother Nature, and a shepherd, student, and confidant of her animals?

This is not where we humans end our spiritual journey. This is where we begin.

Acknowledgments

I WOULD LIKE TO THANK MY MOTHER, Dr. Melinda McClanahan, for her painstaking edit of the lion, elephant, and bee chapters. Mother, you have the brainpower to light up the galaxy. Thank you for beaming some of your starlight my way! I'd also like to extend a heartfelt "Thank you!" to Fiona Knox, who created the most stunning watercolor paintings for each chapter and donated her work as a gift to animal welfare on this planet. Every time I received a painting, I burst into tears. Your talent, Fiona, captured the very soul of each species, and I am in awe of your gift behind the brush. A hundred buzzing thanks go to Michelle Black, the bee-witching brainy lady who also helped edit and inspire the bee chapter. Thank you, Michelle, for keeping me buzzing long after my batteries had run flat. I want to thank the creator of the Language of Miracles Online Institute, Leslie Bower, who brought my work from the written page to the wonderful world of webinars, and my devoted director, Jane Elisabeth Tollefsen, who created Ark Angel TV and continues to lovingly host my webinars all over the world. I'd like to thank Ark Angel's biggest supporters, Dr. Melinda McClanahan, Catherine Brown-Swain, Elaine Checkley, and fearless Rita Black, who has made the pilgrimage to the gorillas and orphans in Rwanda possible.

Rita, your heart is so big, all five hundred orphans can fit in your heart with room to spare. I'd also like to extend a heart-felt thank you to Gregory Abelar, who not only coordinates my *No Horror for Animals* fundraisers in Hollywood, he even "goes as me" every Halloween dressed in drag as "Angela" in his black wedding gown. And no thank-you page could be complete without thanking Dr. Bernie Siegel, who lifted me up on the wings of his love. Your support, Bernie, completely transformed my life. I'm also grateful for the hawk eyes of Elissa Rabellino, my razor-sharp copy editor, and Barbara Fisher, who designed the book's gorgeous cover. But most of all, I want to thank Jason Gardner, my editor, for his fearless wild spirit. And bless you, everyone at New World Library. You are all true to your name. New World Library is helping foster what could and should be our next "New World," a world filled with love...and wild animals.

Resources

PLEASE SUPPORT THE FOLLOWING organizations to help promote the ideals presented in this book.

TIGERS

Please give generously to tiger conservation by supporting the World Wildlife Fund.
www.worldwildlife.org

POACHING/TRAFFICKING EDUCATION AND PREVENTION

To help educate rural African children about wildlife conservation to curb the poaching of elephants and lions, and to help prevent lion bones from being sold as tiger bones on the black market, please support Ark Angel.
www.ameliakinkade.com/ark_angel

ELEPHANTS

To help preserve elephants and stop poaching, please support the following organizations.

African Elephants

The David Sheldrick Wildlife Trust
www.sheldrickwildlifetrust.org/index.asp

Amelia's Ark Angel Society
www.ameliakinkade.com/ark_angel

World Wildlife Fund
www.worldwildlife.org

Asian Elephants

Elephant Nature Foundation
www.elephantnaturefoundationuk.org/elephant-nature-foundation

Elephant Family
elephant-family.org

Lions

To help lions, please support Drakenstein Lion Park.
www.lionrescue.org.za

African Wilderness Conservation

Please support the Ajubatus Foundation to promote wilderness conservation in Africa.
www.africanconservation.org/explorer/ajubatus-foundation

Marine Wildlife

Please support the Sea Shepherd Conservation Society.
Paul Watson
www.seashepherd.org

Whales

Please support the Great Whale Conservancy.
Michael Fishbach
www.greatwhaleconservancy.org

Wildlife

www.bornfree.org.uk

Bibliography

Ackerman, Diane. *I Praise My Destroyer*. New York: Vintage Books, 2000.

Barker, Raymond Charles. *The Power of Decision*. New York: Tarcher, 2011.

Barth, Friedrich G. *Insects and Flowers: The Biology of a Partnership*. Translated by M.A. Biederman-Thorson. Princeton, NJ: Princeton University Press, 1985.

Blackiston, Howland. *Beekeeping for Dummies*. 2nd ed. Hoboken, NJ: Wiley, 2009.

Campbell, Don. *The Mozart Effect*. New York: Avon Books, 1997.

Castaneda, Carlos. *Tales of Power*. New York: Simon and Schuster, 1974.

Emoto, Masaru. *The Hidden Messages in Water*. Translated by David A. Thayne. Hillsboro, OR: Beyond Words Publishing, 2004.

Epstein, Donald M., and Nathaniel Altman. *The 12 Stages of Healing*. Novato, CA: New World Library, 1994.

Fishbein, Morris. *The Medical Follies*. New York: Boni & Liveright, 1925.

Frisch, Karl von. *Bees: Their Vision, Chemical Senses, and Language*. 3rd ed. Ithaca: Cornell University Press, 1971.

———. *The Dance Language and Orientation of Bees*. Translated by Leigh E. Chadwick. Cambridge: Belknap Press / Harvard University Press, 1967.

Grant, Robert J. *Edgar Cayce on Angels, Archangels, and the Unseen Forces*. Virginia Beach, VA: A.R.E. Press, 2005.

Greive, Bradley Trevor. *Priceless: The Vanishing Beauty of a Fragile Planet*. Kansas City, MO: Andrews McMeel Publishing, 2003.

Heidborn, Tina. "Dancing with Bees." *Max Planck Research*, February 2010. https://www.mpg.de/789446/MPR_2010_2.pdf.

Hills, Carol. "Thailand's Tiger Temple Saga Isn't Over Yet." *USA Today*, June 3, 2016. http://www.usatoday.com/story/news/world/2016/06/03/thailands-tiger-temple-saga-isnt-over-yet/85334156/.

Maeterlinck, Maurice. *The Life of the Bee*. Translated by Alfred Sutro. New York: Dodd, Mead and Company, 1913.

Matthews, Simone M. *Shealla Dreaming: A Journey to Unlock the Secrets of the Universe*. Tempe, AZ: Soul Star Publishing, 2012.

Mindell, Arnold. *The Shaman's Body: A New Shamanism for Transforming Health, Relationships, and the Community*. San Francisco: HarperSanFrancisco, 1993.

Nordhaus, Hannah. *The Beekeeper's Lament: How One Man and Half a Billion Honey Bees Help Feed America*. New York: HarperPerennial, 2011.

Rochat, Lesley. "Why I Swim with Sharks." LesleyRochat.com (blog). http://www.lesleyrochat.com/2013/why-i-swim-with-sharks.

Seeley, Thomas D. *The Wisdom of the Hive: The Social Physiology of Honey Bee Colonies*. Cambridge, MA: Harvard University Press, 1995.

Shwartz, Mark. "Elephants Pick Up Good Vibrations — through Their Feet." *Stanford News Service*, March 5, 2001. http://news.stanford.edu/pr/01/elephants37.html.

Sparrow, Gregory Scott. *I Am with You Always: True Stories of Encounters with Jesus*. New York: Bantam Books, 1995.

St. Germain, Maureen. *Beyond the Flower of Life*. New York: Phoenix Rising Publishing, 2009.

TRAFFIC. "CITES Turns Up the Heat on Tiger Smugglers." www.traffic.org. March 14, 2013. http://www.traffic.org/home/2013/3/14/cites-turns-up-the-heat-on-tiger-smugglers.html.

TRAFFIC. "New Study Reveals Scale of Persistent Illegal Tiger Trade." www.traffic.org. March 7, 2013. http://www.traffic.org/home/2013/3/7/new-study-reveals-scale-of-persistent-illegal-tiger-trade.html.

Ulanov, Ann Belford, and Barry Ulanov. *The Witch and the Clown: Two Archetypes of Human Sexuality*. Wilmette, IL: Chiron Publications, 1987.

Wenner, Adrian M., and Patrick H. Wells. *Anatomy of a Controversy: The Question of a "Language" Among Bees*. New York: Columbia University Press, 1990.

About the Author

ANIMAL COMMUNICATOR AMELIA KINKADE is the author of several books, including *Straight from the Horse's Mouth* and *The Language of Miracles*. She is the president of Amelia's Ark Angel Society, a charity that educates children in rural Africa about wildlife conservation to stop poaching before it starts. She is also the founder of Ark Angel TV and the Language of Miracles Institute online. Amelia lectures and teaches workshops in the United States, Canada, Mexico, England, Scotland, Sweden, Germany, France, Norway, the Netherlands, Switzerland, Austria, Portugal, Italy, Poland, the Canary Islands, Brazil, Zambia, Rwanda, and South Africa, where she trains animal lovers from all walks of life, including doctors and vets.

Amelia's unique abilities have been the focus of hundreds of magazine and newspaper articles in such publications and media outlets as the *New York Times*, the *Chicago Tribune*, *Good Housekeeping*, *Cat Fancy*, *Dog Fancy*, Boston's *North Shore Sunday*, London's *News of the World*, *Bild der Frau* in Germany, *Annabelle* in Switzerland, and the *Freizeit Kurier* in Vienna.

She has appeared on such television programs as *The View*, *The Other Half*, *The Ellen DeGeneres Show*, *ABC News*, *Extra*, *The Jenny Jones Show*, *The BBC News*, *Beyond Belief with George Noory*,

Carte Blanche in South Africa, and numerous news broadcasts in the United States, Europe, and Australia. She has been heard on over four hundred radio programs from Memphis, Tennessee, to Cape Town, South Africa. A BBC documentary was created about her work with elephants in Kruger National Park, and a BBC children's programming tour was created for her youngest, most open-minded fans.

Amelia's true passion is leading her annual Sacred Harmony Safaris in Africa and assisting organizations that rescue elephants, cheetahs, penguins, great white sharks, lions, and rhinos. She helps troubleshoot problems for tigers, primates, elephants, and countless breeds of exotic as well as domestic animals. In 2002, she was honored to accept invitations to Buckingham Palace to work with the household cavalry of Queen Elizabeth II and to "whisper" with the hunting horses of Prince Charles. Amelia is also privileged to work with Olympic show-jumping horses. Her two superstar horse clients won the gold and silver medals at the Longine Global Champions Tour in Rome and Vienna in 2016.

www.ameliakinkade.com

A portion of the publisher's proceeds from this book will aid Ark Angel Society.